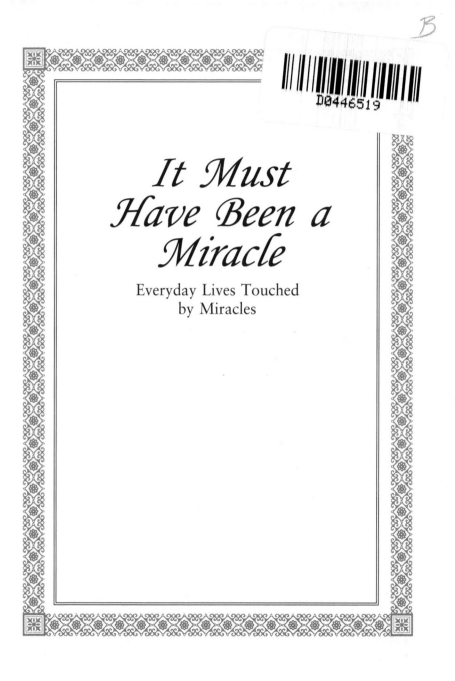

# It Must Have Been a Miracle

Everyday Lives Touched
by Miracles

*Berkley Books by Kelsey Tyler*

THERE'S AN ANGEL ON YOUR SHOULDER
IT MUST HAVE BEEN A MIRACLE

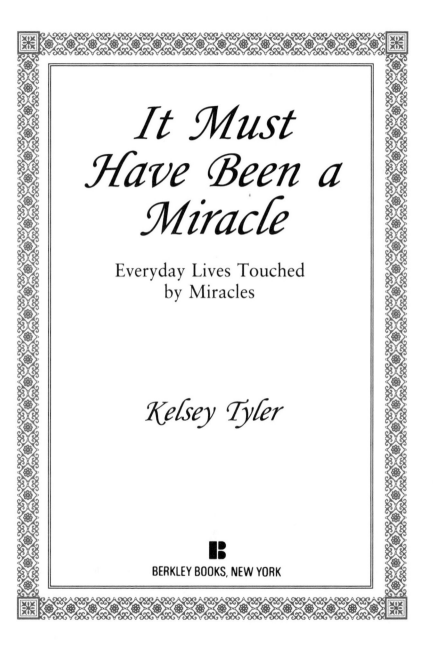

# It Must Have Been a Miracle

## Everyday Lives Touched by Miracles

### Kelsey Tyler

BERKLEY BOOKS, NEW YORK

IT MUST HAVE BEEN A MIRACLE

A Berkley Book / published by arrangement with
the author

PRINTING HISTORY
Berkley trade paperback edition / April 1995

ISBN: 0-425-14825-4

BERKLEY®
Berkley Books are published by The Berkley Publishing Group,
200 Madison Avenue, New York, New York 10016.
BERKLEY and the "B" design
are trademarks belonging to Berkley Publishing Corporation.

PRINTED IN THE UNITED STATES OF AMERICA

10  9  8  7  6  5  4  3  2  1

# Acknowledgments

*I*t has been a privilege to put this collection of miracle stories together, one that would not have been possible without the help of many people.

First, I would like to thank my agent, Arthur Pine, for dreaming up the idea of writing about miracles. Brainstorming with you on this book is what made it happen.

Also, I would like to thank the people whose stories make up this collection. You are honest, hard-working, private people who took a risk by sharing your stories with me. As a result, people all over the world will be touched by your miracles.

A special thanks goes to my editor, Elizabeth Beier. Thank you for your eternal enthusiasm and your amazing way of turning my work into something beautiful.

Next, thanks to Renee Gildehaus, who allowed her own life to be uprooted while she staged a mock preschool at my home so I could hide away and put these stories on paper. My children love you, Renee, and so do I.

As with past projects, I want to thank my husband for understanding me and loving me, anyway. And my parents for their never-ending support.

Finally, I want to thank Gina Hammond for making the transition from Los Angeles nothing short of miraculous. Truly, I thank God for your friendship and always will.

# Dedicated
## to

My husband and precious children, whose
presence in my life is also a miracle,
and whom I love more with each passing day.

Lisa,
who has been there for me as long
as I can remember.

Gina,
whose heart is so like my own.
Thank you for sharing
my dreams and disappointments.
You're the best!

And to Almighty God . . .
the
Wonderful Counselor, Everlasting
Father, and Prince of Peace,
who is, indeed,
still working miracles
among us.

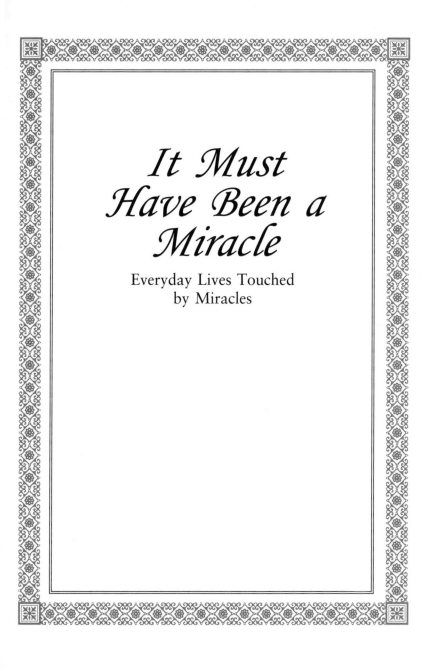

# It Must Have Been a Miracle

Everyday Lives Touched
by Miracles

# Foreword

*"A miracle is an event which creates faith. That is the purpose and nature of miracles. Frauds deceive. An event which creates faith does not deceive; therefore it is not a fraud, but a miracle."*

—*George Bernard Shaw*

We are, all of us, looking for a miracle.

The passing grade, the awaited phone call, the necessary career move, the healthy cry of a newborn baby.

"It's a miracle," we say when the moment comes to pass.

And perhaps it is.

But for some of us, life has become a series of days in which we barely get by. Crime plagues our neighborhoods, wearisome jobs put distance between us and our dreams, our children are ill, our marriages rocky, our finances tight. When this is our life, we are desperately in need of the one thing that will pull us through: Faith.

Faith in our fellow man, faith that goodness will prevail, faith in happy endings. And especially faith in miracles.

The Bible notes a time when Jesus said to a blind man, "According to your faith will it be done." The blind man had great faith, and moments later he could see.

As we rush headlong toward the Twenty-first Century, we are a society desperately in need of hope. Certainly there is nothing like a miracle to bring hope to our lives, meaning to our existence. A supernatural reassurance that indeed someone is looking out for us after all. Amidst these often troubled times, as a nation we are beginning to renew our faith in miracles.

We look around us and see the paralyzed walking, sick people well again, loved ones reunited. The very thing that should never have happened in many cases *is* happening. Miracles abound! Those who believe know that miracles are real—and also that there is nothing new about them.

People have experienced the wonderment of miracles since the beginning of time. But in recent decades we witnessed what seemed to be the end of an innocent age, and we seemed to forget that miracles ever existed at all. We found ourselves caught in an increasingly materialistic, crowded and violent world where sadly there was scant room for even the possibility of miracles. And that may be why we seem, these days, at the brink of change.

Suddenly there seems to be room for miracles.

Once again there is hope in our eyes as we look to the past and recognize certain phenomena for the miracles they might have been. And not just to the past, but to the present and even the future. There is breathing room once more, a flickering light in our personal caverns of darkness. For us all there is hope as we recognize the miraculous among the mundane, as we learn to believe in miracles.

In this way, we allow for the possibility that whether we are close to our God or not, he is close to us. And perhaps his calling card is nothing short of a miracle.

In some cases, the miracles we have begun to notice are simply strange and highly unlikely coincidences, incidents that in a more cynical era might have gone unnoticed. But today, in a world where hope is an utterly precious commodity, people are recognizing that something unusual, something worth feeling good about, even something life-changing, might be happening next door or across town. Maybe even in our own lives.

We are beginning to understand that anything is possible when we believe in miracles.

# Introduction

*D*ictionaries define *miracles* as events that appear unexplainable by the laws of nature and so are held to be supernatural in origin or acts of God. But over the years the word has taken on a broader definition. Hollywood has given us miracles performed by everyone from Santa Claus to home-run hitters. Pinocchio would not be a real boy, the Little Mermaid would not be a human with legs, and Sleeping Beauty would still be sleeping if not for one of Disney's cinematic miracles.

Yet perhaps the most intriguing miracles are those that we truly cannot explain. They were not created by an artist or a storyteller, but they pepper history in a way that causes us to take notice.

Noah and the ark, Daniel in the lion's den, Jonah in the belly of a great fish, the young David slaying the giant Goliath with a slingshot, Moses parting the Red Sea, Jesus walking on water.

But miracles did not cease to exist after biblical times. In fact, it's quite possible that miracles are still happening to us today; that what appears to be a unique occurrence or a coincidence of immeasurable proportion might instead be nothing less than a miracle.

This is a collection of stories about ordinary people who, like many of us, found themselves in need of a miracle. But rather than give way to defeat, these people clung to their faith and believed in the miraculous. They believed in miracles and so, it seems, experienced one.

Some stories in this collection have been told before, passed down through the ages to those who would believe. Others are more obscure, told in passing and now captured in this collection. And still others are the stories of people whose lives are not uncommon but whose experiences certainly are; people who defied their circumstances and rose to a place no one thought they could reach.

These stories all have one thing in common: all of them involve real people whose lives were changed by what may have been a miracle. And within their stories is something that all people need a great deal more of and more often: Hope.

When we believe in miracles, things are not as dismal as they seem. There is light amidst the darkness, a flicker of promise in the still night of despair. Hope springs eternal; faith is our sustenance. If only we would believe as these people did.

Read their stories and see if you, too, believe.

*A Note to the Reader: In putting this collection together, I had the privilege of talking with most of the people whose miracle stories are detailed in this book. In some instances, the names of the people involved have been changed to protect their privacy. In these cases, as well as several stories that are in the nature of folklore, names are fictitious and are not intended to represent specific living persons. On the few occasions when it was impossible to contact secondary people involved, the details were provided by a person who witnessed the event in question firsthand and believed the story—including the parts involving secondary people—to be both truthful and completely credible. However, it is not the intention of this book to prove the validity of miracles. Instead these stories have been written for your pleasure, to evaluate and take at face value.*

# ONE

# Match Made in Heaven

For Rob and Andy Kaler the summer of 1968 was supposed to be full of carefree fun in the sun. But what would happen while their family vacationed in the south of France would change Rob's life forever.

That summer Rob was fifteen and Andy fourteen. Most days their parents would play tennis at the club where they were staying or involve themselves in organized activities, leaving the boys to spend their days at the beach. Rob and Andy were thrilled with this freedom and were careful to act responsibly. Both boys were avid swimmers and by midsummer had made several new friends along the shore.

One afternoon just after lunchtime, a woman and several young blond girls walked down the beach and set up not far from where Rob and Andy had their towels.

"Must be new," Rob whispered to his brother. Andy nodded. Neither boy had seen the family before.

The teens watched as two of the girls—who looked about seven and four years old—climbed into a rubber raft and set out into the water. "Wonder if they know about the riptides?" Andy asked.

Rob looked concerned and narrowed his eyes. The ocean had cleared of most people; by watching the waves he could see why. The riptides that came up at about this time were particularly strong that day. When he glanced back toward the small rubber boat, he was shocked.

"Look!" He pointed toward the boat. "They're being sucked right out to sea!"

He jumped up and raced toward the woman who had brought the young girls.

"Your girls!" he shouted when he was still several yards away. "They're in trouble!" Rob motioned toward the ocean, where the two little girls were now frantically waving toward the shore for help.

The woman saw what was happening and began to panic. "Oh, no! Help!" she shouted hysterically, her head swiveling as she looked for someone nearby. Then she turned to Rob. "I can't swim!"

Rob did not hesitate for a moment. He pulled off his shirt, kicked off his sandals, and ran for the water. Seconds later he was beyond the surf and could feel himself being sucked into the current. Never had the water tugged so desperately at his body. By straining with all his energy, he could force his head high enough out of the water so that the girls were visible. The current was taking him straight for them.

Within a minute or two he was at their side. Both children were terribly frightened, crying and clutching the sides of their rubber raft. The raft had begun to take on water, and each second was being drawn farther from shore.

"Shh," Rob told the girls. "Stop crying and stay still. We're going to be all right."

The girls' screams quieted to whimpers.

Rob took a deep breath and grabbed the edge of the raft. Turning toward shore, he began to kick with all his might. Although he was only a hundred yards or so from shore, the tide was so strong he felt he was making almost no progress at all. The older girl saw his difficulty and began to cry aloud once more.

"We're going to drown!" she screamed.

"We will be fine. Now be quiet," Rob said, still forcing himself and the raft toward shore. This time Rob's voice had an immediate calming effect on the girls. He was able to focus all his attention on reaching the shore.

Ten minutes passed and it seemed they had barely moved ten yards closer to shore. Rob could feel his muscles tightening and his energy draining. He glanced over his shoulder and saw the two girls, their white-blond hair matted onto their faces, their pale blue eyes wide with fright. He would not give up. If they drowned, then he would, too.

Summoning every bit of energy he had, Rob began kicking even harder, lunging forward with each stroke of his free hand and yanking the raft between strokes. The current was so strong, he felt as if he were pulling the raft straight up a hill. Still he continued.

Meanwhile, a crowd had gathered on the beach. Andy stood to one side, terrified that his brother had not yet reached the shore. Rob was a brilliant swimmer, and if it was taking him this long to pull the girls safely back to shore, something was terribly wrong. Andy had heard of currents that literally pulled people underwater to their deaths. He prayed that this was not the case as he kept his eyes riveted on his older brother.

Alongside Andy, strangers had circled the girls' mother, attempting to comfort her and hold her up while the girls made painfully little progress toward shore. There were no boats in sight, and although the lifeguards had been called, this was a private beach and none had arrived yet.

Thirty minutes passed and Rob could tell he was getting perceptibly closer to shore. He could feel the adrenaline coursing through his body and forcing him forward, even if only a few inches at a time.

"Please God," he prayed silently. "Help me get these children back to shore."

Never had Rob thought of himself as a hero. At school he was about to enter the tenth grade, and although he was quite athletic, he had never been called upon for anything like this. He well knew that if he gave in to the fatigue that racked his arms and legs, he and the girls would probably all drown. All the progress he had made so far would be wiped out in one moment's driving riptide. He pursed his lips in determination and continued forward.

The boys' parents had heard a commotion on the beach and headed down to see what was happening. When they found Andy and saw the fear in his face, they, too, were horrified. They looked out and saw that their son was a hundred yards offshore, but still not close enough to be sure of reaching the beach safely.

"I'm going out, too," the boys' father, Raymond, said.

"Dad, don't do it!" Andy shouted. "The current's too strong. Besides, Rob might need you when he gets to shore."

"He's right, Ray," Rachel, the boys' mother, said. "Besides, Rob's a wonderful swimmer. He'll be all right."

For the next thirty minutes, twenty people lined the shore awaiting Rob's and the girl's safe return. The boy was clearly exhausted, and the children frightened. But finally it looked as though they might make it. When they were only ten yards away, Rob's father swam out and pulled the trio safely to the sand.

The girls' mother swooped them into a waiting towel, while the crowd surrounded them. Raymond lifted Rob into his arms and took him onto the beach, where he set him gently in a chair. Rob's hands and legs were swollen and his face was ashen. He closed his eyes and began to moan. "Son!" Raymond said. "Are you all right? Can you hear me?"

Rob opened his eyes groggily. "Water," he said. Instantly Andy ran up toward the club and returned with a cup of water. After several sips Rob sat up straighter and opened his eyes fully. He looked around, past his parents and brother toward the area where the little girls' mother had been. The crowd had disappeared.

"That's funny," Rachel said, taking her son's hand and stroking it gently. "They didn't even stop to thank him."

"Oh, I'm sure they meant to," Raymond said quickly. "They probably wanted to get the girls indoors and out of the heat."

Rob nodded and closed his eyes again. He was exhausted, but he had survived the ordeal and he was humbly thankful. Only he knew how close he had come to giving up and letting his body mercifully sink under the waves.

Throughout the rest of the week the village people got word of Rob's heroic rescue and began treating him like a celebrity. People would point to him and talk in whispers, and several times people came up to him and congratulated him on saving the lives of the young girls.

He learned from several of them that the girls' father was a very wealthy merchant in town and that he disapproved of Americans. This puzzled Rob, but he tried not to think about the man. He had to have known where the boys were staying, and yet he made no attempt to contact Rob or to thank him in any way for saving his daughters' lives.

After several more days the Kaler family packed their things and returned home to Detroit, Michigan. As they boarded the airplane, Rob glanced once more toward the airport. Secretly he had hoped that the girls' father might have chosen this time to thank Rob in person for his rescue. But when he saw no one, he decided to put the incident out of his mind.

Twenty years passed and Rob finished school and college. His younger brother married and had two children, but Rob became an attorney and remained single. He dated occasionally, but for one reason or another never wound up in a serious relationship.

"It's time you find yourself a wife, brother," Andy joked once in a while.

But Rob would only shake his head. He was more serious than his younger brother and did not easily make close connections with people. He was thirty-five that year, and he had long since decided that his life was full regardless of his single status.

That summer he decided to vacation alone at the same spot where his family had spent the month twenty years earlier. The anniversary of the day he had rescued the little girls was approaching, and he wanted to spend it on the same beach.

"I don't know what it is," he told Andy. "I feel drawn to that place."

"Something to do with saving those kids?" Andy asked.

Rob shrugged. "I don't know. It's just something I can't get out of my mind. I have to go back there."

Rob decided to stay at the same hotel and spend time thinking about his future. For several days he walked the beach and swam the surf. He made little conversation with anyone; after nearly a week he felt well-rested.

Finally Sunday arrived, the twenty-year anniversary of his hour-long rescue. Late that afternoon Rob walked down the beach and sat near a tree just up the shore from the spot where the girls had first gotten pulled out to sea.

Suddenly Rob realized he wasn't alone. Several feet away from him a beautiful young woman with blond hair and blue eyes was quietly watching him.

"You're Rob Kaler," she said softly.

Rob's eyes widened and he stood up, slowly moving toward the woman. "I'm sorry," he said. "I don't believe I remember meeting you."

The woman smiled shyly and looked away. "We never met on a formal basis," she said. "My name is Anna Guten, daughter of Maurice Guten."

Instantly Rob understood.

"You were in the boat," he said excitedly. "The day I rescued you!"

Anna nodded. "I was four years old, my sister eight. And we had just set out for a ride in the waves when the current took us out to sea."

"And before anyone knew what was happening," Rob continued, "you two were in big trouble."

The girl was quiet a moment. "I have wanted to meet you, to thank you for what you did that day. I know you risked your life to save us."

Rob smiled. "How did you know it was me, here on the beach?"

"Townspeople talk. It's a small place and they never stopped talking about how Maurice Guten's daughters were rescued by an American. When you returned, several people remembered you. I was hoping to find you here since this is the anniversary of that day so long ago. When I saw you, and saw that you were American, I took a chance."

Rob nodded. Her story made sense. He had told some of the people at the resort who he was, and a few of them who still worked there had remembered the incident. There were only five hundred people in the seaside town, so it was very possible that Anna would hear about his presence.

"I want to apologize," Anna said. "For my father. He is a very stern man, stuck in his ways. Sometimes I wonder if he even really cared that you rescued us that day. I know he never thanked you, and all my life I've wanted to do something about that."

"And now you have," Rob answered.

He was touched and quite taken with the young woman's beauty. She was twenty-four now, but he noticed that she was not wearing a wedding ring.

"Would you like to have dinner?" he asked her. For some reason he felt comfortable with her, as if he'd known her all his life.

She smiled and nodded in answer. The two spent the rest of the afternoon talking about the lives they had lived for the past twenty years. He learned that Anna was a very lonely young woman. Her father had never treated her like his other daughters and had let Anna know that he did not believe himself to be her father. He thought Anna's mother had had an affair and that Anna's real father was an American tourist. For that reason he hated all Americans and had refused to thank the young boy who had rescued his children from certain death.

Since then, Anna's mother had died and her other sisters were married and living on their own. As she spoke, Rob felt his heart going out to the woman. When the evening was finished, Rob knew he wanted to marry Anna. He made plans to see her the next day and the next. By the end of the week, he shared his feelings with her.

"Marry me," he told her, taking her hands in his own. "Leave this lonely place and come back with me to the states."

Anna smiled, tears in her eyes, and agreed. When she shared the news with her father, he seemed utterly unemotional.

"Be gone, then," he told her, waving her off with a brush of his hand. "But if you marry the American, then don't bother coming back here ever again."

Anna was saddened but not surprised by her father's response. Later that week she and Rob left for the United States.

Rob's family could hardly believe what had happened. Rob had left for vacation a confirmed bachelor and returned two weeks later engaged to a beautiful young woman. But when they learned that she was one of the children Rob had rescued that summer at the beach, they were stunned.

Rob and Anna married and in the next few years had a little girl, Amy, who had golden hair and sea-blue eyes like her mother. People who knew the couple often talked about the love they shared, marveling at the way they seemed almost a part of each other.

"Don't you ever fight with each other or have a bad day?" Andy asked Rob once.

But Rob shook his head. "I was thirty-five when I met her," he said. "I guess I'm just making up for lost time. I love her like no one in my life, Andy. In many ways it's like a miracle."

"What's that?"

"Who would have thought? That all those years ago I was saving that little girl to be my very own some day. It's really nothing short of a miracle."

# TWO

# Love Beyond

*L*ife was just beginning to fall into place for twenty-four-year-old Christine Skubish in the spring of 1994. She had a wonderful relationship with her father and had reached a point where she was living out the things he'd taught her. She had completed her education at California Paralegal School in Northern California and was the mother of a beautiful three-year-old boy, Nikky. But most of all, after years of uncertainty, she had worked things out with Jay.

Christine met John Joseph Conn—Jay—when the two were thirteen and attending Kramer Middle School in Placentia, California. Immediately they were fast friends.

Jay was Christine's first crush, a clean-cut surfer boy with sandy-blond hair and a perpetual tan. He lived down the street from Christine and was her friend through difficult years of transition in both their lives. Together they did homework, took long walks, and eventually shared their first kiss. There was no separating them, and Christine's father believed he understood.

"I know what you share with Jay," he once told Christine. She was his oldest child and the two had always been close. Christine knew she had an ally in her father, and she listened intently as he spoke.

"Once in a while two people meet and there is something so unique about what they share that neither will ever be the same again," he told her that day. "Even if you go your separate ways one day, you'll never forget him, honey."

Christine smiled at her father's words. "But I'm not going away. I'm going to stay right here, and one day I'll marry Jay. Wait and see."

Larry Skubish laughed. "Well, I'm one father who won't be surprised when the day comes."

Instead, the separation between Christine and Jay was only months away. Larry was with the Army, and in 1985 he was transferred to a base near Portage Township, Indiana, where his family had been anchored for years. Every summer Christine and her brother had spent a month or more with their cousins in Indiana, and they knew the area as if it were a second home. But the idea of leaving Jay was heartbreaking for Christine.

"Promise me you won't forget me," Jay told her one evening when the two were sitting outside her house in the days before she moved. By that time her parents had separated and her mother was making plans to move to Northern California with Christine's brother. Throughout the heartbreak of those times Jay had always been there for Christine, listening to her and helping her see through the pain. She knew as she sat beside him that night that she would do whatever was necessary to remain close to him.

"Ah, Jay." She hugged him tight. "I could never forget you. I'll write and we'll visit in the summertime. Nothing will change; you'll see."

Childhood promises are easily forgotten in the course of busy high school years, but Christine and Jay remained in contact. Although they dated other people, they continued to write to each other and twice shared visits during the summer months.

"You don't mind, do you, Dad?" Christine said as she planned one of the trips back to Southern California. "I'll miss you, but I really want to see Jay."

"Honey, you know how I feel about Jay. He's a class act, a great kid. And what you two have is something some people never have in a lifetime."

The break in this seemingly solid friendship came after they graduated from their separate high schools. Jay made plans to attend college in Southern California, while Christine, a bright girl with good grades and leadership qualities, was accepted at Purdue University in Indiana.

"I thought we'd be together after we graduated," Jay protested when he heard about her decision. "This Purdue thing is going to mess everything up."

But Christine was adamant. She had grown independent since her days of living down the street from Jay, and she wanted to experience university life without being tied to a serious relationship. "We have the rest of our lives to spend together, Jay. You're my best friend and I still love you. But I need to do this for me."

"When you're ready, I'll be here, Chrissy," he told her then. "Waiting for you."

For the next several years, Christine and Jay spoke only on occasion. They both dated other people; in fact, Christine became seriously involved with a young man she met at Purdue. Although she still thought about Jay, she didn't imagine they would ever find their way back into each others' lives again.

Then, just before completing her sophomore year at Purdue, Christine and her boyfriend broke off their relationship. She was heartbroken but certain that they'd done the right thing. The young man was not the kind of person she wanted to marry, and despite the pain of ending the relationship, she felt an inner peace. Suddenly she wanted to see Jay more than anything else. He had known her since she was a child and certainly he would be there for her now. She took money from her savings account and purchased a plane ticket. Then she called Jay.

"Jay? It's me, Chrissy. I'm coming home."

Jay was stunned. He knew she was busy at Purdue and that she was seeing someone quite seriously. He figured she'd be married next time he heard from her.

"I can't believe it. What happened?"

"We broke up. I'm through with school for the summer and I miss you so much. Can I see you, Jay? Please?"

She was rambling and Jay began to laugh. He, too, had dated in the past two years, but there was no one serious. He pictured Christine's soft blond hair and her warm brown eyes. Of course she could see him. His voice was soft when he finally answered. "I'm here Chrissy. Still waiting."

They shared a storybook summer—going to the beach, holding hands while they walked through their old neighborhood, and staying up late each night at Jay's parents' house catching up on the past few years. The two were inseparable, and after only four weeks Christine notified her father that she had made a change in plans. She would not be returning to Purdue University that fall. Instead, she wanted to enroll in paralegal school in Northern California.

"I can be near Mom that way, Dad. What do you think?"

"And closer to Jay," he said quietly. "Am I right?"

"Yes, Daddy. I love him. I can't stand being so far away from him."

Larry knew that his daughter would have done brilliantly had she finished at Purdue, but he had known from the beginning how much Jay meant to her. "You have my blessing, honey. You know best about what will make you happy."

Christine's plan was to leave Placentia at summer's end and travel to Northern California to prepare for her coursework at California Paralegal.

Instead, just before the end of summer, Christine found out she was pregnant. Devastated and confused by what her future would hold, she abruptly returned to Indiana to be with her father and said nothing of her pregnancy to Jay.

"I don't understand," he told her as she packed her bags. "What did I do? Why won't you talk to me?"

But Christine just shook her head. "It's not you, it's me," she told him, shunning his attempts to hold her. "We're moving too fast and I need time to think."

"But I thought you wanted to get your paralegal training and get married. What's happening to us, Chrissy?"

Christine only shook her head and pulled away. She had no idea how she was going to break the news to her father about her pregnancy, but she could not fathom getting married so soon and having a child all within the next year. She was certain of one thing, however. She would not consider having an abortion. She and Jay had made a mistake and now she was pregnant and would have to accept the consequences. But Christine believed with all her heart that the tiny baby she carried had a right to live. And since the child was a part of Jay, she knew she could never bear to give it up for adoption. She determined to return to Indiana, talk to her father first, and then break the news to Jay.

Instead, Christine's strange behavior turned Jay away. After she left for Indiana, he stopped calling her and resumed his previous dating life. He was hurt and believed she had abandoned him. Although he ached for her every day, he had decided to go on with his life.

Assuming that Jay no longer cared about her, and confused about what to do next, Christine did not force the issue of their broken relationship. She refused to tell Jay that he was about to be a father. When Nikky Anthony Skubish was born in January of 1991, Jay had no idea.

At about that time Christine moved to Northern California as she had planned and enrolled in the paralegal school. For the next two years she made no effort to contact Jay and went about getting her education.

Then, one night in 1993 shortly after Nikky's birthday, Christine was sorting through old photographs when she came upon one that showed her with Jay as young teenagers. Tears filled her eyes, and she wondered at her own stubborn attitude which had driven a wedge between them. Now, with her coursework at paralegal school finished, she could complete her education through correspondence from anywhere in the country. She thought about Jay and wondered what he might be doing, whether he had missed her as she had missed him. Suddenly nothing could stop her, and she impulsively picked up the telephone.

"Jay?" Christine's voice was tentative this time. She knew nothing of what he might be doing, who he might be seeing, only that she needed to hear his voice.

"Chrissy? Where are you?"

She filled him in briefly about her move to Northern California and explained that she was close to completing school and was free to finish the remainder of her degree work by mail.

"I think we need to see you, Jay," she said softly.

"Who's 'we'?" Jay asked.

"We," she paused a moment. "Your son and I."

The first meeting between Christine and Jay and Nikky was filled with tears. Jay held Nikky and kissed him and shook his head at Christine. "You should have told me, Chris. We've lost so much time."

"I'm sorry," she said, burying her head in his shoulder. "At first I didn't know how to tell you, and then it seemed like you just wrote me off. Will you forgive me?"

Jay nodded, gently turning her face so that he could see her eyes. "I told you I'd wait for you, Chrissy, and I'm still here. But this time I'm not letting either of you go."

Christine and Nikky moved to Placentia a few weeks later to be near Jay, and in the spring of 1994 the couple made plans to get married. But first they would caravan up north to get the rest of Christine's things out of storage and allow her to turn in her final project and meet with her instructors at the paralegal school. She only had an internship in Southern California to complete, and then she would be ready to begin working. Before taking the trip, Christine wrote this letter to her father in Indiana:

Dear Dad . . . and the rest of the Skubish crew! As promised, here are the pictures of Nikky. I hope you like them. But as they say, pictures rarely do justice to the real thing. God willing, I'll find a way to fly out for a week or two soon.

Well, we are all healthy here in every sense of the word, meaning body and mind and spirit. And if I'm not, I'm trying to be.

I always hated it whenever I'd fall because I always fall so hard and healing takes time. But I learned long ago that interference on my part always only frazzles things up.

I know that it is wise that once you've placed your life in God's hands it is best to leave it there. There are things that I feel with subtle strength. I can't say I know, only what I feel. I am aware that there is a time and place for everything, and life's meetings, experiences, and challenges are all at some point tied to each other.

For I do believe there comes a time when everything just falls in line. We live and learn from our mistakes, and the deepest wounds are healed by faith.

I am facing a new and unexplored journey, and it is scary, as always. But I will rise to the road now before me with caution, but will be passionate as always in spirit and promise to forever keep my eyes on Jesus.

I love you each one, and think of you often. Take care of yourselves and remember us in your prayers as we will also do for you. Always, Chris and Nikky.

P.S. Daddy, please place this letter in my file for future reference. You never know, I may just wish to put it in my book someday. Thanks.

Jay and Christine's trip began the last week of May; by May 31, they had completed everything they'd set out to do. On that day Jay began the drive back to Placentia since he had to return to work, and Christine—who was driving with Nikky in her own car—made plans to visit a close girlfriend for a few days on the way home. She had planned to be back in Placentia by June 6—the day after Jay's birthday.

Christine left her friend's house in Carson City, Nevada, at just after midnight on June 6, and by two o'clock that morning was seen getting gasoline at a station near U.S. 50, fifty miles east of Sacramento. Then she and Nikky disappeared.

When Jay did not hear from Christine that day or the next, he began to worry. Still, he figured she might have decided to stay a few extra days since she would not likely return to Northern California for some time. He did not know Christine's friend's phone number and did not call to check on her, but by early June 9, Jay was worried sick and he called Christine's father.

Larry knew the girlfriend Christine had been visiting, and after talking with Jay he became deeply worried. He immediately called and learned that Christine had left early on June 6. Moving as quickly as possible, Jay filed a missing person's report, and Larry contacted California Highway Patrol officers. The CHP instantly began searching Highway 50 along the route that Christine would have taken had she been heading back to Placentia.

That particular stretch of Highway 50 is in an extremely remote area, and officers devoted hundreds of man-hours to checking the heavily wooded canyons and mountain areas that surround that section of the roadway. There was no sign of Christine, Nikky, or the car they'd been traveling in—a red Hyundai two-door hatchback—and no break in the case until the next day, June 10. Christine had been missing almost four days.

That morning CHP officers received a report from a motorist that there had been a woman with long hair running naked along U.S. 50 some forty miles away from the area where Christine was last seen getting gasoline. Since that section is so remote, county police checked into the report but did not find anyone where the motorist had reported seeing the woman.

Undaunted, the motorist contacted the CHP once again and when she was told that officers had found no sign of the naked woman, she insisted that she drive with the officers to the section of highway where she'd seen the woman running back and forth.

"Maybe she wasn't naked, but she seemed strange-looking, like she was all one color and without clothing," the woman told the officers.

In addition to the CHP, sheriff's deputies followed along behind to

check out the motorist's lead. Together they looked for signs of someone along the roadway, wondering if there was a connection between
the sighting and the missing young woman who had traveled through
the same area at about the time of her disappearance. Still they found
nothing.

The next day, June 11, the two sheriff's deputies returned to the
same section of roadway, still puzzled by the separate incidents. If the
report of a naked woman alongside the road was in fact the missing
woman, time was running out in which to help her. They wanted to
do everything they could.

This time the deputies saw something they hadn't seen before. Although other officers had combed the area and not found anything
unusual, at 6:30 A.M. the deputies spotted a child's tennis shoe along
the side of the road. The deputies exchanged a curious look and
climbed out of their patrol car. They walked toward the shoe and
one officer picked it up. After they examined it, they looked down
the side of a steep embankment through a dense growth of pine trees.
There they spotted Christine Skubish's red Hyundai.

The officers scrambled down the embankment only to determine
that Christine was dead. Her child also appeared lifeless and was
wearing only his pajamas, but he was curled up beside his mother,
still clinging to her body.

"Hey, can you hear me?" one of the deputies yelled, his voice ech-
oing in the canyon. Suddenly the child lifted his head and began to
cry.

Nikky Skubish was taken to the Intensive Care Unit at Sacramento
Medical Center, suffering from severe dehydration, vitamin defi-
ciency, and minor cuts and abrasions.

That night Larry Skubish was watching a television news program,
when he saw a story about the incident. He called Jay, and both men
immediately booked flights for Sacramento.

When they met at the hospital, Jay broke down in Larry's arms.
"Is it true, Larry? Is she really gone?"

Larry nodded, holding tightly to Jay.

"Things were finally coming together. We were going to get married and be a family. I told her I'd wait for her forever and . . . what am I going to do now, Larry? How can I go on without her?"

The men cried together, and finally Larry said, "You still have your son, Jay. He needs you now more than ever."

Jay nodded and drew in a deep breath. Then he walked down the hospital corridor to Nikky's room, and for the next several days rarely left the little boy's side.

In the days that followed the discovery of Christine's car, the police determined several things. It seemed that Christine must have fallen asleep while she was driving, since there were no skid marks on the road where she went over the embankment. Nikky had somehow survived five days in the wilderness without either food or water. The police also learned that Christine had broken her neck upon the initial impact of the accident, and that she had most likely died within several hours.

"You know that if she had any waking moments after the accident, she spent them praying for Nikky," Larry told Jay one day when they were both in the child's hospital room.

"She prayed whenever she was in trouble," Jay said, staring out the window. "But what about that woman running along the freeway?" He turned toward Larry again. "Doesn't that seem strange to you? Like somehow Christine was still looking out for Nikky?"

Both men had thoroughly discussed the report of a woman running alongside the freeway naked. Was it possible that after she died, Christine was able to alert a passerby to the fact that her son was still alive and needed help?

The men also wondered about the tennis shoe found alongside the roadway. Police determined later that it was not Nikky's shoe, and yet it sat on the highway at the exact point where the child lay clinging to his dead mother awaiting help. Had the shoe not been there, authorities would not have found Christine's car until late that summer when forest crews work on the road.

While Nikky was still in the hospital, Jay would try gently asking his son what happened. Normally the child would cling to his father and cry for his mother. But one time Jay told Nikky that people had been very worried about him, and that they had looked very hard to find him. The child thought a moment and then said something both Jay and Larry will always remember.

"I know. They told me you were looking for me."

Jay paused a moment. "Who told you, Nikky?"

"The angels," the boy said firmly as he reached for his father's hand. "After the tree hit Mommy, we couldn't wake her up. And then they said you were looking for me and that someone was going to find me. They said everything would be okay."

Months after the accident Nikky's angels have been proved right. Although he still misses his mother, he has gotten even closer to his father. And as for Jay, he still feels Christine's presence in his life every day. Especially when he looks into the eyes of Nikky, a child who would be dead but for the efforts his mother made to save his life—even after hers had been taken from her.

# THREE

# A Special Friend

$\mathcal{B}$ob and Sue Nobles had been married nearly five years, when they learned in 1979 that Sue was pregnant. Since they had been trying to have a baby for several years and were both in their late thirties, they were thrilled with the news.

"I hope it's a girl," Bob told Sue, a pretty woman with dark hair and green eyes. "And I hope she looks just like you."

Sue smiled and wondered how she would ever survive the nine-month wait until she could hold their baby in her arms.

"I can't believe it's finally happening," she said. "And you know, I really don't care if it's a girl or boy! I just hope our child is healthy."

Bob placed an arm casually across Sue's shoulders. "Don't worry, honey," he said. "Everything will be fine."

When Nicolette Jane Nobles—Coley—was born in

March 1980, everything seemed perfect. Their tiny daughter was beautiful with a head full of dark curls and delicately etched features. But after several months Bob and Sue began to notice that Coley was not responding to sounds as she should be. They discussed their fears with Coley's pediatrician, but he was quick to offer reassurance.

"Some babies take longer to be noticeably affected by sounds," he said. "And others may have immature eardrums. Either way it's too early to tell, so it's best not to worry at this point."

Bob and Sue tried to feel optimistic about Coley's hearing, but as the months passed, they experimented on their own. Everything they tried seemed to prove that although Coley would smile and cast expressive glances in their direction, she was unable to hear them. At times the couple would get on either side of her and make sudden noises in an attempt to startle her or capture her attention. Other times they would bang pots and pans and noisy kitchen utensils, watching for her reaction. Not once did she seem to hear the sounds around her.

By the time Coley was one year old, Bob and Sue began to notice another difference between her and other children her age. She was silent. Whereas children her age whom they might see in the supermarket or at church would coo or say simple words, Coley rarely uttered any sound at all.

Finally the parents arranged an appointment with a specialist who was able to confirm their fears. Coley had been born deaf and would remain so for the rest of her life. On the drive home from the doctor's office, Coley sat in the back seat playing with a stuffed animal, while Bob and Sue held hands and shared their grief over the news.

"I want so much for her to be like the other kids," Sue said, wiping the tears from her cheeks. "It just isn't fair. She's such a beautiful girl, and now she's going to be different from her peers for the rest of her life."

Bob stared straight ahead, keeping his eyes on the road. "I keep thinking that she'll never hear me tell her how much I love her." He glanced at his wife. "She'll never hear the sound of our voices."

Sue and Bob vowed that day always to be strong for Coley and to expect only the best from her in every situation. They would never allow her to use her deafness as an excuse for doing anything less than she was capable of. They agreed to learn sign language and to teach Coley as soon as possible. And they would also teach her to read lips so that she would have an easier time fitting in with other children in a school setting. They knew there would be times of disappointment and setbacks, but they promised to lean on each other and give Coley the best life possible despite her handicap.

As the years passed, the Nobles lived up to their promise. While she was still a toddler, Coley learned to speak to her parents in sign language, and soon she was making progress in her ability to read lips.

Teaching Coley to make friends with hearing children proved to be the most difficult aspect of helping her learn to live with her deafness. As a toddler, Coley was introduced to lots of children her age but never seemed to fit in with them. Once while at the park, she tried to talk in sign language to a young girl who was obviously able to hear.

"Want to play with my dolly?" Coley signed quickly.

The child gave Coley a blank stare and looked at her hands. "Why are you moving your hands like that?" the girl asked out loud.

Coley looked at the girl curiously, unable to understand her lip movement, and then once again used sign language to ask the girl if she wanted to play. This time the child began to laugh at Coley, assuming that Coley was playing some kind of game.

But the girl's laughter confused Coley, and she began to cry, turning and running to where her mother sat painfully watching the exchange from a nearby park bench.

"It's all right," Sue signed to her daughter, taking her into her arms. "She wants to be your friend, honey, she just didn't understand you."

"She didn't like me," Coley signed back to her mother. Sue's heart went out to her daughter, whose tiny spirit seemed crushed by the encounter.

"No, Coley," Sue signed in return. "She liked you a lot. She just didn't understand you."

But Coley seemed frightened, and Sue thought she knew why. For the first time the little girl understood that she was different from other children, and the thought must have terrified her. After that she refused to make any attempt to communicate with other children. She would play near them and smile at them, but she always remained an outsider.

"What are we going to do, Bob?" a weary Sue complained one night. "I've tried to help her make friends with other children, but she's afraid to make an effort, afraid they won't like her."

"Give it time, honey," Bob said, sitting down at the table across from his wife. "She has a lot of adjusting to do, and she's come so far in such a few years. She'll have friends one day."

Susan was quiet for a moment. "Bob," she finally said softly. "Have you prayed about it, I mean about this friendship thing?"

Bob looked sad as he answered. "Not really. I mean, of course I've prayed for Coley. I've prayed for her since the day she was born. But I haven't really asked God to send her a special friend, if that's what you mean."

Sue nodded. "Well, let's do it. Let's pray together and then let's keep praying every day that God will love Coley enough to send her a special friend."

Bob reached across the table and took Sue's hands. Together they bowed their heads and prayed. Quietly, sincerely, they asked that Coley be watched over and cared for and that God would find it in His heart to give Coley a special friend.

After that, Bob and Sue prayed daily for Coley and the friend she might one day have. Later that year Coley turned five and began attending a school for children with special needs. Academically she excelled far beyond her parents' dreams, but she still struggled socially.

One day she came home with her head high and, much as an adult would, asked her mother to sit with her on the couch and talk for a while.

"I'm deaf, right, Mommy?" she signed.

Sue paused a moment. They had dealt with Coley's deafness since the day she was diagnosed, but they had never discussed with her exactly what made her different from other children. "Yes, Cole," Sue moved her hands gently, her eyes searching those of her daughter's. "You were born without the ability to hear sound."

"And that makes me different, right, Mommy?" she asked.

Sue sighed, feeling the tears well up in her eyes. "Yes, honey. Most children can hear sounds. But there are many children who were born deaf, just like you."

"Even though I'm deaf, I'm still smart and I'm still pretty, and I'm still special. Isn't that right, Mommy?" Coley's eyes shone as she asked the question, and Sue struggled to keep from crying. "And God still loves me, right?"

"Of course, Coley, God loves you very much. You are very special and beautiful and very wonderful and being deaf will never change that."

Coley thought for a moment. Then her hands began to move once again. "It's time for me to have a friend, Mommy . . . But I want a friend who's deaf like me. Is that okay?"

Sue pulled her daughter close and wrapped her arms around her, stroking her silky dark curls. "I've been asking God to send you a special friend, Coley. Maybe that's what He has in mind. A special friend who is deaf like you. We'll just have to wait and see."

The year ran its course, and although Coley made more of an attempt with the other children than she had in the past none of her classmates was deaf, and she finished her first year of school without a close friend.

A few months before her sixth birthday, Coley stumbled upon a picture of a white Persian kitten in one of her storybooks. She was immediately and completely enamored with the kitten and ran to show her mother the picture.

"Mommy, can I please have a kitten like that for my birthday? Please?" Coley was so animated that Sue had to calm her down before her daughter would show her the picture in the book.

"That's a Persian kitten, Coley," Sue said as she looked at the picture. "You want a kitten like that?"

"Yes, yes, yes," Coley signed quickly. "Please, Mommy," she pleaded.

Later that night Sue and Bob discussed the idea of getting a kitten for Coley's birthday.

"She's always loved her stuffed animals," Sue said as she presented the idea. "Maybe that's just what she needs right now. A pet of her own."

"But a white Persian kitten?" Bob asked. "They cost hundreds of dollars, Sue. You know we can't afford that."

Bob was a teacher and Sue worked part-time at Coley's school. With the cost of their daughter's special education, they were barely able to scrape enough money together to meet their monthly needs.

"I know," Sue said. "But maybe we could save for the next few weeks and watch the advertisements in the newspaper. Maybe there'll be one for sale that we can afford."

Bob thought a moment and sighed. "All right, let's try it. But don't say anything to Coley about it. I'd hate to get her hopes up."

For the next seven weeks Sue scanned the newspapers for white Persian kittens and found none for sale. Finally, a few days before Coley's birthday, she and Bob decided they had barely saved enough money to purchase such a kitten if only they could find one.

On the morning of Coley's birthday, while the little girl was still sleeping, Sue opened the newspaper and pored over the classified advertisements. Suddenly she gasped out loud.

"Bob! They're here. The kittens. Persian kittens, white, $200. Can you believe it! That's where we're going to get Coley's kitten."

When the child woke up, they gave her a card and her favorite pancake breakfast and told her that they were going to take her that afternoon to buy a white Persian kitten. Coley's mouth flew open and her eyes grew wide.

"Oh, thank you, thank you," she signed repeatedly. "When do we get him?"

Sue walked over to the phone as she signed, "Let's call them right now."

While Coley waited impatiently watching her mother, Sue dialed the number that had been listed in the advertisement.

"Yes," she said when someone answered the phone. "I'm calling about the white Persian kittens."

On the other line Maria Amado smiled. "Oh, yes," she said. "We have a few left and they're both the same, white kittens with gray markings."

"Oh." Sue's face fell in disappointment, and Coley watched closely, trying to read her mother's lips. "We were looking for one that is completely white. It's for my daughter's birthday."

"I see," Maria said. "Well, there is one kitten that's completely white. I'll sell her to you for fifty dollars instead of the two hundred dollars if you're interested."

"I don't understand," Sue said, her face puzzled.

"Well," Maria paused, "the kitten is deaf. I'm not sure if I'll be able to sell her."

Sue began to shake, and for a moment she was unable to speak. Aware that something strange was happening, Coley began signing frantically. "What, Mommy? What is it?"

"Are you still there?" Maria asked, breaking the silence.

"Yes! Um, just a minute," Sue said. She turned toward her daughter and set the receiver down on the counter. Stooping to Coley's level, she quickly began moving her hands. "The kitten is a girl kitten, and it's deaf, Coley. A deaf white Persian kitten."

Coley's face lit up as Sue had never seen it do before. "That's my kitten, Mommy!" she said. "Let's go get her."

Within an hour, Sue, Bob, and Coley arrived at Maria's house. Maria explained how the other kittens would run and hide when she ran the vacuum, but the white kitten seemed unaffected by the noise. Bob and Sue exchanged a knowing glance, remembering the days when they were trying to figure out what was wrong with Coley.

"Eventually I had the kitten checked by a veterinarian, and she told us the poor little thing was deaf," Maria told them.

Sue held the kitten and handed him to Coley. Her hands began to move. "See, Coley. She's perfect and beautiful and special, just like the other kittens. The only difference is she can't hear."

Coley smiled, snuggling her face up close to the kitten's. Then she looked at her mother and with her free hand said, "Let's take her home, Mommy."

Over the next few weeks there was no separating Coley and her tiny deaf kitten. Every afternoon she would set the kitten in front of her on her bed and use sign language to talk to her. One day Sue watched, trying to understand what Coley was telling the kitten.

"It's okay, Kitty," Coley said, her little hands moving slowly so her kitten could understand. "You don't have to be afraid or lonely anymore because now there's two deaf people in our family. We'll be best friends forever."

Sue walked into the room slowly and sat down next to Coley. "You love her don't you, Cole?" she signed to her daughter.

"Yes, Mommy. She and I are both special because we're both deaf." Coley looked at her kitten, whose soft white face was tilted curiously as she watched Coley's fingers move. Coley looked back at her mother. "She doesn't understand sign language yet, but when she gets older she will. And then it will be easier for her to talk with me."

Coley reached for the kitten and held her close. "Thank you for praying, Mommy. God heard your prayers," she signed. "He gave me a friend who was born deaf just like me."

"Yes, Cole," Sue smiled. "I was just thinking that. God definitely heard our prayers."

# FOUR

# Unseen Hands

*I*t was Christmas 1988, and the Moffitt family had shared a wonderful holiday together at their home in central Arizona. In addition to their presents, the family felt thankful for things that could not be wrapped and placed under a tree. Brian was very happy in his job as a local resort manager, and Ann was four months pregnant with their third child. Their first two, Erica, five, and Brianna, four, were healthy and happy and the source of much joy. In fact, the Moffitt family couldn't have been happier.

After celebrating Christmas at home that year, the family climbed into their Toyota Landcruiser and headed for Payson, Arizona—a small town about ninety minutes away. Since Brian's parents lived in Payson, he knew the roads well and enjoyed the scenic drive.

"It never gets old, does it?" Brian asked his wife, reaching over to hold her hand as they climbed toward

Payson. "God sure knows how to make things beautiful."

Ann smiled and placed his hand on her pregnant abdomen. "He sure does."

The visit with Brian's parents was fun-filled and full of the laughter of Erica and Brianna, but after two days it was time to return home. A light snow was falling as they packed up the Landcruiser and said their goodbyes.

"I hate to drive in snow," Ann said as they climbed in and buckled their seat belts.

"I know," Brian said calmly. "But you're not driving. I am. And I'm perfectly fine with it. Just say a prayer that we get home safely."

Ann nodded and silently asked God to guard their car as they drove home. That done, she did her best not to worry. She stared out her window and admitted that the snow was certainly beautiful. It fell gently and looked like freshly sifted powdered sugar on the ground.

Highway 260, the road that leads from Payson to the Verde Valley where the Moffitts lived, is a two-lane road with an occasional passing lane. From Brian's parents' house the highway climbs slightly until it reaches the small towns of Strawberry, and Pine and then it continues downhill for nearly forty minutes until leveling out in the Verde Valley.

Although traffic was light that morning, Brian drove slowly and carefully, aware that there were patches of ice under the snow-covered road. Most of the cars on the road had snow chains on their tires, and though the Moffitts did not, they felt secure in four-wheel drive and that the Landcruiser had heavy-duty snow tires.

Still, Brian sensed his wife's fears as they began the section of highway that was nearly straight downhill. He glanced at his wife and smiled warmly. "Honey, it'll be okay. Don't worry."

"I know, I know," Ann said. "I just wish we were home, that's all."

"We'll be home soon. Try to relax."

Ann nodded, but she could feel a tension throughout her body. The road seemed especially slippery, despite the fact that Brian was driving in a low gear.

Just as the highway became steep, Brian shifted into yet a lower gear just to be sure they wouldn't lose traction. Suddenly the back of the Landcruiser began fishtailing across the road, swinging from one side of the highway to the other. Brian struggled to correct the truck's steering, but as he turned the wheel, he could feel that it was having no effect on the tires. Suddenly he knew what had happened. The vehicle was in a slide with the tires completely detached from the road.

At that instant the Landcruiser swung sharply toward oncoming traffic, sending the vehicle spinning in a complete circle.

"Oh, Jesus!" Ann screamed, grabbing on to the dashboard. "In the name of Jesus, please stop!"

The Landcruiser stopped spinning and began a fast sideways slide toward the cliff that buttressed the edge of the highway. If the vehicle slid off the road, Brian and Ann knew they would probably be killed since the fall would send them several hundred feet down the hill along rough terrain.

"Jesus, please help us!" Ann screamed again. But deep in her heart she knew they were traveling far too fast and she felt certain that they were going over the edge.

Then just before the drop-off, the Landcruiser slammed to a sudden stop. One of the girls had taken off her seat belt and the harsh jolt sent the child flying across the car into the window.

For a moment there was silence.

Brian looked at his wife in shock, not believing that they had avoided going over the edge of the highway. He was amazed that they were alive.

"Girls, are you okay?" he asked, turning around.

"Yes, Daddy," came a small voice. "I hit my head, but I'm okay."

Relieved, Brian stared at his wife once more. "We must have hit a tree stump or a boulder or something," he said.

"Maybe a guardrail," Ann added.

Still shaky from the closeness of what could have been a deadly car accident, Brian climbed out of the truck. He walked around the vehicle to the side that was not parallel with the cliff. There was nothing in between the Landcruiser and the sheer drop.

"Ann, come here!" Brian said loudly. "Come see this."

Ann opened her door and slid carefully onto the small space between the vehicle and the side of the cliff. "What did we hit?" she asked.

"That's just it. We didn't hit anything. There's not a rock or a piece of wood, no guardrail. Nothing. The truck just stopped for no reason at all."

Ann examined the edge of the road and saw that Brian was right. The truck had been sliding at more than ten-miles-per-hour and had suddenly stopped for no explainable reason. Together they looked down the jagged, rocky mountainside and shuddered at the thought of what might have happened.

"Ann, it's like the hand of God just reached out and stopped us from going over the mountainside."

Quietly Ann remembered her desperate plea for Jesus to help them. She reached over and circled her arms around her husband's waist, resting her head on his chest. "With all my heart I believe you're right. We were stopped by the hand of God. It must have been a miracle."

FIVE

# A Football Hero in Street Clothes

Shervonne Shuler knew she wouldn't be gone for long. She had a few errands to run and would come right home to spend the day with her eighteen-month-old son, Lydell. On afternoons like that one, Shervonne was thankful her uncle lived near her fourth-floor Baltimore apartment. Because that summer day, like many others before it, he had agreed to stay with Lydell while she took care of her business.

However, Shervonne had been gone little more than an hour when her uncle lost track of the small boy, a curious child with a tendency to explore his surroundings. Wandering through the apartment, Lydell wound up in a bedroom in which a screenless window was open. He toddled toward it and peered precariously forty feet down to the street below. Then he smiled and began to climb.

Across the street Donald Hughes, a thirty-year-old labor crew leader with Baltimore's Parks and Recreation Department, heard commotion and glanced toward the apartment complex. Suddenly he realized that people all around him were pointing to a small boy perched on the window ledge. There was nothing between the child and the pavement and at any moment the boy—with his precarious toddler's footing—might fall to a certain death.

"Oh, my God!" Shervonne screamed, running frantically toward the apartment and then freezing in terror. She had returned from her errands only to find her son sitting on the window ledge looking at the street below. "That's my baby!"

Donald's head swiveled around; he saw that none of those who had noticed the child was making a move to help him. At that instant he heard a voice tell him to get beneath the child. *Now.* Immediately Donald began moving quickly and cautiously toward a spot on the street just under where the child was moving along the window ledge. Shervonne Shuler saw the strange man make his way through the crowd, but she was riveted to Lydell, praying that her baby would not fall. What she didn't know was that no one could have been more prepared to help her son than Donald Hughes.

Raised in Baltimore, Donald had been an athlete from the moment he could walk. He played in a number of sports but was especially talented at baseball and football. As Donald began his high school athletic career, it became apparent that if he was to advance beyond that level in any one sport, it would be football. On the football field Donald Hughes was one of the best wide receivers in the state. In his junior year at Lake Clifton High School, he helped lead the team to the state championship, reeling in dozens of catches and scoring in nearly every game. His senior year proved to hold more of the same, and Lake Clifton High finished second in the state.

About that time letters began pouring in inviting Donald—a tall, muscular boy with incredible foot speed—to accept a scholarship and play football on the collegiate level.

"I have a choice to make, Mama," he told his mother one day that year. Donald was the tenth child in a family with eleven brothers and sisters, and he knew he was expected to make money as soon as he was old enough to do so. "I need to know if I should work or go to school and play ball. And I just can't decide."

His mother knew that a college scholarship was a once-in-a-lifetime chance, and although she did not know how she would help support her son, she encouraged him to get his degree. In the end Donald was offered a prestigious job with the city's parks department, and he chose to pursue a career rather than higher education.

"I've made my decision, Mama," he told her one afternoon. "I've got a good job and I'm going to stick with it. I think it's the right thing to do."

"Well, son," she told him. "You know best. Besides, your football years were not a waste. You never know when you might have a chance to be involved in sports again, and you'll always be thankful you did so well when you were in high school."

Donald's mother's words proved to be full of wisdom. Ten years later Donald was at his mother's house when an explosion ripped through the house across the street, sending it into flames. Donald raced to the window and watched as the man who lived in the house struggled outside, overcome by smoke.

"Where are the children?" Donald muttered aloud, watching closely for any sign of the man's five children. "Come on," he whispered. "Get out of there."

Minutes later, when there was still no sign of the children, and the father was being attended by firemen and paramedics, Donald called on his still-blazing foot speed and raced across the street. Running behind the house he tried the back door, which led to the basement. It was sealed shut.

"I could hear something crackling, like it was about to explode," Donald told his family later. "I knew they were in big trouble."

Unconcerned with the danger to himself, Donald kicked the back door of the house in and raced down the basement steps. There were the five children and two other adults, huddled together alongside a gas furnace, which was sputtering and sparking from the heat on the first floor of the house.

"Come on!" he shouted above the roar of fire engines and flames. "Get out! It's going to blow!"

He swept the three youngest children into his arms, cradling them as easily as he had once cradled a football, and motioned for the others to follow him. In a matter of seconds he had succeeded in getting all seven people out of the basement and safely onto the lawn.

Almost at the same instant there was another explosion as the furnace blew up, destroying the basement and setting fire to another three houses.

"You could have been killed, Donald," his sister told him later. "Weren't you even a little scared?"

Donald shook his head. "It was like I knew I was going to get those people out in time. God was with me. I could actually feel him leading me there and helping me with those little kids."

The incident had happened two years earlier, and now, as he moved closer to the apartment building where the toddler was perched on the window ledge, Donald again felt God's presence.

"Move slowly," he told himself. "The timing must be perfect."

At that instant the child moved suddenly and toppled over the edge of the window, tumbling toward the concrete below. Donald kept his eyes on the child and ran hard and fast, timing himself so that he would arrive just under the little boy. He stretched out his arms and tried to imagine he was making a touchdown catch for the biggest game of his life.

Shervonne watched in horror—to her, everything seemed to be happening in slow motion.

"Please hurry!" she shouted. "He's gonna die!"

Just then Donald reached his arms out a bit farther and caught the child safely in his arms. The weight of the falling toddler caused Donald to lose his balance for a moment, but inches before Lydell would have hit the pavement Donald swept him up and tightly into his arms. All around them, the stunned crowd erupted into applause.

Shervonne, terrified by what she had just witnessed, burst into tears and took her child from Donald's arms.

"She didn't even say thank you," Donald told his mother later. "I guess she was in shock."

"Don't worry about a thank-you," his mother said. "God had you there for a reason, and you saved that child's life. That's all that matters."

But several passersby had seen what had happened, and they notified the local media. That night the story of Donald Hughes's heroic effort made the evening news, and the next day the newspapers ran the story in the front section. Shervonne Shuler read the newspaper account, as she finished, she had tears in her eyes. She contacted the parks and recreation department and thanked Donald profusely for saving her child's life, apologizing for her reaction the day before.

"How did you catch him like that?" she asked. "I thought for sure my baby was going to die right there on the street."

"I played football a long time ago," Donald said humbly. "Wide receiver. I guess I just made myself respond like I had all those years when I played the game. The timing, the catch, everything. It was second nature to me."

"Imagine what would have happened if my baby had fallen some other time, when a football hero in street clothes was nowhere to be seen," she said. "It was a miracle, Mr. Hughes. And I can't thank you enough."

When Shervonne finished talking to Donald, she knew that she must still find some way to repay him for saving Lydell's life. She picked up the phone and dialed the mayor's office. After talking with the mayor's press secretary and telling them what happened, the government set a process in motion.

Later that month Mayor Kurt L. Schmoke presented Donald with a special proclamation honoring his bravery and declaring June 10 Donald Hughes Day in Baltimore, Maryland.

At the press conference Donald was typically humble and refused to take credit for what happened. "It was God looking out for that little boy," he said. "I was only there to help."

# SIX

# A Mysterious Voice

*V*icki, six, and Donna, nine, were sisters who were almost inseparable. One of their favorite ways to spend a day was visiting their neighbor, Judi Sharp, and the girls did so as often as possible. The young sisters looked up to twenty-two-year-old Judi, and in many ways tried to be like her.

"Can we go for a walk with you?" one of the girls would say whenever Judi walked around the block.

"Sure." Judi would smile and wave for them to join her. Judi lived at home with her parents, and for years she had enjoyed watching Vicki and Donna grow, and visiting with them. She thought of them almost as younger sisters.

One day Judi needed to drive to Kmart to pick up a few items. Vicki and Donna were visiting and begged to go along.

"Please, Judi," Donna whined. "We're bored and we want to come, too. Please?"

"Yeah, Judi, we'll be good. Come on, let us come."

Judi smiled but shook her head. "No, girls. Not today. I'm only going to the store real fast. I'll pick up the things I need and be right back."

"Judi!" the girls cried in unison.

"The answer's no," she said. "I'm not doing any shopping today, anyway."

But as Judi looked for the car keys and got ready to leave, the girls continued to plead with her. Finally Judi relented.

"Okay you can come along but only if you stay in the car while I run inside," she said firmly. "And you need to ask your mother."

The girls were thrilled with Judi's offer and readily agreed to stay in the car while she picked up the things she needed. Quickly they dashed home, and once they had permission from their mother, they hurried back to Judi's house.

"Is it okay with your mom?" Judi asked as the girls ran up to where she waited by her car.

Vicki and Donna nodded and climbed happily into the backseat of Judi's car. Judi started for the store, but almost as soon as she began driving, the girls began whining again.

"Oh, come on, Judi," they said. "Let us go inside with you. Just this once. We won't bother you. Come on!"

Judi sighed, frustrated that she had agreed to let the girls come with her. "I said no. We made a deal that you'd stay in the car and that's final."

Although the girls continued to try to convince Judi to let them come with her into the store, she remained firm.

"Absolutely not," she said as she parked the car in the Kmart parking lot. "Now stay here. Don't move and I'll be right back."

In less than ten minutes Judi had purchased the things she needed and was returning to the car when she realized the girls were not inside.

"This makes me so mad," she muttered to herself. She knew that the girls were playing a joke on her and were probably hiding near the front of the store somewhere. But she had wanted this to be a quick trip. Now she was frustrated that she would have to spend time looking for the girls, especially after she had ordered them to remain in the car.

"I'll teach them," she thought to herself. She decided to screech out of the parking space as fast as she could so that the girls would think she was leaving them.

"That'll show them what I think about their tricks."

Judi slipped the key into the ignition and revved up the engine. She put the car into first gear; since there were no cars parked in front of her, she planned to drive quickly forward to catch the girls' attention and then speed out of the lot. Then she'd circle back and pick up the girls. After that they would be sure not to do something like this again.

Just as she moved her foot off the brake to begin to go forward, she heard a distinct voice from the back of the car.

"Put the car in reverse," she heard the voice say. "Go backward!"

Immediately Judi obeyed, not knowing why or who had spoken the words, but being unable to deny the voice's power. As she backed up five feet, she suddenly saw Vicki and Donna in front of the car crouched low and giggling. They had been hiding by the front grill of the car the entire time.

A wave of nausea washed over Judi, and she felt her body grow weak. Had she sped forward as she'd planned, she would have run over the girls and killed them both.

Unaware of the danger they had been in, the girls came skipping and giggling toward the car and climbed inside.

"Tricked you, didn't we?" Vicki asked.

Judi slipped the car into park once again and turned around. She was shaking. "That wasn't funny, girls. I told you to stay in the car until I got back."

The girls' faces fell. "Sorry," Donna said softly. "We were just trying to play a joke on you."

Judi was silent the rest of the way home, choosing not to tell the girls about what had nearly happened. Instead, when she got home, she thanked God for the mysterious voice that had caused her to drive in the opposite direction.

"I know I would have killed those girls if I'd driven straight ahead," Judi has said since then. "Wherever the voice came from it was definitely a miracle. If I'd hit those girls, I don't think I could have ever recovered."

# SEVEN

# Heavenly Hindrances

$\mathcal{P}$astor George W. Nubert looked at his watch and took a deep breath. His wife was busy making dinner in the kitchen, and he had ten minutes to get over to the church, light the coal furnace, and be back in time for dinner. Sometimes he felt like he was performing a circus act, twirling plates in the center ring. He had to keep a dozen plates spinning at all times; not one of them could crash to the ground.

But Pastor Nubert didn't mind.

Over the years he had learned to deal with the pressures that came with the ministry. Inevitably his life was surrounded by crises while he was expected to remain calm. Through prayer and discipline, he had discovered one secret to being dependable for those around him. He was organized and punctual beyond reproach. And so although he would rather have sat down and rested for a moment on that cold March evening, he slipped into a jacket and kissed his wife goodbye.

"Be right back," he said. "I need to light the furnace for tonight."

At 6:30 he arrived at West Side Baptist Church on Court Street and LaSalle in the center of the town of Beatrice, Nebraska. The church was something of an anchor, a landmark that everyone in town used when giving directions to outsiders. A stranger could find almost any place in Beatrice as long as they could first find the tall white steeple that marked West Side Baptist Church.

Pastor Nubert made his way inside the church building and climbed down two flights of stairs to the basement. There he lit the coal furnace, making sure it was working before he turned to leave. Next he walked up to the sanctuary where twenty rows of wooden pews made up the seating for Sunday mornings. Glancing at the thermostat, he adjusted it so that the building would be warm in exactly one hour. It was Wednesday. And that year—1950—choir practice was always at 7:30 Wednesday evening.

Glancing once more at his watch, Pastor Nubert quickly left the church and headed home for dinner. He intended to be back at his usual time, no later than 7:15 P.M.

Martha Paul had been the choir director at West Side Baptist Church in Beatrice for sixteen years; as far as she could remember she had never been late to choir practice. Without fail Martha arrived at least fifteen minutes early.

"That way I have time to get the hymnals ready," Martha liked to tell her husband. "I can be sure there's enough sets of choir music, get the lights turned on, and still have time to catch my breath."

Martha had often impressed upon her choir the importance of being on time, reminding them that nothing could be accomplished until every choir member was in his or her place ready to sing.

"A choir is not one or two voices," she would say. "The plan is not to arrive at seven-thirty but to begin singing at seven-thirty."

That particularly cold Wednesday evening in March, 1950, Martha had every intention of being at church as usual by 7:15. This was to be a special practice since it was the last rehearsal before the church performed its annual Easter Cantata. In addition to the fourteen choir members there would be a trio of teenage girls joining them. The trio had been working on a musical piece for the cantata and that night would be the first time the two groups would practice together. Martha knew that as a result there would be music to arrange, seating assignments to work out, and a handful of other details that needed her attention. More than any other Wednesday it was crucial that she be at church especially early that night.

But she had run into a problem.

Her daughter, Marilyn, had been attending junior college and working part-time to pay tuition. That evening she returned home from her afternoon job and gave a weary nod to her mother.

"I'm going to sleep for a while," she had said. "Wake me up for practice."

Marilyn, nineteen, was a pianist and was scheduled to play the piano for the Easter Cantata. Although she had missed choir practice on occasion, her attendance was crucial that evening. So at 6:45 Martha went upstairs to Marilyn's room and leaned inside.

"Wake up!" she announced. "We're leaving in twenty minutes for practice."

Marilyn moaned and rolled over once in bed. Certain that her daughter was awake and would now get up and get ready for practice, Martha returned to the kitchen.

At 7 o'clock, when Marilyn had still not emerged from her room, Martha trudged back up the stairs. The young woman lay on her bed, still sound asleep.

"Marilyn," Martha said loudly, moving toward her daughter. "What's wrong with you? You need to wake up right now and get ready for practice. We have to leave!"

Slowly Marilyn turned over in her bed, obviously still very much asleep. Martha felt the girl's head and found it cool. Marilyn typically had plenty of energy, and Martha couldn't remember the last time she had come home from work only to fall into such a deep sleep.

"Marilyn!" Martha said in a still louder voice. She placed her hand on the girl's shoulder and shook her gently. "Marilyn, wake up!"

Gradually Marilyn's eyes opened, and she narrowed them as she tried to focus on her mother.

"Mama?" she mumbled.

"Marilyn, please wake up! We're going to be late if you don't get up this instant!"

"I'm up, I'm up," Marilyn croaked, sitting up in bed and rubbing her eyes. "I'll be right down."

But fifteen minutes later, at 7:20, Marilyn was still not downstairs, and Martha began to fume.

"Marilyn!" she yelled up the stairs. "Get down here right now or I'll leave without you."

"Mama? Come here, please," Marilyn said, her voice shaky.

Martha marched up the stairs and stomped into her daughter's room. Her car keys were clenched in her fist, and her purse hung from her forearm. She stared at her daughter in frustration. "Are you ready?"

"Mama, I'm sorry, but I fell asleep again," Marilyn said. "I can't understand it. I've never felt like this. It's like I couldn't wake up. Every time I tried to move out of bed, my eyes got heavy and I closed them. The next thing I knew I was asleep."

Martha looked at her watch and sighed loudly. It was 7:25.

"Well, this will really be something," she said. "I ask everyone to be on time for practice, and now my own daughter makes me late." She shook her head. "I know you didn't mean to fall asleep, honey, but if you're feeling okay, can you please get ready quickly?"

Marilyn nodded. "Yeah, I think I'm awake now," she said, shaking her head and opening her eyes wider. "I'll get ready fast as I can."

"All right, then, I'll be downstairs waiting. Please hurry."

Just as Martha turned to leave, the house went pitch black. She groped in front of her until she felt the door frame and steadied herself.

"Great," Martha muttered. "Now we'll really be late."

"What happened?" Marilyn asked.

"Electricity's out," Martha said. "I'll work my way downstairs and see if I can find a candle."

Donna, Rowena, and Sadie had been best friends since grade school. As far back as they could remember, their families had attended West Side Baptist Church, and for years they had sung in the children's choir. Each of the girls loved to perform, and in their private moments they had always dreamed about forming a singing group and being famous one day after they graduated from high school.

Now that they were teenagers, too old for the youth choir and too young for the senior choir, Martha Paul had devised a way to keep them involved. She created the West Side Girls' Trio, a special choir for the three friends in which they could work on musical pieces and perform them occasionally for the congregation.

The number they had been practicing for the Easter Cantata was their most beautiful yet, and none of the girls could wait to present it that evening at practice.

"Let's get there early," Rowena suggested to the others. "That way we can visit a while before practice."

The girls made a plan and arranged for Donna to borrow her father's car and pick Rowena and Sadie up at their homes by 7 o'clock.

That way they could all be at the church by 7:15.

But at 7:10 that evening, after watching out her front window for several seemingly endless minutes, Rowena finally pursed her lips in frustration. Donna was never late when they made plans to do something. She picked up the telephone and dialed her friend's number.

"Hello?" Donna answered.

"Donna? What are you doing? You're supposed to be here to pick me up."

"Rowena, what are you talking about?" Donna said. "I'm waiting for Sadie. I thought she was going to pick both of us up."

"No, that wasn't the plan," Rowena said. "I can't believe this! Now we're all going to be late and no one's going to take us seriously."

"Ro, I'm telling you Sadie is supposed to be doing the driving tonight."

Rowena sighed. She had no transportation other than catching rides from her friends, and she was determined to work out their misunderstandings so that they could get to choir practice.

"Listen, Donna. I'll talk to Sadie and see what's happening, and I'll call you right back."

Sadie answered her telephone immediately and Rowena discovered that she had been right. Sadie, too, was waiting for Donna, since her mother had taken their family car and she had no way to get to choir practice unless Donna could drive.

Rowena called Donna once again and explained the situation to her. "So, if you can't drive us, I guess we won't be going," Rowena concluded.

Donna apologized and promised to ask her father about borrowing the car and call her friends back as soon as possible. At 7:25 Donna called and explained that she had the car keys in her hand, Sadie was waiting outside, and she was on her way out the door. Just before the girls hung up, everything in both their houses went black.

Theodore Charles was not accustomed to being apart from his wife, Anne. The couple had been married fifteen years and had rarely spent a day away from each other during that time. But that spring Anne had some family matters to attend to in nearby Lincoln, and she wouldn't be home until the next morning.

"Don't worry, Theodore," she told him before she left. "I've made plans for you and the boys. You'll be having supper with the Mc-Kinters on Wednesday night while I'm in Lincoln."

Theodore was pleased with this arrangement. The McKinters were a kind couple well past retirement age, and Margaret McKinter was one of the best cooks in Beatrice. He knew that he and the boys, ages eight and ten, would be in good hands while Anne was gone.

They even had plans for after the meal. Wednesday night was choir practice, and he and Anne usually took the boys along with them. The fact that Anne was gone didn't change things. Theodore and the boys would have dinner at the McKinters at 6 o'clock and leave shortly after 7:00 so they would make practice in plenty of time. Theodore enjoyed getting to practice early enough to visit with his friend, Herb Kipf, since both men were busy the rest of the week and rarely had time to talk.

As he'd expected, Margaret McKinter's meal was wonderful, corned beef with biscuits and gravy, and homemade apple pie for dessert.

"I must say, Margaret," Theodore commented after the meal. "You make the meanest apple pie this side of the Blue River."

"Oh, now, that ain't so," Margaret gushed. "That pretty, little wife of yours makes a pie just as fine as any around town. I remember the time when she was just a wee little thing, that Annie girl. Yes, sir, just a little girl with the prettiest dresses and . . ."

Theodore had expected this. Along with Margaret's good cooking she was also quite the conversationalist. Often a person could rest ten or fifteen minutes while Margaret did a fine job of carrying on a conversation all by herself.

That being the case, Theodore was not surprised to find himself nodding in agreement and glancing at his watch as 7:15 slipped past. At 7:25 Theodore silently determined to cut into Margaret's monologue, apologize profusely, and quickly exit with his boys before he missed choir practice altogether.

"And so like I was saying," Margaret McKinter drew in a quick breath, "whenever Thelma does her laundry without the bleach, I'm talking about her underclothes and all the rest, and then hangs them out to dry on the . . ."

Suddenly everything in the McKinter house went dark, and for the first time in nearly an hour there was utter silence in the room.

Gina Hicks was unsure about what to do that evening. She very much enjoyed being a member of the West Side Baptist Church choir and planned on singing a solo in the coming Easter Cantata. Certainly the choir director would expect her at practice since the performance was less than two weeks away.

But then there was her mother to consider.

Norma Hicks was a charter member of the Ladies' Missionary Group which met one Thursday each month at a different home. That month the women planned to meet at the Hicks' home, and the meeting was set for the following night.

"Gina, I know you need to go to practice," her mother had said earlier in the evening. "But I could really use your help. Besides the cleaning, I have some baking to do, and I'd like to get it all finished tonight."

Gina's younger sisters and brother would be taking their baths and getting ready for bed, and Gina knew there was no one else to help her mother. Still, she struggled with her decision. She lived so close to the church she could hurry right home after practice to help her mother. But maybe her mother really needed her, and in that case she would definitely stay home.

Gina looked at the clock. 7:20. There was still time to get to the church before practice. She began searching for her coat when just then she heard her mother struggling to break up an argument between her two sisters.

Gina sighed softly.

"Mom!" she yelled across the house. "Don't worry about things. I'll stay and help."

After all, she figured, God might want her to sing in the choir— but first he'd want her to help her mother. She began humming the melody to her solo number and headed toward the kitchen. Quickly she dialed her friend and fellow choir member, Agnes O'Shaugnessy.

"Aggie, I won't be there tonight. Tell Mrs. Paul I'm working on my number, and I'll get with her about it later."

"Okay. Mary and I are just about to leave. We'll let her know."

Gina hung up the phone, but just as she began washing dishes, there was a distant roaring sound. Suddenly the windows began rattling and the ground beneath her feet began to shake.

Norma came flying down the stairs with the younger girls racing behind her. "Oh, dear, Lord!" she cried out. "What in Heaven's name was that?"

At that instant they were enveloped in black.

Mary Jones and Agnes O'Shaugnessy were young mothers who always carpooled to choir practice at West Side Baptist Church. Usually by 7 o'clock they had finished with dinner and gotten their toddler-aged children ready for bed so that their husbands would have no trouble taking over while they attended practice.

That Wednesday it was Mary's turn to drive and she arrived at Agnes's house at 7:15. Agnes lived just two blocks from the church, so usually the two women talked for a few minutes before leaving for practice. But on that night Agnes was caught up in the final segment of "This Is Your Life," and she motioned for Mary to sit down.

"This is great," she said. "You've got to see this guy."

The program was one of the neighborhood favorites, and Mary soon found herself hooked. Even after the phone call from Gina Hicks, Mary and Agnes continued to watch the program. Before either women realized what had happened, it was 7:25.

"Oh, no!" Agnes gasped. "We're going to be late. I'm so sorry, Mary. I lost all track of time."

Mary stood up quickly, eyes still turned to the final moments of the television show. Just then Agnes's husband, Paul, joined them with the baby in his arms.

"Aren't you going to be late, girls?" he asked, looking at the clock.

"Nah," Mary said. "Besides, I love this show, and we'll still be there by 7:30. The church is just around the corner."

In less than a minute the credits began rolling on the screen as the program ended and both women said goodbye to Paul and headed for the car. Just as they opened the car door they heard the sound of a terrifying explosion, the force of which shook the ground and nearly knocked them off their feet.

"What in the world was that?" Mary said, straining to look in the distance toward where the sound had come from.

"I don't know, but we'd better get to practice before we're in deep trouble with Mrs. Paul," Agnes said, getting into her car. "Come on, let's go."

*     *     *

Pastor Nubert had finished dinner by 7 o'clock that evening and was helping his wife with the dishes. Susan, their six-year-old daughter, was already dressed and waiting by the front door, so their evening was right on schedule. The pastor smiled. He was looking forward to choir practice since the cantata was coming up so quickly. Everyone was excited about the performance, and it brought an even greater purpose to their gathering together and singing.

"Should be a good turnout tonight," he commented to his wife.

Before she could answer, Susan walked into the kitchen.

"Daddy, I'm thirsty," she complained.

Pastor Nubert looked at the clock on the wall. 7:05. They needed to leave in the next two minutes if they wanted to arrive by 7:15.

"Honey, can't you wait until after practice? We'll have punch and cookies when we're done singing," he said, stooping to her level and brushing a lock of hair from her eyes.

The little girl shook her head adamantly. "My throat hurts and I want a drink now, please," she said politely. "Please, Daddy."

The pastor sighed. "All right, but we have to leave in just a minute. Drink it quickly, okay?"

Susan clapped her hands happily. "Yes, Daddy. I will."

He walked to the refrigerator and pulled out a pitcher of red punch, then poured some into a cup and handed it to her.

"Thanks, Daddy," she said, turning around and walking out of the kitchen. Pastor Nubert watched as the child rounded the corner into the living room and then tripped on the throw rug, dumping the red drink down her white pinafore dress. Immediately the liquid seeped into the beige rug, and Susan cried for help.

"I'm so sorry, Daddy. I didn't mean to." Tears had formed in her eyes, and the pastor's heart went out to her. He moved quickly to the little girl's side. "It's okay, sweetie, we'll clean it up."

In an instant the child's mother joined them with a rag and a bucket of water, working as fast as she could to dilute the stain on the carpet and clean off Susan's dress.

"You'll need to change, dear," she said patiently.

The pastor looked at the clock once more. 7:13.

"We're going to be late," he muttered as their daughter left the room.

"Everybody should be late once in his life," his wife said with a smile. "Don't let it kill you, George."

He sighed again and began helping with the clean-up. "You're right. Go help Susan. We'll get there when we get there."

Fourteen minutes later, just as the Nuberts had finished cleaning up the mess and were preparing to leave for practice, the house suddenly shuddered and the lights went out. They were left standing in utter darkness.

"What is it, George?" his wife whispered. "What do you think happened?"

The pastor held his car keys in his hand and led his family carefully through the unlit house to the front door. "I don't know. Let's get down to the church and see if the lights are off there, too."

Herb Kipf had finished dinner and was working on a letter he was writing to the secretary of another Baptist church across town. He often helped out with paperwork in the church office and that included writing letters.

At age twenty-nine Herb was a machinist and a bachelor who lived at home with his parents. He often worked long hours and nearly every day volunteered some of his time down at West Side Baptist Church. He'd been a member of the congregation all his life, and he'd sung in the choir since he was twelve.

In fact, most of the choir was made up of a core of people who had sung together for the past seventeen years. Even after many members left to fight in World War II, every original member had returned and continued on as part of Beatrice's West Side Baptist Church choir.

"Herb, aren't you going to be late for choir?" his mother called to him that evening. "It's ten after seven."

Herb glanced at the clock in his bedroom and was surprised to see that the time had slipped by so quickly. He had planned to be at practice by 7:15 so he could visit with Theodore Charles and his other friends. But now he'd be doing well to get there by 7:30. He wrote more quickly, and by 7:25 he sealed the envelope, stamped it, and stood up to leave.

Racing down the stairs of his parents' home, Herb shouted goodbye to his family and ran outside to his car. But just before he drove away, his mother burst through the front door and motioned for him to roll down his car window.

"What is it, Mom? I'm in a hurry," he yelled.

She jogged to the car, and Herb could see that she looked deeply distressed. "Herb," she said breathlessly. "Gladys just called and it's the church. It blew up! Just a minute ago, at 7:27."

Herb's face fell and his stomach turned over. If the church blew up at 7:27, it could mean only one thing. Many of his closest friends had been inside. He nodded to his mother and headed for the church, praying as he drove that at least some members of the West Side Baptist Church choir had somehow survived the explosion.

As he approached the church, Herb could see numerous fire trucks and police officers and dozens of people gathering on the sidewalk to see what had happened. Herb stared at where the church should have been and was horrified. The building had been leveled and was nothing but a smoldering pile of splintered wood and crumbled bricks. He moved his car slowly around the emergency vehicles and saw the towering white steeple. The twenty-foot high section of the building had been severed from the church in the explosion and now lay exactly where he and the other singers usually parked their cars.

"Dear God, who was inside?" Herb whispered in horror as he made his way quickly from his car to the fire chief.

"Ernie!" Herb called frantically. He could hear people screaming and crying as they stared at the flattened church, and he tried not to imagine how many of his friends had been inside the building when it exploded. Sirens wailed through the night, and the air was filled with heavy smoke and settling debris. It had been dark for a couple of hours, and it was difficult to see clearly.

"Thank God," the fire chief said as he made his way to Herb and put an arm on his shoulder. "I thought you must have been inside. Don't you have choir practice tonight?"

Tears filled Herb's eyes as he nodded. "Yes. I was late. But the others . . . Ernie, they must be inside. It's after seven-thirty. What happened?"

"The whole thing just blew up. Probably a natural gas leak. The steeple sliced through the power lines, knocked out power all over town. Windows are blown out, too. Up and down the block." Ernie bowed his head a moment. "I hate to tell you this, but if anyone was inside they didn't have a chance."

"Have they looked?" Herb strained to see the area where the church once stood. "Someone might need help inside."

Ernie shook his head. "They've given a quick check, Herb. There wouldn't even be any bodies to identify. It looks like a bomb went off. And anything in the basement is buried under tons of rubble."

The fire chief looked intently at his friend, not sure if he was up to the task he was about to give him.

"Herb, there's a lot of frantic people standing around, and they need some answers. Please, walk around and gather all the choir members you can find. We need to know who's missing."

It was the most frightening task Herb had ever attempted. He took a deep breath and headed toward the church looking desperately into the night for the faces of choir members among the crowd. Debris cluttered the area and Herb had to step over piles of shattered church pews and roof tiles as he began his search.

Just then he saw the three teenagers who had planned to join them that night, Donna, Rowena, and Sadie. He was filled with relief as he reached them and pulled them into a group hug.

"Thank God," he said.

Donna was crying too hard too talk, and Rowena seemed stunned. "We got mixed up about who was driving," she said, staring at the flattened church. "We were ten minutes late. Just ten minutes!"

Herb pointed the girls toward the fire chief and told them they needed to wait there. "We have to find out who was inside," he said.

At that Rowena began to sob.

"Rowena, keep hold of yourself," Herb said. There was no time for hysterics, not with so many people still unaccounted for.

"Pray, Rowena," he said. "Just, pray."

The girls followed Herb's orders, and he continued through the crowd, which was growing constantly. Just then he saw Theodore Charles with his two young sons huddled next to him. The men were such good friends, and Herb began crying unashamedly in relief.

"Theodore!" Herb yelled. "Over here!"

Theodore spotted Herb, and with his sons in tow he walked quickly to meet him. "We were late," Theodore said. "Mrs. McKinter talked too long." He looked at his friend intently. "Otherwise we'd be dead."

"I was late, too," Herb said. "Writing a letter, time just got away from me." He paused a moment. For the first time he considered the truth. He should have been inside the church when it exploded. Every other Wednesday night as far back as he could remember, he had arrived at choir practice fifteen minutes early. He hugged his friend tightly and sent him toward the fire chief.

For fifteen minutes Herb maneuvered frantically through the crowd. He found Pastor Nubert, his wife, and their daughter, Susan. There were quick hugs exchanged, and Herb pointed them toward the fire captain with the others. A few minutes later he found Mary Jones and Agnes O'Shaugnessy, and three retired women, each of whom came separately and had a different reason for being late to practice that evening. Soon afterward he found a young couple who had only joined the choir the year before. They had received a long-distance phone call, which had made them late that evening.

Finally Herb came upon the choir director, Martha Paul, and her daughter, Marilyn.

"Martha!" Herb hugged the crying woman and let her rest on his shoulder for a moment. "I thought for sure you'd be inside."

"Marilyn couldn't wake up," she sobbed. "I tried and tried to get her up, but she just kept sleeping." She looked up at Herb, her eyes red and her face tear-stained. "Do you know that in sixteen years I've never been here later than seven-twenty?" she asked, her eyes filled with awe.

"The church blew at 7:27," Herb said gravely, pointing Martha and Marilyn toward the others. "Let's go join the others. We need to know who's still missing."

Herb felt as though he were in the middle of a strange and twisted dream. First there was the horror of seeing the church leveled by an explosion, and then the miracles, one after another, of finding each choir member alive. How was it possible that so many people had been late for so many different reasons?

There were fourteen choir members, three teenage singers, and three children who should have been at choir that night. After a quick count, Herb was stunned to learn that only one person was missing.

"Gina Hicks?" he yelled so that the other choir members could hear him. "Anyone seen Gina?"

"She couldn't come tonight," Agnes said happily, wiping tears from her eyes. "She called and said she had to help her mother."

That made twenty people. Every choir member was accounted for.

Just then Erma Rimrock, a retired woman who had been a member at the church for forty years, approached the huddled choir.

"Thank God, you're all alive," she said. Then she turned to Pastor Nubert. "Pastor, last week my brother and I purchased the old closed-down Methodist Church down the street as an investment. I want you to know you can hold services there as long as you need to. The rest of the congregation has decided we'll be here tomorrow to salvage what we can from the mess. And with a little cleaning at the other building we should be able to meet this Sunday."

The pastor was stunned. There was no explanation for anything that had happened that night, including Erma's offer. He hugged her and thanked her, and then turned back to Herb.

"We're all accounted for?" he asked, still amazed.

Herb nodded and looked at the faces in front of him, each struggling with the nearness of disaster as they stood silent and shivering in the freezing March night. For nearly a minute no one said a word as they realized the certainty of the miracle they had been a part of.

"I think we should join hands," Herb said softly. The choir separated itself from the milling crowd and found a spot in the middle of Court Street where they formed a circle.

"Do you understand this?" he asked them. "Every one of us was late tonight. Every single one of us."

"Let's pray," Pastor Nubert suggested, and instantly everyone in the circle bowed their heads.

"Dear Lord," the pastor's voice cracked with emotion, and he struggled to continue. "Lord, we know that you saved us tonight from certain death. By delaying each of us just ten minutes, you have proved yourself beyond a doubt, and we thank you."

The pastor squeezed the hands of his wife and daughter and looked at the other faces around him. Then looking upward, he spoke in a voice that was barely audible. "Thank you, God. We will not forget this."

# EIGHT

# The Gift of Gardenias

*R*enee had nothing else to do that winter in 1929, so when her friend saw her at school one day and asked her to come over for dinner, she shrugged and readily agreed.

"My brother's having the football team over," her friend explained. "If you come, at least I won't be the only girl."

Renee laughed and after talking with her friend a while longer made plans to see her that evening. Although Renee did not follow football, she knew that her friend's brother was on the professional team called the Bergen Flames, which was based in Hillsdale, New Jersey. Since it was long before the days when professional football players would be paid vast sums of money, most people thought little of the professional teams. Still, Renee was intrigued and she made sure to do her hair carefully before walking to her friend's house down the street.

That evening as the house filled with nearly thirty football players, Renee felt herself growing shy. She had just turned twenty and had always been quiet around boys, especially when they were in large groups as they were that night. After a while she separated herself and sat by the fireplace to warm her feet. While she was there, a handsome football player came over and introduced himself.

"I'm Attilio Mastalli." The young man grinned, his eyes sparkling in the light of the fire. "But everyone calls me Tilly."

Renee couldn't help but laugh, and with the ice broken the two talked through much of the evening. Tilly was just eighteen years old and determined to play football as long as possible. Renee listened intently, and when the evening ended, since Renee lived just three blocks away, Tilly offered to walk her home.

"Know what I don't like about the winter?" Tilly said as they made their way to Renee's house.

"What?"

"No gardenias."

"Gardenias?" Renee asked curiously.

"Gardenias are the best. Someday I want a home with my very own gardenia plant. There's nothing like the smell of gardenias in the summertime."

Renee smiled at her interesting companion. The next day when he called to take her for a ride on his horse, she wasn't surprised.

"There's an attraction there," Renee told her friend a few weeks later, after she and Tilly had dated several times. "But neither of us wants to get serious right now."

Since their families were both poor and Tilly's mother was ill, the couple waited eight years before getting married. When they did, Tilly brought Renee a gardenia to carry down the aisle.

"Now nothing can separate us, Renee," he told her. "This is the happiest day of my life."

Throughout the next twenty-eight years, Tilly and Renee shared a relationship few people ever have. Tilly even got his wish—not long after they were married, they planted a gardenia bush in the yard of their home in Hillsdale, New Jersey.

Then, shortly after his fifty-four birthday, Tilly was passed over for a promotion at the school where he was the head maintenance worker.

"The kids loved him, the faculty loved him, everyone loved him," Renee told her close friend sometime later. "The administrator was the only one who had something against him."

When it became clear that Tilly wouldn't be getting the promotion, he began suffering symptoms of stress. He had headaches and chest pains and complained about feeling tired. Renee was worried about him and arranged for him to see a doctor.

"You need to take it easy, Mr. Mastalli," the doctor told him. "But I don't think there's anything seriously wrong with you."

Then on a sunny afternoon in 1964, just one week after the appointment with the doctor, Tilly suffered a massive heart attack and died.

Renee rushed to the hospital to be by Tilly's side, but there was nothing the doctors could do. The love of her life was gone forever. Without Tilly, Renee plummeted into a deep depression that nothing could ease.

For weeks after his death students sent letters to Renee telling her what a wonderful man Tilly had been and stating how badly they missed him. But nothing helped Renee's grief.

Over the next several months Renee lost weight and rarely left the home she and Tilly had shared. Then late that year she began seeing friends and spending more time socializing. She even went on a few casual dates with a male friend of hers. But her heartbreak over losing Tilly was still so great that she broke things off with the man.

"I don't know when I can see you again," she told her friend one night. "I still have so much of my past to deal with. You see, Tilly and I were married for nearly thirty years. I guess I just don't know how to stop loving him after all that time."

That week was perhaps the darkest of all for Renee, who felt as if she'd made an attempt to live again and failed. She still missed Tilly so badly that she thought she might never leave home again.

That was the middle of winter—at the end of that week she woke up one morning, bombarded by the heavy smell of gardenias in the air. Puzzled, Renee climbed out of bed and wandered through the house. There was snow on the ground and outside everything around her was frozen. Still, as she made her way from one room to the next, she was overwhelmed by the smell of Tilly's favorite flower.

Quickly she went to the telephone and dialed her friend and neighbor, Lisa.

"Please, Lisa. Come over right away," she asked her friend. She did not mention the gardenias because she wanted to see if the smell was only in her imagination. Since it was so strong, she knew that if she wasn't imagining it, Lisa would recognize it as soon as she walked into the house.

"Hey, where are the gardenias?" Lisa asked as she opened the door bundled in a coat and boots. "It's wintertime. No one's supposed to have gardenias."

Renee stared at her friend strangely, and Lisa realized that something was wrong. "What is it, Renee?"

"There aren't any gardenias in the house. None at all. And there can't be any on the bush outside because it's frozen solid."

Lisa looked around and suddenly an expression filled her face as if she understood.

"It's Tilly, Renee," she said. "He must want you to know that he's fine and that everything's going to be okay. You can go on with your life."

"Do you really think so?" Renee asked, sitting down and steadying herself in the chair.

"Yes. How else can you explain this smell? It's so strong it can't be anything else."

Renee nodded slowly. "You're right." Then she began to cry softly. "It's time for me to let go, I guess."

At that instant the smell of fresh gardenias disappeared from the room. Renee looked at Lisa to see if she had noticed.

"It's gone," Lisa said simply.

"Yes. As soon as I said it was time to let go."

Renee never again smelled gardenias in the dead of winter as she had that cold winter of 1965. Soon after that day she began socializing with her friends again, and in time her depression disappeared completely. Although she has male friends, she has never remarried.

"There will never be anyone like Tilly again," she told Lisa some time later.

As if to remind herself of that fact, she has kept a gardenia bush every year without fail. Each summer when the flowers bloom she is taken back to that winter day when she was not sure whether she could live without the man she had loved for so long. And Renee remembers the smell of gardenias, and how by some miracle Tilly Mastalli was able to give her the strength to go on.

# NINE

# Invisible Protection

$\mathcal{M}$elanie Parsons and her friend Tricia Andrews had been looking forward to New Year's Eve for months. The girls were seventeen and for the first time had been granted permission from their parents to attend the all-night party that preceded the annual Tournament of Roses Parade along the streets of Pasadena, California. When morning came, the two friends would watch the parade and then return home.

The girls and their parents believed the plan was both simple and safe. They would travel together in Melanie's car and set up alongside a dozen other friends who would also be lined along the parade route. They did not drink, and so planned to refrain from the alcohol-induced revelry that would certainly be going on around them.

Melanie was not concerned. She and Tricia had been attending an active high school youth group at her local Christian church, and she had recently com-

mitted her life to God. Regardless of how crazy things might get
around them, she did not foresee any problems.

At first the night went as planned. She and Tricia had met up with
their friends and the group laughed and danced to the music that
filled the street from all directions. Despite the darkness, crowds of
people walked along the parade route dressed in flamboyant attire
and waving flags. Others openly tilted champagne bottles and beer
cans while hooting in preparation for the approaching midnight hour.
Although Melanie would not be drinking that night, she knew that
some of the girls in the group would be. She silently hoped no one
would get sick or hurt. Not one to worry for long, Melanie forgot
her concerns and began enjoying herself and the mood of celebration
around her.

About that time a diminutive man walked past Melanie and her
group of friends. Abruptly he turned, set his eyes on Melanie, and
slowly approached her. As he reached her, he handed her a yellow
sticker that read "Jesus loves you." Melanie smiled as she took the
sticker.

"Thanks," she told the man, who appeared to be by himself and
detached from the partying taking place around him. "I already know
that." The man nodded and smiled serenely at the teenage girl. Then
he turned away and proceeded down Colorado Boulevard.

"That was strange," Melanie told Tricia as she pulled her aside.

"What?" Tricia looked around confused.

"That man." Melanie pointed to the sticker which she placed on
the sleeve of her shirt. "He just walked up to me and gave me this."

Tricia shrugged. "It's New Year's Eve. I guess that means there'll
be all kinds down here tonight."

"Yeah, I guess," Melanie said, looking after the man once more
and seeing that he was no longer in sight. She smiled. "At least it's
true."

Tricia nodded and grabbed Melanie's sleeve. "Come on. Everyone's waiting for us."

As the girls returned to their group of friends, Melanie dismissed her thoughts of the man. As the evening progressed, people began cruising Colorado Boulevard in their cars, greeting those lined along the parade route, and lending their music to the party scene before moving slowly along the street. Melanie and her friends joined in the fun, waving to the people in the cars and enjoying the excitement.

When the cars lined up were bumper to bumper and barely moving, a hatchback with two good-looking young men pulled up in front of the girls.

"Hey, wanna ride?" one of them called out.

Melanie, always the vocal one in the group, laughed out loud. "Right!" she shouted over the roar of noise that filled the street. "Like we'd take a ride with a total stranger."

The young man smiled. Melanie and Tricia exchanged a knowing glance, silently agreeing that he was indeed very handsome. "Oh, come on. We're just circling the parade route. Climb in through the hatchback, we'll take you once around and bring you back here."

Melanie was skeptical. She eyed the car they were driving and saw that the hatchback was open. What harm could come if she and Tricia sat in the back and rode once around the parade route? Traffic was moving so slowly that they could always jump out if they didn't want to stay with the guys.

"Well," the driver of the car said, grinning as he ignored the honking horns from the cars he was holding up behind him. "You coming or not?"

Melanie looked at Tricia and shrugged. Grabbing her hand, she leaned toward her friend. "You only live once—come on!"

Tricia grinned, moving alongside Melanie and climbing gracefully into the rear of the hatchback. Melanie was always impulsive, but even so, taking a ride from two strangers was completely out of character for her. Still, it was New Year's Eve and the traffic was moving so slowly there seemed to be no harm in what they were doing. At first the girls had a wonderful time, waving to the hundreds of people set up along Colorado Boulevard. They laughed and linked arms and pretended to be part of a parade vehicle as the car moved slowly through Pasadena. Melanie guessed that the boys' hatchback was creeping along at barely five miles per hour. Their feet could almost touch the ground safely. She felt certain she and Tricia were safe.

But when thirty minutes had passed, Melanie suddenly noticed that the crowd that lined the street was thinning and there were no longer markers indicating that they were on the parade route. At about that time the driver of the car whispered something to his friend, and both laughed out loud. Melanie looked over her shoulder and saw that both young men were drinking and that there were several empty beer cans along the floor of their car.

Just then the car came to a stop at an intersection, and Melanie instantly realized that they were heading away from Pasadena. Although the boys had the radio turned up very loud, she suddenly heard a voice say, "Get out! They're taking you to the beach to rape you."

Melanie looked through the windshield and saw that the hatchback was about to enter the westbound Ventura Freeway—a route that eventually would lead to the beach.

"Quick!" she shouted at Tricia. "We're in trouble, get out!"

Tricia sat stunned and made no move to jump out of the car. But the driver of the car had heard Melanie's scream, and immediately pressed his foot down hard on the accelerator. The car jolted through the intersection and toward the freeway ramp.

In a split-second decision Melanie knew she would rather die on a

roadway in Pasadena than be taken to the beach and raped. She pulled her feet up under her and dived out of the back of the moving hatchback before Tricia could stop her.

The traffic light had just turned green and cars from all directions came to a screeching halt as Melanie's body slammed onto the pavement and slid into the middle of the intersection. Although a number of cars were traveling fast and headed right toward her, none of them harmed her. Later, one of the passersby would say there seemed almost to be a protective shield around the girl as she landed in the road untouched by the heavy traffic.

A motorcycle police officer saw what happened and instantly was at Melanie's side. He had attended enough accidents to know that the girl was probably seriously injured.

"Don't move," he said, climbing off his motorcycle and kneeling by her side. "I'll call for help."

"My friend!" Melanie shouted, tears streaming down her face. "They're going to rape my friend."

The officer looked up and saw the hatchback that the girl had jumped from moments earlier. The car had temporarily pulled off to the side of the road when the girl had jumped, but now the driver was attempting to enter the freeway once again. Immediately the officer climbed back onto his motorcycle, flipped on his red lights, and in a few seconds pulled the car over.

As soon as the car stopped, Tricia climbed out the back and ran toward Melanie, who was still in the middle of the street where she was being helped by several people who had seen what happened. Tricia was crying when she reached her friend.

"My God, why did you do that, Mel?" she asked, standing over her friend and running her hand nervously through her hair. "You could have killed yourself!"

"They were going to rape us, Tricia. I heard it. Someone told r

they were going to take us to the beach and rape us."

Tricia's face grew pale. "Who? I didn't hear anything."

Melanie pointed toward the freeway signs. "Look. They left the parade route a long time ago, and they were just about to take us on the freeway. They're drinking, Tricia. As soon as we got on the freeway, we would have been dead. The hatchback was up and we could have flown right out of there. Don't you see?"

Tricia looked back at the car where the police officer was administering a drunk-driving test to the young man behind the wheel.

"Melanie, you're right. I can't believe we were so stupid." Tricia was terrified as she knelt by her friend's side. "Are you okay?"

For the first time since jumping from the car, Melanie rolled onto her back and sat up. She was wearing long white denim jeans and her eyes grew wide as she ran her fingers over her knees. She had dived right onto the pavement and skidded several feet along the asphalt before coming to a stop, yet the knees and fronts of her jeans were completely clean and unharmed.

Suddenly Melanie remembered that as she hit the pavement she seemed to have lost all sense of feeling in her body. There had been no pain, no fear; only a certainty that she had done what she had to do to save her life.

Now as she remembered the strange sensation of landing on the road without feeling pain, she looked at the palms of her hands. She had seen her hands sliding along the street and knew they would be torn apart from the rough road. But as she examined them she found that they, too, were unharmed. Her skin was as soft and unscratched as if she had never touched the road.

"I'm fine," she said, her voice little more than a whisper. "Can you see this, Trish? I'm *perfectly* fine."

Tricia was watching her friend with wide eyes. She had seen the way Melanie had jumped from the car and landed harshly on the

pavement. It was impossible that she would be unmarked by the fall. Melanie stood up and looked herself over once more. There was not even any dirt to brush off her body, and she felt perfectly fine. Too stunned to wait for the police officer, she motioned for Tricia to follow her, and the girls set off walking back toward their friends. They were silent much of the way until at last their group came into sight. At that moment Melanie stopped and glanced down at her shirt sleeve. There was the sticker, also completely unscathed by the jump.

"Jesus loves me," she said out loud, her voice almost trancelike. Then she looked at Tricia. "You know what happened tonight just doesn't happen. I jumped from a moving car and I'm perfectly fine." She paused for what seemed like nearly a minute.

"Tricia," she finally said, taking the sticker from her sleeve and holding it carefully in her hand. "It was a miracle what happened tonight. That's why that man gave me this sticker. I think God knew what was going to happen, and he looked out for us."

Tricia reached out and hugged her friend tightly, still shocked by the sight of Melanie jumping into traffic only to walk away with no sign of the fall. "Thank God," she whispered, her eyes filling with tears at the thought of what might have happened to them. "Thank God."

# TEN

# Beyond Coincidence

Jim and Eleanora were sixteen when they met while attending high school in Canton, Ohio. That day the blond, blue-eyed teenager was running late for class; when she walked into Jim's homeroom he pretended to faint and fell off his chair onto the floor.

If Jim's introductory act did not win Ellie's heart, it definitely caught her attention. For the next few years until graduation the two were an item, attending dances together and building a very special kind of friendship.

"One day you'll wear my ring, Ellie," Jim would tell her. "And then you'll be mine forever."

Eleanora would laugh the way only a teenage girl can and bow her head bashfully. "Oh, Jim! That's such a long way off."

"I don't care. One day you'll wear my ring, and that'll be the best day of my life."

But after high school Jim began commuting by bus

to a job at a meat packing plant some distance from his home and the couple lost track of each other. For two years they neither saw nor heard from each other.

Then, shortly after her twentieth birthday, Eleanora was tidying her parents' house when the phone rang.

"I still say you'll wear my ring one day, Ellie," the caller said.

"Jim Karman!" She could hardly believe he had called after such a long time. "I thought you forgot about me."

Jim began his courtship passing by Ellie's house each night and serenading her with his harmonica. Ellie was thrilled with his renewed interest, and almost overnight the relationship between them grew until they knew they could never be apart. A year later, on August 24, 1957, Jim made good on his promise and placed a small gold band on Ellie's hand in a wedding ceremony attended by dozens of friends and family.

"This isn't the ring I want you to wear," Jim told Ellie shortly before their wedding date. "But it will have to do until I can afford to buy you the one you'll wear forever."

Over the next few years Jim saved every chance he had until finally he and Ellie went to Zales in downtown Canton and picked out a beautifully designed white-gold wedding band that was nearly half an inch wide. Jim arranged for the jeweler to engrave it with their initials and wedding date; the inside of the ring read: JAK-EMA-8-24-57.

"Now and forever this ring will be a reminder to you that I've loved you since the first day I saw you, Ellie," Jim told her as he placed it on her finger that afternoon. "And I'll love you till the day I die."

The marriage between Jim and Ellie Karman was everything they dreamed it would be. Two years later their first daughter, Michele, was born, followed by Debra three years later and their son, Anthony, two years after that. The family was closely knit, spending weekends and afternoons camping and fishing the lakes in their area.

Then, in 1971, the Karman family went fishing at Clendenning Lake, eighty miles south of Canton in Harrison County. It was a remote lake with a circumference of several miles, and it was a Karman family favorite. The lake was surrounded by a wide rim of rocks that made fishing a bit tricky. Fishermen had to maneuver their way along fifty yards of slippery boulders before reaching the water and casting their lines. But Jim and Ellie believed the rocks kept the lake less populated and resulted in a greater catch each time they went. That fall was no exception, and as the day progressed the Karmans began reeling in one succulent catfish after another.

By then Michele was twelve and Anthony, the youngest, was seven, and everyone in the family knew how to have fun on a fishing trip. Eleanora would set up a fishing line for the children and help them catch crawdads from between the rocks.

Finally the sun began to set that day, and the Karmans stopped fishing for a picnic, bundling into warmer clothes because of a chill in the fall air. When the meal was finished, no one wanted to go home; since the fish were biting so well, Jim and Ellie agreed to stay longer for some night fishing. They retrieved their lantern from the car and fished until nearly midnight.

Giddy from the long day and the excitement of catching so many catfish and crawdads, the weary Karman family made its way across the rocks toward their car. By then the temperature had dropped even further, and Jim flipped on the car's heater so they could all have a chance to warm up.

Two hours later, when they were nearly home, Eleanora suddenly gasped out loud.

"My wedding ring!" she cried. "It's gone!"

Jim glanced across the car at his wife's hand and saw that she was right. Where the ring had been her finger was now bare.

"Jim, we have to go back. I need that ring."

Jim sighed sadly. "Ellie, it's after two in the morning. The kids are beat and we have to get to bed. I can't go all the way back there tonight."

"Oh, no! I can't believe I lost it. My hand must have gotten cold, and somehow the ring must have fallen off when I was casting out."

Jim was silent a moment. The lake was so vast, the shore so long and covered with hundreds of rocks. Her ring could have fallen between the rocks or been washed out into the lake. There was no way they would ever find it now; he was certain of it.

"We have to go back tomorrow, then," Eleanora insisted. "Jim, you *know* what that ring means to me."

Jim nodded. "Yes, I know, honey. But I have to be at work in the morning."

Eleanora's eyes filled with tears, and her fingers began to shake. "What'll we do?"

"Let's go back next weekend and see if we can find it, all right?"

Reluctantly Eleanora agreed and waited what seemed like an eternity until the following weekend. First thing Saturday morning the family piled back into the car and returned to Clendenning Lake to search for the ring.

Although Jim thought he could lead the group to the same spot where they'd been fishing the previous weekend, the task was more difficult than he'd anticipated. The lake had very few landmarks, and since the rocky shore looked the same all the way around the water, the best he could do was guess at where they had been.

For several hours they hunted for the ring, turning over rocks and running their hands through the shallow water. But the ring was nowhere to be found. Before sundown a defeated Eleanor walked toward Jim and allowed him to pull her into a hug.

"It's gone, Ellie," he said softly. "You have to accept it."

Eleanora nodded, her chin quivering as she tried to fight back tears.

"It meant so much to me, Jim," she said, her voice breaking. "I'm so sorry I lost it."

"You don't need a ring to know how much I love you, you know?" She smiled weakly. "Of course."

"Come on," he said, taking her hand. "Let's go home."

After that Jim bought Eleanora another ring, but she was still crushed by the loss of the band Jim had saved to buy so many years earlier.

As the years passed, Eleanora never forgot the ring, often joking that someday someone would catch a fish, cut it open, and find her ring inside.

"I just wish we'd engraved our phone number in it and not the wedding date," she would say, only partly serious. "That way they could call me when it happens."

But realistically, Eleanora knew the ring was gone for good. The seasons affected Clendenning Lake greatly, causing the water to recede thirty feet in some points each winter and spring before returning to its higher level in the summer.

Twenty years passed and eventually Jim retired. In 1992 he began playing daytime bingo once a week at a local church hall. Eleanora was still working but occasionally she joined him for a game of night bingo. Although their children had grown and left home to pursue their own lives, Jim and Eleanora still went fishing nearly every weekend.

"The thing you'd like about the day crowd at the bingo hall," Jim would tell Eleanora, "is that everyone there is into fishing. That's all we talk about."

In fact, Jim had developed a friendship with one woman in particular. Jo Berry worked days at the church selling bingo cards. Early in their friendship Jim and Jo discovered that Jo and her husband had fished at many of the same lakes Jim and Eleanora had fished in. Each week Jim and Jo would exchange fishing tales, sharing stories about the biggest catches, the newest hot spots, and the ones that got away. They learned that they lived just ten minutes from each other; on several occasions Jo and her husband would attend night bingo and sit alongside Jim and Eleanora.

On June 22, 1993, a day when Jim would normally have played bingo at the church, he decided not to go so that he could take care of some business. Instead, he encouraged Eleanora to go without him. She had the day off, and since there was nothing else that needed her attention she decided to go.

"Find out who caught the most fish last weekend," he called out as Eleanora left for the afternoon.

Eleanora was in line to purchase bingo cards and was pleased to see that Jo Berry was the one selling them.

"Where's your honey?" Jo asked lightly. "He hasn't missed a Monday bingo session in months."

"Things to do," Eleanora said, pulling money from her purse to pay for her bingo cards.

"Well, tell him I caught the biggest catfish of my life last weekend at Clendenning Lake."

Eleanora chuckled. "Listen," she said. "If you cut that thing open and find a wedding ring, it's mine. Lost it there twenty-two years ago."

Suddenly Jo's face went slack and her mouth hung open. "What?" she asked.

"I said, if you find a ring in that fish, it's probably mine. I lost my wedding ring at that lake twenty-two years ago."

"Ellie, you're not going to believe this. That fish didn't have a ring inside it, but I found a wedding ring at that lake fifteen years ago."

"Really?" Eleanora asked, her face brightening. "Well," she continued, shrugging off the possibility, "there's no way it's my ring. It's been gone too long. I'm sure it's at the bottom of the lake somewhere by now."

"Wait, describe your ring."

Eleanora looked strangely at Jo. "It was a wide band, white gold with etchings on the top and bottom. And it was engraved."

"Oh, my word, Eleanora, you aren't going to believe this! I have that ring!"

Quickly Jo recounted how she had found it.

Fifteen years earlier Jo and her husband, Steve, had made an annual springtime trek to Clendenning Lake to search the shores for fishing lures. The lake typically receded so far that the rocks no longer lined the shore, and people were able to climb past the rocks and walk along the sandy shoreline. That afternoon in 1978 Jo and Steve found very few useable lures, but they did find a wedding ring lying partially buried in the sand.

"Look at this," Jo had said to her husband that afternoon.

Steve had made his way toward his wife and examined the ring and its engraved markings on the inside. "A wedding ring," he said. "I'll bet someone's been missing it."

Jo had then examined the ring once more and placed it in her pocket.

"What are you going to do with it?" Steve had asked.

"I don't know for sure, but it's obviously a nice ring. I can't just leave it here on the beach."

When they returned home, Jo thought through her options. She could place an ad in the newspaper that covered the Clendenning Lake area. But then people from hundreds of miles away fished at the lake, and there was no telling if the person who lost it would ever see the newspaper. She was also hesitant because of the date on the ring—August 24, 1957. If the person had lost the ring in the 1950s, they would certainly have stopped looking for it by now. In the end

Jo decided her only option was to put it aside.

"I know I'll never find the owner of that ring," she had told her husband. "But it meant something to someone, and I can't just throw it out."

She placed it in a jar with other odds and ends and never thought about it again until Eleanora Karman stood in front of her that June afternoon at the bingo hall.

"Wait a minute," Jo said as a dozen people in line listened to the exchange between the two women. Jo summoned another worker to the table to take her place. "I'll be right back. I'm going home to get that ring."

Fifteen minutes later Jo returned to the bingo hall with a large white gold wedding band on her finger. She walked up to Eleanora, who was sitting near a group of people who had heard the women talking about the ring. Eleanora and the others were now waiting anxiously to see if it was indeed the missing ring.

At home Jo had checked the initials on the ring and knew instantly that it was Eleanora's missing wedding band. Grinning wildly, she approached Eleanora and held up her hand.

"Looky here," she said.

Eleanora was shocked. She stood slowly and moved toward Jo, never taking her eyes from the ring. It was the very ring Jim had saved up for, the one he had given her that day in downtown Canton when he had promised that it would be a sign of his never-ending love for her. She would have known the ring from across the bingo hall, but she reached out and removed it from Jo's hand, turning it over in her own.

"It's my ring," she said finally, tears falling onto her cheeks.

As she said the words, the people around her broke into a loud round of applause. Several of them had glistening eyes themselves at the sight of Eleanora's happy tears.

"Is this unbelievable or what?" Jo said. "You lost the ring twenty-two years ago, I find it seven years later, and now fifteen years after *that* we play bingo together, and all this time I've had your ring sitting in a jar in my house."

At that moment the pastor of the church heard the commotion and approached them. He listened to the story behind the ring, and then Eleanora asked him if he would bless it.

"Mrs. Karman, I don't believe that's necessary," the pastor said. "If the good Lord helped you find that ring after all these years, I'd say that ring has already been blessed."

Again the crowd erupted into applause, and Jo and Eleanora embraced.

"Thank you doesn't seem like enough," Eleanora said, laughing through her tears. "I've never forgotten this ring, even after all these years. And now it's mine again."

Later Jim and Eleanora considered the odds against what had happened. The lake was eighty miles away from their home. It was absurd to imagine that a neighbor would visit the same lake where she'd lost her ring and find it there after seven years of high and low tides. Not to mention that they would then befriend that neighbor and that one day Eleanora would mention the missing ring in front of her.

"Even if that lake was completely dry and we searched up and down the length of it every day for a summer, we very well might never have found that ring," Jim told his wife as they wondered over the wedding band once more. "It should have been several feet under sand after all that time."

"But it wasn't. And now it's mine once more."

The couple was silent for a moment. "Jim, do you believe in miracles?" Eleanora asked him.

"Of course," he said as he pulled Eleanora close. "I told you that ring was a sign that I would love you forever. Now it's found its way back."

Eleanora nodded, running her finger over the ring's engraving. "And since we can't explain it, I guess we best just thank God it's come home." She kissed her husband on the cheek. "Oh, and don't worry. This time I won't let it out of my sight."

# ELEVEN

# Healing Hands

*I*n 1981, newly married and fresh out of Bible college, Cheri and Ralph Brune began making plans to be missionaries in Africa. They spent that next year taking training courses on the African diet, socialization process, and other important details that would aid them in their four-year stint on another continent.

When they had nearly completed their education and had already been assigned to a village in a remote tribal area, Ralph had an idea. He had been trained in Bible education and knew well the message he and Cheri would present to the tribal people. But he had never studied the power of healing through prayer.

"I think I'm going to take that course," Ralph told his wife one afternoon.

Cheri nodded and shrugged her shoulders. "Why not?"

The two had discussed the course, and Cheri, pregnant with their first child, had decided she would not have time for the additional work. But Ralph was intrigued. If he was going to tell the people about God's love, then he'd better be prepared to tell them about his healing power as well.

Although raised in the Christian church and well-versed on scripture, Ralph had never thought much of the preachers who did healing demonstrations. Many of them had proved to be frauds over the years. Even worse, a number had been swindlers who only performed trickery in exchange for donations. And so to consider the true healing nature of God was a new idea for Ralph.

He began the class at about the same time that Cheri visited a doctor for what had become a persistent and painful lower and middle back pain.

"I'm afraid I have bad news for you, Mrs. Brune," the doctor told her as the two sat in his office after her examination. "The X rays show that you're suffering from the early stages of scoliosis."

The doctor went on to explain that scoliosis was a disease that caused the spine to begin to curve unnaturally, forcing the body to become severely hunched and causing excruciating pain in its victims. When the disease occurs in children, it can be managed with a series of braces since the child's skeletal frame is still growing. However, when it strikes an adult, there is nothing that can be done.

"What can I expect?" Cheri asked, fighting tears. The news was devastating. She and Ralph had so many plans for the future. If she was going to be strong enough to bear children and live the rugged life of a missionary in Africa, she would need a healthy back.

"The pain you're experiencing will get worse. Within the next two years you will be able to notice the curving in your spine. I'm sorry."

Cheri nodded in resignation and returned home to share the news with Ralph. He sympathized with her and then told her his own news. He had met twice already with the class on healing through prayer. He told her he was impressed with the stories he was hearing. Not stories of tent revival healings or televised miracles. But quiet stories of health changes that in his opinion could be nothing less than modern-day miracles.

That night as they were falling asleep, Ralph sat up in bed and spoke to Cheri in the dark of their room.

"Would you mind if I pray for your back, Cheri?"

Cheri shrugged, already partially asleep. "Sure. Do I have to move?"

"No. You're fine."

Cheri was lying on her side, a position that favored her painful back. As she lay, falling asleep, Ralph spent thirty minutes holding his hands above her back and praying silently that God would heal her condition.

Each night for a week he continued this routine. Just as they were about to go to sleep, he would sit up, place his hands over Cheri's back, and pray specifically for God to heal her scoliosis. On the seventh night something strange happened.

Ralph had been praying for his wife for ten minutes when suddenly he spoke.

"Cheri?"

"Yes?" She was still awake.

"Do you feel anything?"

"Just your hand moving up and down along my spine."

Ralph's eyes widened in surprise. "Cheri, I haven't touched your back."

Cheri sat up quickly and turned to look at Ralph. "That's not funny!"

Ralph shook his head. "I'm serious, Cheri. I haven't touched you. The only reason I asked if you felt something was because I had my hand over your back and at that moment I was feeling something warm passing beneath my hand."

"What do you think it was?"

"I don't know. But I'm going to keep praying."

Cheri yawned and lay back down on their bed. "It can't hurt. Besides, I know God *could* heal me if he wanted to. I just don't know if that's part of His plan for us. Modern miracles and all."

"By the way, how's your pain?" Ralph asked.

Cheri paused a moment and then sat upright once more. "You know, actually I can't feel it."

There was silence between them for a moment as they considered the warmth that had passed along Cheri's back and the feeling of a human hand moving up and down her spine.

"Do you think," Cheri asked quietly, "I might be healed?"

"I think we need to see how you feel tomorrow and in the meantime keep praying."

Two weeks later, after Cheri and Ralph had flown to Portland to visit her parents, she visited a doctor who had known her as a child. She brought with her the X rays and diagnosis from the previous doctor. Upon initial examination of the records the Portland doctor agreed with the diagnosis: severe scoliosis, which appeared to be progressing rapidly.

Then, upon Cheri's request, the doctor took another set of X rays and performed an additional examination of her spine.

"I don't know how to explain this," the doctor said as he reentered the examination room. "Cheri, there's no sign of any scoliosis at all. Your back is perfectly normal."

Cheri was stunned. She remembered the night when she had felt a hand moving gently along her back. "Could it somehow have reversed itself?" she asked the doctor, wanting to be absolutely sure about what had happened.

"No. For a person to have scoliosis as severely as you did in these last X rays"—the doctor held the photographs up to the light and shook his head—"you would definitely have had scar tissue, even if it had somehow reversed itself."

"Then how do you explain it?"

The doctor put the films gently on a nearby table and smiled at Cheri. "I've learned over the years that there are some things we on Earth cannot explain when it comes to medical healings. I like to call them miracles."

Cheri shared with the doctor the incident weeks earlier when Ralph had been praying and she had felt a hand on her spine at the same time that he felt a warmth passing beneath his hand. To Cheri's surprise, the doctor nodded.

"Yes, when we hear of this type of thing, and we don't hear about it very often, there is often a warmth associated with it. It doesn't take a lot of believing on my part. After all, the human body itself is a working miracle. That our Creator would continue to work miracles within us is in my opinion quite possible."

Months later when Cheri and Ralph left for Africa, it was in good health and with a deep respect and belief for the kind of prayer that God answers in the form of miraculous healing.

# TWELVE

# Mystery Man on the Beach

*F*rank and Shirley Beyer wanted to wait until their children were old enough to be somewhat independent before the family became missionaries. Confirmed Christians for many years, the couple knew of the potential dangers on foreign mission fields, and they had no intention of taking infants or toddlers into such an adventure in faith.

Finally, in 1968, they decided the family was ready. Their oldest son, Kenneth, was eleven, David was nine, and the youngest, Rebecca, was seven.

"We need to be very careful and be sure to stick together," Frank said as he prepared the family for the five-year trip to South America. "And most of all, we need to trust that God will take care of us while we're gone."

Through the first year there were many times when members of the Beyer family barely avoided injury or illness. Always they believed this was because God was watching over them.

Then on an afternoon when the family had been in South America for one year, they decided to spend a day swimming and sunbathing on a deserted beach. It was a beautiful day with a gentle breeze and a brilliant blue sky. But a powerful undertow made swimming difficult.

As the children headed toward the water, Rebecca found herself fighting to stay on her feet, and she decided to stay in the shallow water that hit just around her ankles.

"Come on out, Rebecca!" Kenneth yelled to her. He and David had gone out farther and were swimming despite the strong pull of the current.

"Yeah, Rebecca, come on and play with us!" David shouted.

Rebecca shook her head firmly. She was not a good swimmer like her brothers, and she was scared to swim in deep water. "No!" she yelled over the sound of the pounding surf. "The tide's too strong."

The boys returned to their own swimming, but a few minutes later they called Rebecca out once more. Finally, they convinced the young girl, and she timidly made her way closer to them, stopping when she was in water up to her waist.

"No farther!" she shouted. "You can come over here and swim with me."

The boys saw that Rebecca had made an effort, and they joined her, splashing and swimming with her for the next fifteen minutes.

"I'm tired," Kenneth said to the others. "Come on, let's go back to shore."

The others agreed and together they started to go in. Kenneth and David had to work to swim against the strong undertow, but they began making progress and heading for the shoreline. When Kenneth realized that Rebecca was not with them, he turned around.

"Come on," he said. "Stay with us."

Rebecca shook her head. "It's too strong. I'll catch the next wave and ride it in."

The girl waited, looking out to sea and spotting a wave that seemed the right size to push her into shore. She got into a diving position and jumped in front of the wave expecting to be carried to shore. Instead, the undertow pulled her beneath the surface of the water and dragged her farther out to sea.

When Rebecca was able to come up for air, she found that she was in water over her head. Just then another wave came upon her, pulling her under water and dragging her still farther out. Frantically the child tried to swim against the undertow, but her efforts only kept her in place.

Terrified that she was going to drown, Rebecca gasped for air only to be pulled under by yet another wave. By that time the waves were coming so quickly, she had to struggle just to get her head out of the water for a quick breath of air.

Then a towering wave pulled Rebecca deep into the water—although she fought to find the surface she remained buried in the sea.

"I'm drowning," she thought to herself. Years of being at church and learning about God had taught her that the only chance she had was to pray for help.

"Please, God, save me," she prayed. "Please!"

Instantly she was shot into the air for a few seconds, just enough time to gasp for air.

"Help me, God!" she screamed before the next wave knocked her back under the water. By then she was much farther from the shore, and she could see her family standing at the edge waving at her to come in.

Praying constantly, Rebecca stayed under several seconds before she could fight her way to the top and breathe again. This time she looked toward shore and saw a man standing a few feet away from her family. He was looking at Rebecca and shouting at her in Spanish. As the girl was pulled back under water, she was frustrated. She needed help desperately, but she could not understand the man since she did not speak Spanish. Rebecca could feel her body tumbling with the current, and she knew her strength was waning. As she came up again for air, she saw the man once more. Rather than standing directly in front of her, he stood off to the side but still on the shore. This time, although he was speaking in Spanish, the child understood.

"It's all right, child!" the man yelled. "Swim toward me, not toward the shore. Come slowly, and when the waves hit you, don't fight. Just swim toward me."

Rebecca was afraid and unsure about the man's advice. She had been swimming since she'd been pulled out to sea, and her efforts hadn't gotten her any closer to the shore. Still, Rebecca had no choice, and so she obeyed the man. When she would come up for air, she could see him on the sandy shore still yelling at her to be calm and to keep swimming at an angle.

After a few minutes Rebecca realized that, bit by bit, she was making progress and getting closer to shore. Once more a wave knocked her under water, but this time when she came up, she was standing in knee-deep water. Instantly her brothers were at her side helping her to the shore. Gasping for breath, Rebecca looked toward the spot where the man had been standing, but he was gone.

"Rebecca!" her mother called as the boys brought the child to her. "Thank God you're alive. We were so scared!"

Rebecca collapsed on a towel and slowly lifted her weary head. "Where is he?" she said as she coughed up water and struggled to fill her lungs with air. "Where is that man?"

Kenneth and David exchanged a strange look and then looked at their parents.

"Honey, what man?" her father asked, kneeling beside the exhausted child. Rebecca struggled to pull herself up and once again she scanned the deserted beach. "The man who helped me. He was standing over there, and he told me to swim to him."

There were perplexed looks on the faces of all of her family members, and finally her father spoke.

"Rebecca, there hasn't been anyone but us on the beach all day."

"But, Daddy, he helped me. He told me to swim at an angle and I'd be all right. He spoke in Spanish, but I understood everything he said."

Frank took his wife's hand and together with the boys they formed a circle around Rebecca.

"We believe you, Rebecca," he said gently. "I think he must have been an angel sent by God to save you."

Rebecca was shocked. She certainly had seen the man, and to imagine now that he might have been an angel was overwhelming. She began to cry, and her father placed his arm around her.

Then, feeling as if they were in the very presence of God, the Beyer family knelt together and thanked God for the miracle that sent a Spanish angel to rescue Rebecca from certain death.

## THIRTEEN

# Legacy of Love

Since their retirement Ken and Jean Chaney had fallen in love all over again, often taking leisurely drives in the mountainous area adjacent to their central California home. On the afternoon of February 28, 1991, the white-haired couple were enjoying just such a scenic drive, chatting about their three adult children—Madge, Skip, and Jayne—when suddenly Jean began to feel anxious.

"We need to pray for the kids," she urgently told her husband of nearly forty years as they continued to make their way up the mountainside. "We need to pray."

The Chaneys had raised their children with a strong faith in God, themselves praying that Madge, Skip, and Jayne would carry those beliefs with them into adulthood. Instead, each of the three rebelled against their parents' faith. As the children grew older, the heartbreak of their rebellion was compounded by something Jean considered tragic: The love between the Chaney siblings had dissolved, and they were no longer a close-knit family. The separation had not been the result of any single conflict; rather, years of bickering and indifference had turned the children into strangers. As they were accustomed to doing, the Chaneys prayed in hushed tones for Madge, Skip, and Jayne that February afternoon as dark clouds filled the sky and a light rain began to fall in the Sierra Mountains.

"Lord, whatever it takes," Jean prayed. "Let us be a family once again."

The drive that day should have taken Ken and Jean just one hour as they traveled from Fresno through the Central California Sierra Mountains to their retirement home in Mariposa County. But after taking care of business at the Internal Revenue Service in nearby Fresno, Ken and Jean decided to veer off Highway 41 and take a longer, more scenic route home. Since retiring, the couple had spent many hours exploring in their 1984 Ford Thunderbird but had not driven along North Fork Road until that afternoon.

Sometime around five o'clock that evening, unsure of which road would lead them to Oakhurst and eventually Mariposa, the Chaneys stopped in North Fork for directions. Nearly an hour later, after driving steadily up North Fork Road and around several narrow, twisting turns, Ken suggested they turn back.

"Oh, Ken, not now," said Jean, who at sixty-eight was not as adventurous as she had once been. "The road's too narrow. I don't think we could turn around if we tried."

"All right, we'll keep going."

As they continued up the hill, snow began falling, and within the hour the Chaneys realized they hadn't seen anything but trees and mountainous terrain for the past twenty-six miles.

Suddenly the Chaneys' car hit a patch of ice and began skidding uncontrollably across both lanes before slamming into a snowy embankment on the opposite side of the road. The car was partially buried in a large snowdrift. Ken Chaney's mind flew over his options. He could leave Jean and venture along the road in search of help, even though they hadn't seen anyone or even another car for an hour. Or he could wait with her until someone happened to drive by.

The decision was an easy one for Ken. After four decades of staying at Jean's side, Ken knew this was no time to leave. They would stay together until someone found them.

"I'm not afraid, Ken," Jean told him, reaching over and taking his hand in hers. "Just worried about the children. I have so much more to tell them."

The Chaneys huddled together for warmth and slept intermittently throughout the night. The next morning they found that snow had piled up against the car, making it impossible for them to open either door. Unsure of what would happen to them, Jean reached into the glove compartment, pulled out several scraps of paper and a pen, and began writing:

Friday, March 1, 1991, 6:30 A.M.

Dearest Madge, Skip, and Jayne,

Well, here we are in a winter wonderland! We have been here since about 6:00 or 6:30 last night. We skidded into a snowdrift on the wrong side of the road and couldn't get out. Before you think we are completely crazy, let me tell you what happened. . . . It was raining when we started, and it wasn't cold, so we never imagined we would run into snow. After we came over Mile High Curve, your dad wanted to turn back, but the road frightened me and I didn't want to turn back. One more time when I should have listened to your dad!

From an early age Jean Wright had disliked listening to the advice of others, something that didn't change even after she met Ken Chaney and the two fell in love.

"I love him," she would tell her friends shortly after the two met in 1948. "But I don't have to listen to him."

Jean was a twenty-five-year-old bookkeeper when she had met Ken Chaney at a popular Italian restaurant in Goshen, Ohio. By then, Jean had developed a fierce independence—she didn't care what other people thought of the choices she made.

There had been something slightly rebellious about spending that first evening in Ken Chaney's company. Ken was in the process of divorcing his wife after ten years of marriage and three children. But that wasn't the only thing that gave the man a tainted reputation. He was also known among his peers as a loud, fighter-type whose most obvious physical trait was the chip on his shoulder.

Ken had grown up a sensitive and emotional child in a time when boys were expected to be every bit as macho as men. By the time Ken was an adult, the constant teasing from his childhood peers had left him something of a hell-raiser.

Jean saw none of that. In her eyes thirty-two-year-old Ken was tall, dark, and handsome, a friendly man with warm brown eyes and a dashing smile who needed someone to believe in him. The challenge was almost as irresistible as the man, but Jean made certain not to get too close to Ken in the early days of their friendship. After all, he was not yet legally divorced. For all her tendencies toward rebellion, Jean still considered herself a good girl, and that meant staying away from married men.

Privately, Jean felt herself falling for Ken.

For his part, Ken was instantly taken with the petite, blue-eyed woman with the pale blond hair. The two continued their friendship discreetly for the next several months and then in February, 1949, shortly after his divorce became final, Ken and Jean married at the United Methodist Church in Gnadenhutten, Ohio.

Years later, trapped inside their snow-covered car, the Chaneys spent hours remembering their early days together. When a comfortable silence fell over them, Jean once more took time to continue the letter to their children:

> At first, we joked around about our mis-adventure. Then we began to realize that we were on the road that isn't maintained during the winter. Truly a miracle if anyone comes by. We spent the night singing hymns and choruses. I should say him singing and me croaking! And quoting Bible verses and catnapping. We would run the heater for about five minutes every couple of hours. So here we are, completely and utterly in God's hand!! What better place to be!!! If He wants to take us home—Hallelujah. May He be glorified!!

In May, 1955 a job transfer had moved Ken and Jean Chaney from snowy Ohio to the warm climes of Southern California. By then the couple had a two-year-old daughter named Madge who made the move with them. Together the young family moved into a trailer in Redlands, a small town where Jean's aunt also lived. The woman was a Christian, and it was in her company that the Chaneys first discovered their hunger for a deeper faith.

In the years after the Chaneys had rededicated their lives to the Lord, they moved to San Bernardino, where Jean became a homemaker and Ken worked as a carpet layer. The couple believed in sharing their faith with others, and many times during the next few years Ken would get off work and drive several hours to the Mexican border to deliver building materials and Bibles to missionaries there. Jean was equally involved in the church prayer support group.

Life was good for the Chaney family; four years later their son, Skip, was born. Then after another four years, they were blessed with the birth of Jayne. Early on, the three Chaney children became accustomed to their parents' involvement in church activities.

So strong was the faith the Chaneys developed during those days that decades later, as they sat stuck in the mountains, their car gradually becoming entombed in snow, the couple did not panic. Instead, they shared fond memories, laughing about times gone by and reflecting on the future. And during lulls in their conversation, Jean continued to write to their children:

> I love you all so very much! So many things I want to say . . . remember what is so dreadful today will be forgotten next year. Please be a family!! And look to our dear Savior for all your needs. He loves you even more than we do!! And let my grandchildren know that I love them—for ever and ever.
> Friday, March 1, 11:00 A.M.
> Snow is up to windows. Doors won't open. I love you all and don't really want to leave, but His will be done.

The rebellion of the Chaney children against the beliefs their parents held so dear had begun in the 1970s. In 1971 Madge graduated from high school and immediately moved to Ohio to live with relatives. She had grown away from her brother and younger sister and had stopped attending church. Reluctantly Ken and Jean allowed her to go and began focusing their attention on Skip.

That year Skip entered high school and began to associate with a group of troublemakers. Almost overnight Skip lost interest in his appearance, ignored his family, and shunned his parents' faith. His actions sent Ken and Jean to their knees daily in prayer for each of their children. But by then they were especially concerned for the baby, Jayne.

Jayne had been born with a heart murmur and a weak bronchial system that left her ill and frail through much of her childhood. When she entered junior high school, the family moved to Antelope Valley, where the desert air was free of the allergens that had plagued Jayne in San Bernardino. There, for the first time, Jayne found a two-year respite of good health. At a time when her parents expected her to be thanking God for her good health, Jayne instead rejected her parents' religious beliefs altogether.

It wasn't until 1979, when Jayne suffered a serious bout of ulcerative colitis, that her faith in God had been restored. She had been in the hospital near death that year when Jean convinced her that her only hope was to turn to God. When Jayne had agreed, Jean was filled with joy.

"God has a plan for our children," Jean had told Ken that year. "One day they will all be a family again."

Perhaps the most significant answer to the couple's constant prayers had come just two weeks before their fateful drive in the mountains. On February 14—Valentine's Day—the Chaneys celebrated Ken's seventy-fifth birthday at the San Bernardino home of Skip and his wife, Carole. For the first time since his teenage years, Skip seemed clearly a changed man. He had been sober for quite some time and showed real interest in his parents and their church involvement. Carole remembered that when the Chaneys left for Mariposa the next morning, they had seemed more content than ever.

"Answered prayer," Jean whispered to Carole as they pulled away.

It was the last time they would see Ken and Jean alive.


March 2, Saturday
We spent the day and night reciting scripture, singing and

praying for everyone we ever knew. All of you were prayed for many, many times. The third day and so far we aren't hungry. Found two little packages of jelly and a stick of gum in the glove compartment. Saving them. We reach out the window and eat snow. Daddy is feeling bad about not showing up at work this morning. One thing for sure, a situation like this sure draws you closer to Jesus!! When I feel hysteria rising up in me, I just start praising Him and talking to Him and the serenity comes. What a loving and kind Savior we have. Your dad and I are having such a good time in the Lord!! We sing, we laugh, we pray, and our love for Him and for each other swells until I can hardly contain it. We both say, whatever the outcome, we wouldn't have missed this experience! We realize that not a single soul knows where we are (but God), and like I said, who better to know?!

As Jean wrote those words, North Fork Road had been closed for more than twenty-four hours because of severe snow conditions. It was the first time the California Department of Forestry had closed the road in four years of drought.

In fact, as the Chaneys predicament grew more serious with each hour, Californians across the state were rejoicing in what was later called the "March Miracle", a three-week long snow and rain storm that dumped more than ten inches of much-needed moisture onto the parched state.

Normally when forest rangers closed a road because of bad weather, they checked it first for stranded motorists. But because the Chaneys had missed their turnoff twenty-six miles before, they were on a stretch of the road that was not maintained during winter and was rarely traveled even in the best conditions. Roads that were not maintained during the winter were not checked before closures were made.

The Chaneys were stuck on a section of North Fork Road that makes a fifty-mile scenic loop. Prior to their mishap, the Chaneys probably thought they were traveling toward Oakhurst and Mariposa when actually they had unintentionally been traveling in a gigantic circle. They were at the peak of that circle, at an elevation of 6,750 feet, when they lost control of their car and became stuck.

Sunday, March 3, 11:00 A.M.

The snow is coming down heavy and piling up fast, but our faith is still holding. The gas is on empty, so we aren't starting the car up for heat anymore. Praise the Lord for an old wool blanket that Ken used for moving! The Lord is sustaining us!! Praise His name!!

National Weather Service records later indicated that snow fell at record rates that first week of March. By the third and fourth days officials estimated the Chaneys' car could have been buried under as much as twelve feet of snow. By then Ken and Jean's days had probably evolved into a quest for God's peace and their own survival.

Ever mindful of her children, Jean had found every available scrap of paper in the car in order to continue writing to them. Meanwhile, Madge, Skip, and Jayne continued in their separate lives, completely unaware of the danger their parents were in.

Monday, March 4

It is pouring rain. Praise Him. It is helping to melt the snow! It had gotten almost to the top of the car. We're wondering if anybody has missed us yet. We thought maybe there would be helicopters or snowmobiles out looking. But I have a feeling that so far, no one has missed us. How would they know where to look? You dad and I have learned so much! Oh, how I love you all and really don't want to leave you. But I know that God knows what He is doing. I wish I had more paper. I would like to write each of you individually.

That same day the couple's church friends began worrying about Ken and Jean. The week before taking the trip to Fresno, Ken had been hired to do parttime work at the local hardware store in Mariposa. The job was his way of staying active and remaining involved in his small community. In Mariposa, a town of only a few thousand people, word of mouth was much faster and more effective than any form of mass media. So it was that several of the Chaneys' church friends were well aware that Ken had missed work the day before. When they did not show up for morning service or an important church meeting that afternoon, several of their friends grew concerned. Shirking commitments was not something Ken would ever do.

Because they were newly retired and enjoyed spontaneous outings, there was no reason for anyone to think something was wrong until that Sunday. Yet from where they sat trapped in the Thunderbird, their situation becoming more desperate with each hour, the Chaneys felt certain that by then someone would have missed them and started searching for their car.

March 5, Tuesday

More snow last night. The Lord is really sustaining us! Only sound up here is an occasional plane. We keep listening for helicopters or snowmobiles, but nothing. We are still praising Him—praying and thinking about all of you and thanking Him for such wonderful children! I cry when I think of you. I love you so much!

By the sixth night, as the snow continued to bury their car, the Chaneys began having difficulty distinguishing between night and day. In addition to their lack of nourishment, it became nearly impossible for them to get water because the car windows were often frozen shut. At about the same time the car ran out of gas completely, and they were no longer able to use their heater for warmth.

Buried alive under an increasing amount of snow, Ken and Jean should have been experiencing the early signs of hypothermia—numbness in the toes and fingers, an inability to concentrate, and a false feeling of warmth. Instead, Jean continued writing to her children with no obvious sign of numb fingers or disrupted concentration. Instead, the couple felt enveloped in warmth.

"The heat is from the Lord," Ken told his wife. "Even here, He is with us."

During that first week of March, both Skip and Jayne tried separately on several occasions to call their parents. However, because of the couple's involvement at church, neither of them thought it strange when no one answered. And because of the chasm between them, the brother and sister never spoke about their concerns with each other.

### March 6, Wednesday

This will be our seventh night here. The gas is all gone, so no more heat. It froze everything solid last night, and when we tried to roll the windows down, they wouldn't go, so no snow. So we just prayed and sang. And I asked the Lord to come in with His love and surround us with heat. The sun came out and melted and dried up everything in the car. We had been feeling so damp. Praise Him!! What a wonderful God we serve! As I am writing this, it is actually hot! He is really sustaining us. We have eaten one little packet of jelly between us, Rolaids, and Tic-Tacs. Quite a feast!! I love you all so much.

Finally, on the evening of March 6, Jayne Peterson received a call from her parents' church friends in Mariposa saying they hadn't seen Jean and Ken for several days. When the caller mentioned that Ken had missed work that past Saturday, twenty-nine-year-old Jayne felt a knot fill her stomach.

"Something's wrong," she thought to herself. "Dad never misses work."

Immediately Jayne contacted Skip and Madge, learning from Skip that he, too, had not heard from their parents in more than a week. Feeling as if she were working against an invisible clock, Jayne hung up the phone and raced to call the Mariposa Sheriff's Department. She told them about her parents' disappearance; two deputies offered to drive by their home.

An hour later one of the deputies called back. There were no signs of foul play at the Chaney home. Dishes still sat in the sink, empty suitcases were stowed away in closets. Ken and Jean did not appear to have been victims of crime, and they did not appear to have gone on a spontaneous vacation.

After a restless night's sleep Jayne and her husband, Karl, left early Thursday morning for Mariposa, where they filed a missing person's report on their parents. That weekend they frantically went through the couple's checkbook, bank statements, and personal records searching for clues to their disappearance. Throughout their search, Jayne couldn't shake the feeling that something terrible had happened.

By Sunday Jayne and Karl had their first clue—their parents' 1990 taxes were missing. That afternoon they learned from neighbors that their parents had been in contact with the IRS in Fresno. In addition they found a phone number scribbled on a piece of paper near the couple's kitchen telephone. It belonged to the Fresno office of the IRS. Several times that weekend, more than she had in the past decade,

Jayne telephoned Madge and Skip to let them know what was happening.

"Pray for them, will you, Skip?" Jayne pleaded.

There was a pause. "I'll pray," Skip reassured her. "And be sure to call Madge. She's worried sick."

Had Jean Chaney known what was happening, her situation would have been far more bearable. Thrown together in the midst of an unfolding nightmare, her children had started relying on each other and working together.

Miraculously Jean's prayers were being answered.

March 7, Thursday
The nights are the worst. We can't get comfortable. (These old bones like a nice bed!) Last night was the same as before. Everything froze and then today the sun dried everything out. You each mean something different to me. But I love you all the same. God has been so good to us to give us such wonderful children! I love you, I love you, I love you!

The weekend behind them, Jayne and Karl were fairly certain the Chaneys had taken a trip to Fresno, but after that the leads dried up. They were unable to get confirmation from the IRS that any meeting had occurred, and on Monday Jayne found a brochure in her parents' home about property in Mexico.

Perhaps they had gone southwest toward Mexico, she thought. Or maybe the couple had traveled north on a lark toward some unknown destination. Ken and Jean knew people across the country and might have decided to visit one of them without notifying their adult children.

In Ohio, Madge Chaney, thirty-seven, was beside herself with anxiety. Madge had just started a new job as a computer operator. Gradually she had begun renewing her relationship with God, which was so much a part of her she knew she could not ignore it forever.

With her parents missing, Madge spent each spare moment making long-distance phone calls. She contacted her parents' banks to see if they had withdrawn an unusually large amount of money and as Jayne had suggested perhaps taken an impulsive trip. And she checked with their utility companies to see if they'd been paying their bills on time. She also got in touch with an organization that helped people find missing children.

"What do we do if the missing people are adults?" Madge asked them.

The organization had no answer. Frustrated, Madge continued making phone calls until after midnight each night before dropping wearily into bed and getting up at 5 o'clock the next morning for work.

Back in California, Jayne and Karl had visited dozens of their parents' friends by Monday afternoon in an effort to find someone who might know where they were. Their friends were concerned and even donated money to aid in the search, but still there were no leads. The next morning Jayne developed a plan and called Skip and Madge. She would charter a helicopter and scour the mountain roads leading into and out of Mariposa—especially those leading toward Fresno.

By then Skip had convinced himself that his parents were dead. He was so certain of this that Skip said no when his wife, Carole, asked him if they could take their daughters and join Jayne and Karl up in Mariposa.

"They're dead, they're gone!" he shouted, angry tears in his eyes. "What good can we do now?"

But Carole was determined to help out. While Jayne made arrangements to charter the helicopter, Carole packed her bags and began the six-hour drive to Mariposa. By that afternoon Jayne was aboard a helicopter searching narrow, winding roads for her parents' car. But after several tense hours, Jayne finally directed the pilot to land. The search had turned up nothing.

Hours later Carole arrived in town. She had had a hundred flyers printed on fluorescent-yellow paper showing a picture of Ken and Jean and giving details about their car and the last time and place they were seen. That evening, as Jayne and Karl headed back home to get their parents' dental records, Carole placed flyers at post offices, churches, supermarkets, restaurants, and other retail outlets throughout Mariposa. Finally, sometime near midnight, Carole returned to her motel room and fell asleep, exhausted.

By then even Jayne's and Carole's optimism was beginning to wane. The Chaneys had been missing for nearly two weeks, and the prospects of their being trapped in a snowbank more than twenty miles up a remote mountain road was the farthest thing from their minds.

Meanwhile, the Chaneys had spent several hours that day scraping frost off the windows for a single drink of water. Dehydrated, hungry, and freezing to death, the couple was finally beginning to succumb to the severity of their predicament.

"I still have some time," Jean told Ken, struggling to move her pen across the last of her paper. "I have to tell those children how important it is for them to love each other and most of all to be a family."

### March 12

Each day has been the same. . . . Oh, how we take for granted the little things in life! A drink of water for me will never go unappreciated again. And a bite of food—any kind!! Daddy wants Progresso Chicken Noodle soup. . . . He is getting terribly weak. Today is the first day that I have noticed any weakness. I love you all. Please love one another.

The next morning Carole staged a press conference that was attended by several radio and television stations. When it was over, Carole took another two hundred flyers and began the drive to Fresno. Along the way she posted flyers in every small town and at every truck stop or restaurant. She stopped in Oakhurst and North Fork—the same town Ken and Jean had stopped in before taking the wrong turn up North Fork Road.

As she left the area, she unknowingly came to the same intersection where the couple had mistakenly turned left up the mountainside instead of turning right, back toward the Mariposa Valley. For a moment, Carole sat at the intersection and stared up the road to the left.

"Something was telling me to follow the road up the mountain," she told Jayne later. "Why couldn't I have followed my feelings?"

Instead, she rested her head on the steering wheel for several minutes and cried. "I didn't know what to do," she said. "I had to let it go, let the sheriffs do their job, and leave it to God."

Later that night when she walked in the house, she made one simple statement to Skip: "It's in God's hands now."

### March 18

Kids: I can't find the dome light—writing by glove compartment light. Dad went to the Lord at 7:30 this evening. It was so peaceful, I didn't even know he left. . . . The last thing I heard him say was, "Thank the Lord. . . ." I think I'll be with him soon.

For the next two months Jayne and Karl continued to drive to Mariposa each weekend in search of their parents. Throughout those weeks, life somehow went on. Carole and Skip celebrated his first year of sobriety, his young children attended school, and they returned to work.

But as the days passed, something amazing began to occur. Madge, Skip, and Jayne began to depend on each other. It was more than just the search for their parents. They were becoming friends.

Although Skip thought Ken and Jean were dead, Jayne and Madge held out hope that somehow their parents had perhaps taken off on a last-minute trip from which they could return at any time. But even they experienced times of deep depression as March ended and they trudged through April. Madge remembered how her father would pick up hitchhikers just for a chance to tell them about Jesus, sometimes bringing them home for a warm meal.

"Dad did anything he could to help people get to know the Lord," Madge remembers. "What if this time they picked up the wrong person?"

Jayne agreed. Their parents could have been beaten or murdered and left somewhere on the side of the highway. There were nights when none of the adult Chaney children could sleep because of the terrible images they conjured up.

The breakthrough finally came on May 1. That afternoon the stormy weather eased enough to open North Fork Road and allow a surveying team up along the fifty-mile scenic loop, which by then had been closed for two months.

Twenty-six miles up the road they discovered the Chaneys' Thunderbird, still half buried under snowdrifts ten feet high. The frozen bodies of Ken and Jean were inside, still side by side. On the car's front seat, arranged neatly near Ken and Jean in chronological order, lay the envelopes and torn notebook sheets that contained Jean's final words to her children.

The Chaneys had lived eighteen days trapped in the snow, a fact that at first troubled Madge, Skip, and Jayne.

"The tragedy of them suffering such a long time was so paralyzing at first that we couldn't see past that to Mom's real message," Madge told a friend. "Mom and Dad didn't care about their lives. They knew where they were bound. They cared about us. All they wanted was for us to love God and love one another."

Today the Chaney siblings understand the peace their mother felt before her death. Indeed, her reassuring words have proved to be a legacy of faith and love for Madge, Skip, and Jayne. Each of them believe it would please their parents to know that their final days of praying for them were not in vain.

The changes in their lives took place almost immediately after they learned what happened to their parents.

After reading her mother's journal, Madge left Ohio and moved to California, where she rented a house next door to Jayne. The two sisters have since joined Skip several times for holidays and special occasions. Also, the three Chaney siblings have rediscovered their faith in God, another answer to Jean's final fervent prayers.

"We lost our parents, but we found one another," Jayne told her husband later that year. "Can you see what their death has done, Karl? The three of us finally understand how important it is to be close to one another. What happened on that mountain happened for a reason. Maybe it was God's way of answering Mom and Dad's prayers."

But there was more.

As long as Madge, Skip, and Jayne could remember, their parents had prayed that when their time on Earth was through they might leave together. After analyzing their mother's diary several times, they were convinced that Ken and Jean did, in fact, die on the same day. Together in death as they had always been in life.

So much to say and so little time. Please, please be a family. Love one another and the Lord. Be grateful for one another— for every drink of water and bite of food. Appreciate what you have, and life will take on new meaning. Hug and love my grandbabies. I can't see. Bye. I love you. Jesus love you all!!

# FOURTEEN

# Touched by Angels

*F*or years Patricia Kluksdahl had known what she wanted to do with the gold cross she kept carefully in a small box in her bedroom. Her mother had given it to her when she was a small girl, and on several occasions she had taken it out of the box and shown it to Eric.

"One day it will be yours, son," she would tell him.

"Can't I have it now, Mom?" Eric would ask, holding the cross and turning it over gently as he looked at it.

"When you're older, Eric. Don't worry, the time will come."

On Christmas Day 1993, when Eric was twelve years old, Patricia decided the time was right to let the boy have the precious gold cross. She wrapped it in colorful paper and set it under the Christmas tree. That morning the cross, which dangled from a beautiful gold chain, was Eric's favorite present.

"Mom, it really means a lot to me to wear this," he said. "I'll take good care of it, I promise."

"I know you will, son," Patricia said, tousling Eric's hair. "And when the time comes, you can pass it on to your son or daughter."

After that Eric wore the gold cross proudly to school every day so that each morning and afternoon when Patricia dropped him off she was touched to know that her son was wearing the same cross she'd worn when she was a schoolgirl.

One snowy winter morning two months after Christmas, Patricia and her son were running late to school. As they rushed to slip into their coats and grab Eric's lunch and school books, Eric forgot to put on his cross.

"Mom," he said urgently as they started out the driveway. "I forgot the cross. Please let me go back and get it."

Patricia pulled back up toward the house and handed Eric the keys to the house. "Hurry!" she urged. "Otherwise we'll be late for sure."

Eric nodded and ran toward the house. A minute later he ran back out, the cross necklace clutched tightly in his hand.

"Better put it on," Patricia advised as she hurried toward the school.

"I will. Soon as I get to class," he replied.

Patricia didn't think about the incident again until the next morning. She had gone outside to start the family truck so it would be warm for the drive to school, and when she returned, Eric was on the couch crying.

"Eric?" Patricia said, moving quickly toward the boy. Although Eric was a sensitive boy compared to his peers, he rarely cried, and his mother knew something must be very wrong indeed for him to be so upset.

"Mom, I lost the necklace yesterday at school," he said, his eyes deeply troubled. "It means so much to me, Mom. And I looked everywhere for it, but it's nowhere. I'll never find it!"

"Eric, are you sure you've checked everywhere? Your locker, your classrooms, your book bag? Every place you were yesterday?"

The boy nodded. "I even checked the lost-and-found, and no one's turned it in. I'll never find it now, Mom. I can't believe I lost it."

"Eric, did you check outside the school at all?"

Eric nodded. "I looked all around our parking spot, and it wasn't there, either," he answered.

His mother always parked in the same section of road, directly in front of the local grocery store and across from the junior high school. Eric had searched the road thoroughly before his mother picked him up the day before just in case he had dropped it on the road.

"I thought I might find it at home, so I didn't tell you until now."

Patricia sat next to Eric and wrapped her arms around him as he sobbed even harder. Her heart went out to the boy and she clung to him as she wiped the tears off his cheeks.

"I'm so sorry, Mom," he said, his words coming in short bursts as he tried to talk between the sobs. "I loved that cross. And you've had it since you were a little girl. It was so special to you."

"Oh, Eric. Don't be so upset, honey," Patricia said softly. "I know you didn't mean to lose it."

Eric looked up at his mother. "What can we do, Mom?"

"Well, if you've looked everywhere and can't find it, then the best thing we can do is pray."

The boy nodded and together he and his mother bowed their heads as she prayed that if it was Jesus' will He would send guardian angels to light their paths and show them where Eric had dropped the necklace. As they prayed, Patricia felt a sudden peace wash over her, and somehow she knew that God had heard their prayers and would answer them.

"Now, don't worry about the necklace," Patricia said as Eric dried his eyes. "If it's God's will that we find it, we'll find it. If not, then someone else will find it and it will be special to them."

Eric smiled, his eyes red. "Thanks, Mom. That's a good way to look at it."

As Eric and Patricia set out for school, she had a strong feeling that they would somehow find the necklace that morning. She said nothing of her thoughts to Eric, though, since she didn't want to get the boy's hopes up.

"Light our way, Lord," Patricia prayed silently. "Please let us find that necklace."

They turned in front of the school and moved along the curb toward Patricia's regular parking place. Just at that moment she saw a glistening flash of gold from the section of road where she always parked.

"Eric!" she shouted to her son. "It's your cross. There it is!"

Patricia parked quickly and hurried out of the car and there on the ground was Eric's cross. It was laid out flat, as if someone had arranged it carefully in such a way so that it would be seen. Patricia picked it up and saw that the soft gold had not been run over by a car, despite the constant string of traffic that crossed that spot. The necklace was in perfect condition.

"Mom," Eric said as he climbed out of the car and stared at the necklace in his mother's hand. "That's impossible. I checked here very carefully yesterday, and my cross wasn't here. I'm *positive*."

Patricia considered the possibilities. Had her son dropped it from his hand the morning before, the cross necklace would have landed in a heap on the ground. Certainly it would not have been carefully laid out as it was when she found it.

Eric started laughing and Patricia joined him, hugging him tightly.

"Thank you, Jesus," she whispered.

Eric smiled and looked up to the sky. "Yes, thank you, God."

Later that day Eric talked to his mother about what had happened.

"You know what it was, don't you, Mom?"

"What, Eric?"

"My guardian angels found my cross and put it there on the road so we'd find it," he said confidently.

Patricia considered her son's words. "Yes, I think you're right. I don't know how else to explain what happened, but it's a miracle."

Eric fingered the cross which was safely around his neck once again and smiled at his mother. "That means my cross is probably the only one in the world that's been touched by angels."

# FIFTEEN

# Brought Back to Safety

*D*onna Patterson was anxious and ready to get out of the house for a while. Although it was March, it was still freezing cold outside, and she and her children had spent much of their time inside.

"Who wants to take a walk?" she asked as she climbed into her coat. It was very dark outside, and Donna's Philadelphia neighborhood was not very safe. But she had lived there long enough to feel secure. And that evening she planned to walk no more than once around the block.

Donna looked into the faces of her four children and saw that none of the older three was excited about the idea of a walk. Jasmine, five, and Justin, seven, shook their heads.

"We want to watch TV, Mom," they said. "Don't go for a walk tonight."

Donna looked at her oldest son, Colin, fifteen, and the boy shrugged.

"Not tonight, Mom. Okay?"

"Sure," she said. "But you watch Justin and Jasmine, all right? I'll take Loni."

Her three-year-old son had a lot of energy, and Donna found his riding toy. Even though it was cold, the child could ride alongside her for one block without it bothering him. It would be good for both of them. She took the child's hand and together they left the apartment.

Once outside Donna and Loni had not traveled far when the child no longer wanted his riding toy. Donna sighed and picked up the toy. As she did, she glanced behind her. She was only about half a block from home, and suddenly she saw Justin and Jasmine walking up the street. They were acting sneaky, darting in and out of the shadows as if they were trying to catch up to their mother and surprise her, so Donna decided to play along.

Turning back toward the direction she'd been walking in, she and Loni continued down the street. When they reached the intersection, Donna turned around and looked for them again. This time she didn't see them.

"Hmm," she said out loud, and Loni looked up at her.

"C'mon, Mommy," the child said. "Walk."

Donna stood unmoving, staring back toward her house and straining to see the children. She wondered if perhaps they had gotten scared of the dark and decided to go back home. Then the thought occurred to her that perhaps someone had snatched them. The neighborhood was often a frightening place, and crimes were committed around them each day. Suddenly Donna began to panic.

"Jasmine!" she called out. "Justin!"

There was no response, and Donna could feel herself beginning to actually shake in fear. Quickly she turned around, tightened her grip on Loni's hand, and began heading back toward the apartment.

As they walked, Donna noticed a man across the street who was headed in the same direction. Donna wondered where he had come from, since the few times she had looked back to check her children she hadn't noticed him. Although she was preoccupied with finding Justin and Jasmine, Donna noticed that the man across the street kept looking at them. Since she did not recognize him as someone who lived in the neighborhood, Donna began to be suspicious of the man and picked up her pace, sweeping Loni into her arms. In one hand she held the riding toy and decided she would use it in self-defense if necessary.

"What's wrong, Mommy?" Loni asked, aware of his mother's nervousness.

"Nothing, honey. We're going home now."

As Donna and her son neared the corner of her apartment building, the man began crossing the street at an angle headed in their direction. Terror raced through Donna's body, and she wondered if she could reach her apartment on time if he tried to accost them.

At that instant a thought came to Donna.

"Pretend you see your father at the front door and talk to him," a voice seemed to say.

Instantly Donna acted on the suggestion.

"Hi, Dad!" she yelled, waving in the direction of her apartment, still four units away. "Have you seen the kids?"

Almost at once the man who had been headed straight for her turned around and started walking in the opposite direction. Donna breathed a sigh of relief. She had tricked him into thinking that her father was really at the door and could see them as well as the strange man who had nearly caught up to them.

Donna ran up her apartment steps and dashed inside. Her fears alleviated, Donna saw that Justin and Jasmine sat on the floor watching television as they had been when she left.

"Why did you guys come back home?" she asked. "Were you afraid of the dark or did something scare you? What?"

The children looked blankly at their mother and then at each other.

"What do you mean?" Justin asked.

"You were outside, following behind me. I saw you, so don't act like it wasn't you. Why did you come back inside?"

Colin looked at his mother then and shook his head.

"Mom, they've been right here the whole time," he said simply. "They didn't want to take a walk, remember?"

"That's impossible," she said, moving slowly toward the chair. "I *saw* both of you. You were following behind us, and when I couldn't see you anymore, I decided to turn around."

Then Donna remembered the strange man. For the next thirty minutes she tried to explain to Colin about the man and how threatened she had felt.

"Mom, maybe the kids you saw were angels and the only way they knew to get you to come back home was to make themselves look like Justin and Jasmine?"

Donna stared at her son. She had been thinking the same thing, but she had been afraid to sound crazy.

"I don't know, son. But I'm sure I saw the kids outside tonight."

Donna told everyone who would listen the story about what happened on her walk, but it wasn't until sometime later that she became sure that a miracle had occurred that night. That was when she found out that the man who had been trailing her was an escaped felon from the state prison. Until his recapture, he had carried a gun, robbing people in Donna's neighborhood at gunpoint.

"I believe he intended to rob me, and then kill me and Loni,"

Donna told her friend later. "And by some miracle two children who looked just like mine led me back to safety while *my* children were inside the apartment the whole time. It must be a miracle because things like that just don't *happen*."

# SIXTEEN

# "Someone Loves Me"

$\mathcal{B}$etsy Monroe was taking a coffee break at the office where she worked in Harrisburg, Pennsylvania, when she saw a car race into view, hit the curb, and flip into the air. The sedan rose ten feet up before landing on its roof and crushing the car's passenger compartment. Racing toward the telephone to call an ambulance, Betsy shouted to her co-workers for help.

"Whoever's inside that car doesn't have a chance," she thought to herself as she dialed 911.

Sandy Lee Jones, twenty-eight, had been especially tired that day. It was August 1991, and the weather was hotter than Sandy had ever remembered. But the heat had little to do with Sandy's lack of energy. That summer she was in the middle of a divorce proceeding and had been fighting feelings of hopelessness, depression, and fear.

Her emotions had become so debilitating that some

time earlier she had made a decision to turn her life over to God. She found a church where she could learn about the Bible, and soon connected with two people who had offered to pray with her.

"I don't know what I'd do without you," Sandy told her church friends. "I'm so afraid, so lonely. But I'm starting to understand that my life doesn't have to be over. There is still a future for me and my son."

Part of Sandy's depression was caused by the fact that since the divorce she had become uncertain about what the future held for her son, Don. At times the thought of raising him by herself was overwhelming.

"Sandy, you know God has a plan for you," her friends would tell her. "You just need to trust Him and realize how much He loves you."

"Well," Sandy would respond. "At least someone does."

But even with that knowledge, Sandy had a hard time feeling loved. And that August she had experienced many sleepless nights. As she sat at work one afternoon, a strange, heavy feeling came over her, and she knew she could not stand to stay in the office another minute.

"I need to go home," she told her supervisor. "I guess it's the stress getting to me."

The supervisor let her leave, but instead of going home, Sandy went to see her ex-husband. He was not happy to see her, and their conversation left Sandy feeling worse than before. She was exhausted and she suddenly felt as if she couldn't take another step.

"I need to lie down," she told him. "Just for a few minutes until I have to get Don from school."

The man she had once loved stared at her as if she were a stranger.

"Absolutely not!" he said. "You'll have to rest somewhere else."

With tears blurring her vision, Sandy picked up her purse and left without a word. She got into her car and headed back toward work, her mind consumed with the negative things in her life. She told herself if she could not even rest at her ex-husband's house, then she wouldn't rest at all. She would ignore her depression and lack of sleep and instead go back to work and finish the day.

About that time she stopped at a red light and shut her burning eyes for a moment's rest. But instead she fell asleep and when she opened her eyes, her feet were off the pedals and her car was headed through the intersection out of control.

Jolted into reality, Sandy slammed her foot toward the pedals but instead of hitting the brake she hit the accelerator without realizing it. Believing that her brakes had failed, Sandy screamed for help.

"Oh, God!" she shouted. "Help me, please."

With her accelerator pressed unknowingly to the floor, Sandy's car picked up speed and was traveling approximately fifty-five miles per hour when it hit a curb and became airborne.

For what seemed like minutes, the car twisted and flipped in the air before slamming upside down onto the pavement. Sandy was flooded with the deafening sound of metal twisting and scraping along the pavement and glass breaking. Horrified, Sandy realized that the car had landed on top of her and now pinned her to the ground as it slid along the roadway. Finally the car came to a stop and silence filled the air as slowly Sandy opened her eyes. She was trapped in the flattened driver's area, but she could mover her arms and legs and she felt no pain.

"I'm alive," she cried softly. "Dear God, thank you, I'm alive."

Without realizing it, Sandy had crashed her car across the street from where she worked. Almost as soon as the car stopped moving, she could see her co-workers running from their building toward her. They recognized the car as belonging to Sandy, and one man urged everyone to stand back and not touch anything.

"The car's crushed," one of her friends whispered. "She can't be alive; there's no way she could have lived through that."

"Sandy!" one man shouted. "Are you okay? Can you hear me?"

"Yes. Get me out, please." Her voice was weak. The man tried to calm her and promised to call her family to inform them of the accident.

Just then rescue workers arrived and began the task of trying to free Sandy from the wreckage. They determined that the car had been traveling very fast, since it skidded two hundred feet after landing. After examining the passenger compartment and the destruction surrounding the driver's seat, two rescue workers stared at each other in disbelief.

"She should be dead," one muttered. "Doesn't make sense."

For fifteen minutes paramedics worked to extricate Sandy from the wreckage. Her body was still strapped to the driver's seat, but the impact had crushed the car so that she lay facedown on a layer of windshield glass with the weight of the car on her back. The workers knew that even though she was alive, there was a strong chance that she'd broken her neck or back. After all, the car had landed on top of her and literally pinned her to the ground.

When they had created enough room, one worker crawled into the flattened car and carefully pulled Sandy out.

"Tell me what hurts." His voice was gentle, and Sandy began to cry as she took her first look at her car.

"Nothing hurts. I'm fine."

The workers exchanged another incredulous look. Usually when a seriously injured accident victim felt no pain, it was because a broken neck had severed the spinal cord. They laced Sandy quickly and efficiently to a back board and rushed her into the ambulance.

Not until Sandy had been checked over at the hospital did news of her condition become widespread. Although the doctors wanted to keep her overnight for observation, Sandy's neck and back were fine.

Other than a bruised leg, she had suffered no injuries.

The next morning a doctor entered her room and grinned at her. "What's your connection?" he asked.

Sandy looked puzzled. "Connection?"

"You must be tight with the Man Upstairs, because that accident should have killed you, young lady. No doubt about it. At the very least it should have broken your neck. But here you are with nothing more than a bruise."

The doctor held up a pair of beige high-heel pumps.

"Recognize these?"

"Sure," Sandy hesitated, not sure what he was getting at. "They're my shoes. I was wearing them yesterday when I had the accident."

"Well, according to the paramedics they were neatly arranged just outside your car window when they arrived on the scene." He paused and glanced skyward. Then he looked back at Sandy and smiled. "I'd say somebody up there loves you."

Suddenly the depression and weight of her personal problems lifted, and Sandy felt a burst of joy. She was alive when she should have been dead. She had a wonderful son whom she loved dearly, and she had friends who cared about her problems as well as a good job.

She would survive this difficult time and grow stronger as a result. And she knew that the doctor was right. The shoes must have been a small sign that God had His hand on her as her car flipped into the air and landed on her back. Indeed, someone did love her, and now, with a new lease on life, she would never forget it.

# SEVENTEEN

# Mysterious Strangers

*F*rom the time she was a little girl, Christine Clark could feel God's protective hands around her. She and her siblings were raised with Christian values in a family where attending church and believing in God was a way of life. But like so many, Christine fell away from the ideals she'd been taught as a child and didn't return to them until she was thirty-five, married, and with a family of her own.

"Somehow everything is new to me, all the things I've known for years," Christine confided in her husband, Earl, one day. "I really know God now, and everything about Him seems suddenly real."

Her faith became so strong that it came as no surprise to Earl when Christine formed a group in her hometown, Bryan, Ohio, called the Christian Woman's Prayer Breakfast. Over the years as the group continued to grow, Christine was very vocal about the need for women to meet together and pray.

"Our children, our marriages, our schools, and our community," she'd tell her audiences. "All of them need our prayers."

Christine was aware that even agnostic scientists had been able to prove prayer changes things, even if they couldn't explain why. Since that was the case, she was determined to start a chain reaction of women's groups meeting for that very purpose.

Over the years, with the help of many other women, prayer breakfasts began sprouting up in other Ohio towns and eventually throughout the midwest and the United States. Eventually the group came to be called the Christian Woman's Club, and it included an active chapter in Washington, D.C.

"If there is any place where we need people who will pray for this country, it's at the Capitol," Christine told her husband.

Earl smiled at her. He was proud of her hard work and the way in which her desire to pray with other women had caught on around the country. "Go get 'em, Christine," he would tell her. "Get the whole country down on their knees."

"Earl, one day I want to go to Washington, D.C. and see for myself that women there are praying, too," she said. "Maybe when the kids are grown and moved away."

Earl thought a moment. "That's a long time from now and a long way from home, dear," he said. "But you never know. Maybe one day you will have that chance."

The opportunity came more than two decades later in the winter of 1977 not long after Christine's sixtieth birthday, long after she had accepted the position of president of the prayer group. That January, Christine was invited to speak at the group's annual nationwide meeting in Washington, D.C.

"You don't care if I go, do you, Earl?" she asked, holding up the invitation excitedly, her eyes sparkling as they hadn't done in years.

Earl chuckled. "Well, I guess you'll find some way to go no matter what I say," he said. "That's a lot of travel to do by yourself, but I'm sure you'll be fine." He paused and pointed to the telephone. "Well, don't stand around thinking about it. Better get yourself some plane tickets."

One month later Christine and four of her friends from a nearby chapter of the prayer group left for the meeting with plans to stay four days and tour the capital. The trip went far better than Christine ever expected. She was greatly encouraged by the excitement among her peers to continue meeting each week for prayer and to involve more women in the process. She was also proud of herself for traveling so fearlessly after so many years of staying close to home.

"I know I'm not a worldly traveler," she told her friends after a day of meetings that week. "But I wasn't afraid to come here, and I have peace about the trip home. God's brought me this far, and He'll see me back safely."

Christine planned to return to Ohio that Saturday, but Friday morning the weather forecasters began announcing that a terrible snowstorm was traveling across much of the Midwest, including Ohio. That afternoon Christine called home and talked to Earl about the reports.

"Is it true about the weather, Earl?" she asked. Earl was surprised that Christine sounded so calm, and he cleared his throat.

"Yes, dear," he said. "It hit last night and it looks like a bad one. Everything's closed down. Maybe you better stay in Washington, D.C., for a few days."

"Oh, Earl. I don't think that's necessary," she said. "I've had a great time, but I'm ready to come home."

Earl sighed. "Listen, Christine, there's absolutely no movement anywhere in town. The turnpike's closed from here to Indiana, and the radio announcer is warning people to stay off the roads. When does your plane leave?"

"Early in the morning."

"No, Christine. That just won't work. You'll have to stay at least another day until they can clear the roads."

"Earl, I want to come home," Christine said, her voice confident and certain. "If my plane leaves for Toledo, I'm going to be on it."

Earl shook his head. "Don't be stubborn, Christine. It's not worth getting stuck out there in the snow."

"I know that. But they won't fly into Toledo if it's unsafe. Don't worry, I'll be fine. And I'll call you if there's any change in plans."

Saturday morning, an hour before she needed to be at the airport, Christine called the airlines and asked about her flight.

"It's not great flying conditions, but we're planning on taking off as scheduled," an airline representative told her.

At the same time Christine's friends, who lived several hours from Bryan, Ohio, contacted the airline they were flying on and discovered that their flight was canceled. They would have to wait until late Sunday night in order to leave Washington, D.C.

"You're going to go anyway, aren't you, Christine?" her friend, Nell, asked.

Christine nodded. "Yes." She was quiet a moment, for the first time feeling a slight hesitation in her resolve to get back to Ohio. "Why don't we all pray that everything will go all right for me on the way home?"

Having prayed together as a group for several years, the women did what came naturally to them. They formed a circle and asked God to grant safe travel to Christine as she flew and then drove back to her hometown.

Christine arrived at the airport with plenty of time and was surprised to see that only ten people were on the airplane when it took off.

"Is this normal?" she asked one of the flight attendants. "There's hardly anyone on the plane."

The woman shook her head. "Everyone else canceled because of the weather. I guess you're one of the brave ones."

The pilot announced during the flight that they would have perfect flying conditions throughout the trip since the storm had finally ended.

"But you're in for a tricky drive once you land," he said. "It's twenty degrees below zero, and there are drifts of snow ten feet high across most of Ohio."

When the plane landed in Toledo, Christine was surprised to find the airport virtually empty, with lights dimmed and no heat. Christine wrapped her arms around herself and began shivering. She was wearing only a lightweight dress and a long sweater and was unprepared for the freezing temperatures that awaited her outside. She found a pay phone and quickly called Earl.

"I'm in Toledo, have you heard about the roads?" she asked.

"Yes, the turnpike's open but only one lane each way. They're still advising people to stay off the roads," he said. "Honey, why don't you spend the night in a motel out there and make the trip tomorrow morning."

Christine thought a minute. "If the turnpike is open, I want to come home, Earl. It's only two in the afternoon, and I'll be home long before dark."

Earl was surprised at Christine's independence. She had never traveled much by herself and now she was acting as confident as a veteran traveler. "You have a good feeling about it, don't you?"

"Yes, Earl. The ladies and I prayed about it. I'll be fine. God will get me home safely."

Carefully Christine made her way across the snow-packed parking lot to her car. She stared at the vehicle in disbelief. There were snowdrifts around and on top of most of the cars in the lot. But hers had no snow on it. She smiled knowingly and climbed inside. The moment she turned the key, the car came to life.

"As if it had been sitting in a warm garage," she told Earl later, "instead of standing idle for days in freezing weather."

Rather than worry about what conditions she might encounter on the ride home, Christine thanked God for letting her car start so easily and began singing hymns they had sung at the conference. She was filled with joy at the memories she'd made and the new friendships that had blossomed as a result of the national meeting.

As she exited the airport, she had to decide whether to turn right or left. Either way would lead her to the turnpike but the distance was far shorter to turn left. She stared toward the left and saw that snow filled the road. Then suddenly a car came from that direction and Christine decided that the road must be opened if that car had made it through. Carefully she turned her car left, feeling the tires slipping beneath her.

The route she had chosen took her along a narrow road that was not well-traveled, and as Christine inched along atop a foot of packed snow, she saw towering drifts on both sides of her. As she continued she could see cars completely buried in snow and several which had overturned into the ditch that ran the length of the road.

Since everything was covered with snow, Christine became disoriented and missed turning onto the street that would take her to the turnpike. Instead she continued straight ahead unaware that she was traveling into a dangerously remote area. When she had traveled nearly half a mile, she saw a mountain of snow blocking the road ahead of her. Christine felt a twinge of frustration. The snowdrift made it impossible to continue in that direction. The road was narrow and bordered by snowdrifts, so Christine stopped the car and tried to imagine a way to turn around. Looking over her shoulder there seemed to be a clear spot on the right side of the road, so she slowly backed into it.

Almost instantly the back wheels of Christine's car began spinning wildly. Although she rarely drove in winter conditions, she knew enough to understand that she was stuck. Her tires had lost traction with the road. She sat a moment, still calm and certain that God would help her out of the predicament she suddenly faced.

She thought about her options. She was sixty years old, and she knew she would be unable to push her car out of the snow. She could remain inside the car with the engine running, allowing the car's heater to keep her warm. But what if she ran out of gasoline? And what if the road had been closed and no one traveled that way for several days. She closed her eyes and again asked God for his help. When she opened them, she turned and looked toward the right where the snow still blocked the road. There, seemingly stuck in the snow, was a car with two men inside.

At that instant the men climbed out of the car and walked in her direction. They wore similar long gray coats and matching caps and as they approached her they neither waved nor spoke. Christine glanced to her left, in the direction she had come, and was puzzled. There had been no other cars on the road, and she wondered how their vehicle had suddenly appeared. Then she looked again at the two men who had nearly reached her car.

Just then the men stopped moving and stared at her. There was peace in there eyes, and as they exchanged eye contact, Christine felt reassurance. Her car was still running, but she had taken her foot off the gas pedal. At that instant her car lurched forward, and as if it was being moved by the hands of a giant the car slid back onto the road. Suddenly, without having touched the steering wheel or gas pedal, Christine was facing the right direction.

Jolted by the sudden movement, Christine put her foot on the gas pedal and found that the car responded with ease. She looked in her rearview mirror to see if the men had climbed back into their car, but they were gone. There was no sign of them or their car, and Christine felt a burst of adrenaline race through her body. The road was just one lane because of the snow and the drift blocking the way prevented anyone from traveling beyond it. So there was no way for the men to get out of that area except to travel behind Christine in the same direction she was driving.

Instantly Christine knew what had happened.

"They were angels," she muttered to herself. "Sent by God to turn me around get me headed in the right direction."

In her opinion, there was no other explanation.

Christine made the rest of the journey without incident, and when she walked through the front door she quickly thanked God for looking out for her.

When she walked into the house, Earl approached her from one of the back rooms and saw what seemed to be an unnatural glow about his wife's face.

"What is it?" he asked. "Has something happened?"

Christine smiled warmly. "Yes, Earl. Come sit down. I have to tell you about my miracle."

# EIGHTEEN

# Pictures from Heaven

Kathryn was thirteen when she met Kenneth Smith. He was tall and muscular, a seventeen-year-old construction worker who had come to Kathryn's house to work for her father. She was a brunette, petite but mature for her age, and she and Kenneth became friends quickly.

Long after the work was finished at Kathryn's house in Taylors, South Carolina, Kenneth continued to stop by. Often he would eat dinner with her family, talking with her and her parents long into the evening.

"That Kenneth is a good one, he is," her mother told her on several occasions. "I really like that boy."

Kathryn would blush at the suggestion. By then she had strong feelings for Kenneth but knew that she was too young even to formally date him.

"I want to marry you one day, Kathryn," he told her after they'd been friends for more than a year.

Kathryn looked shyly at the only boy she had ever

loved and smiled. "Ah, Ken, how long do you think we'll have to wait?"

It was 1941 and people commonly got married in their teenage years. But Kathryn wasn't yet fifteen, and she had visions of having to wait four years before she and Kenneth could be together like they wanted to be. Six months before her fifteenth birthday, she and Kenneth approached her parents. By then they loved Kenneth as if he were their own son, and they were very pleased with the idea of him marrying Kathryn. But they wanted the young couple to wait at least a year before planning a wedding.

So on June 6, 1942, shortly before Kathryn's sixteenth birthday and just after Kenneth turned nineteen, the two were married.

"I'll never leave you, Kathryn," Kenneth told his young bride that day. "I'm going to take care of you forever."

But even as they celebrated, the United States was being drawn into World War II, and just thirteen weeks after their wedding Kenneth was drafted and ordered to report to active duty. He was devastated at the thought of leaving Kathryn, and he made certain that she was settled back at her parents' house before they said their tearful good-byes.

"I'll come home soon, Kath," he told her. "I promise."

Kathryn nodded through misty eyes and clung to him. She knew nothing of the war or why it was being fought, only that people died in wars. And she couldn't bear to imagine losing Kenneth now. "Please," she whispered. "Please be safe."

Kenneth was selected to be a member of the Army's Quartermaster Corps in the 608th Battalion. As he set out for Fort Lee in Virginia, where he would be trained as a mechanic, he was heartsick about leaving Kathryn but thrilled about one aspect of his departure. He was leaving alongside Joe Grifford, one of his closest boyhood friends.

After receiving their training, he and Joe were sent to France in

1943. In a letter to Kathryn he told her that their division would be in charge of retrieving disabled military vehicles from the battlefield, bringing them back to makeshift garages, and repairing them for battle. It was a dangerous job since the battlefield was likely to be littered with mines, but he promised to be careful.

"Joe and I will watch out for each other," he wrote. "Don't worry. I'll be home as soon as I can."

Over the next three years Kenneth and Joe worked alongside each other through numerous heated battles in Europe. There were times when they saw members of their corps torn apart by the sharpened shards of underground mines.

On occasion Kenneth would send pictures back to Kathryn along with his letters. "We're hanging in there, Kath," he'd write. "There is death all around us. But we're pulling through. We keep watching out for each other, and the Lord watches out for us, too. I am thankful for my camera; otherwise I would be unable to believe this is really happening around us."

Many times the pictures were of Kenneth and Joe, working together on a damaged vehicle or trudging through a battlefield littered with bodies. It was a horrific three years during which Kenneth wrote to Kathryn on a regular basis.

Then, suddenly, in October 1945, the letters stopped.

The war was over and all around the country American boys were returning to their hometowns. Daily listings of soldiers being released for home were printed in every newspaper across the United States—including the newspaper in Taylors, South Carolina.

Each day Kathryn would race for the morning paper and scan the list of names desperately looking for Kenneth's. When she didn't find it, she would wait impatiently for the mail hoping that her husband's letters had perhaps been lost and would finally arrive that afternoon.

But the holidays arrived and still there was no word from Kenneth.

"Daddy, what if something happened to him?" Kathryn asked that Christmas, voicing her deepest fears.

"Honey," her father said, taking her hand. "Ken is a smart man. He survived that whole wretched war. Now, don't go thinking something happened to him in these last few days. He'll be home any time now. Just wait and see."

But Kathryn was still frightened. The soldiers were returning home by ship on sometimes rough seas. There had been several stories of men who had survived the entire war only to drown at sea when one of the homeward-bound ships went down. She began spending more time in her room, praying that God would let Kenneth come back to her.

Then, early in the morning on January 8, 1946, while she was still sleeping, Kathryn's brother burst into her room.

"Wake up!" he ordered, his excited voice little more than a whisper. "Come on, Kath, right now! Wake up!"

"What? What's happening?" Kathryn rubbed her eyes and struggled out of bed, shivering in the cold despite her long flannel nightgown. She opened her eyes and stared at her brother.

"Come on." He took her hand. "I have to show you something."

For a moment she froze. "Is it good or bad?" she asked him softly. "Please tell me that."

"Oh, Kath, for heaven's sake, it's good! Now, come on!"

Kathryn imagined that perhaps her brother had found an early copy of the newspaper and finally located Kenneth's name. With that idea in mind, she nearly jumped from her bed and raced down the stairs behind her brother to the first floor of her parents' house. At the bottom of the stairs, her brother suddenly stepped to the side.

There, still in his uniform and smiling wildly with tears in his eyes, was Kenneth.

"Oh, dear God!" Kathryn's hand flew to her mouth and she began to cry. "You're alive."

"Kathryn," Kenneth said as the two embraced, clinging to each other. After what seemed like several minutes they pulled away and looked at each other. Kenneth had been gone more than three years, and at age twenty-two he had become a man. His shoulders were broad and his face more defined, and Kathryn felt suddenly shy in his presence. She, meanwhile, was nineteen now and more beautiful than she had ever been as a young teenager.

"I haven't heard from you in so long, Ken," she said. "I thought you were dead."

"Ah, Kath, I'm so sorry. A bunch of our letters didn't make it because we were traveling back home. It was a long journey. And, well, there's something else. . . ."

Kathryn could see the pain in Kenneth's eyes and she was immediately concerned. "What? What happened, Ken?"

Her husband stared at the ground and was quiet a moment, unable to talk because of the emotions that welled up inside him. "It's Joe," he said finally. "We were cleaning up; one of the last missions right before we shipped out. He stepped on a mine, Kath. He never had a chance."

Kenneth spent the next few hours telling Kathryn how he and Joe had never done a mission without the other except on that afternoon. Joe had agreed to help another soldier in their corps so that the division could finish quickly and ship out sooner.

"We promised to be with each other, to look out for each other. But when he needed me most, I wasn't there."

"Joe," Kathryn soothed him, running her had over his short-cropped hair. "You couldn't have known."

Kenneth nodded and opened his duffel bag. Inside were several large envelopes of pictures.

"We began developing our own pictures there in the garage," Kenneth explained. "I think I must have hundreds of pictures."

He sorted through the collection until he found one particular picture of him and Joe. "I'll remember him forever, Kathryn. He was like a brother to me. A best friend."

Kathryn took the picture carefully. "At least you have these. So you'll never forget."

Kenneth nodded somberly. "As horrible as that war was, I don't ever want to forget. We made history over there, Kath. Me and Joe made history."

Indeed over the next several decades Kenneth never forgot Joe nor their years in World War II. As Kathryn and Kenneth became the parents of five children, Kenneth pulled out his World War II pictures often. The children would climb on his lap or cuddle close beside him, and he would tell about the brave deeds done by the soldiers, and always he would show them the pictures of he and Joe.

"Nothing more special than a close friend," he would tell them. "Joe died for this country, and I'll never forget him."

Sometimes Kenneth allowed the children to use his precious pictures for school projects, illustrating the horrors of World War II and the realities of life on the battlefields of Europe. Later, when his children had children of their own, he continued the legacy, sharing his tales with them and showing them his World War II pictures. Kenneth vowed that one day even his great-grandchildren would know that their great grandfather had made history, serving in World War II where he had lost his best friend on the battlefield.

Then one day in 1983, one of Kathryn and Kenneth's teenage granddaughters came to live with them in South Carolina. Kathryn, then fifty-eight, and Kenneth, then sixty-two agreed to move into the basement and give their granddaughter their room. One afternoon Kathryn came home to find that their granddaughter had already moved her belongings into their former bedroom and had scattered them throughout the room. She had also removed pictures from the wall and moved other things from the closet. In addition, she had thoughtlessly thrown out many of her grandparents' belongings in an attempt to make room for her own things.

Frustrated, Kathryn hurriedly removed everything that belonged to her and Kenneth into the basement so that their granddaughter could get settled.

Later that year Kenneth began looking for his World War II pictures so he could use them for a grandson's school project. When he did not immediately find them, he called for Kathryn.

"Honey, please help me find those pictures. They were in our room all those years, and now they're nowhere," he said.

Together they searched the attic, basement, closets, and throughout every inch of space in their small two-bedroom home. The pictures had been in an old worn box filled with envelopes of pictures from the forty-two years they'd been married. There were pictures of children, grandchildren, special occasions, and landmarks in their lives. But now those and every picture Kenneth had taken during World War II were completely gone.

"I've got to find those pictures, Kathryn," Kenneth said later that evening after they had searched all day for the box of photos. "Those are all I have to remind me of Joe."

Kathryn felt a sinking feeling in the pit of her stomach. She had an idea about what might have happened to the pictures, and she decided it was time to tell Kenneth. She reminded him of the time when their granddaughter had moved in and told him that she had brought her things into their former bedroom in somewhat of a hurry.

"She threw many of the things in our room away, Kenneth," Kathryn said softly.

"And you think . . ." he began, unable to finish.

Kathryn nodded. "She must have thrown our photographs away."
Over the years Kathryn had rarely seen Kenneth cry. He had cried
when he left for service in World War II, and cried when he came
home and told her about Joe's death. But since then she could not
remember having seen him cry. Now, though, as they sat together
realizing that a lifetime of memories might be gone forever, tears
welled up in Kenneth's eyes.

He stared at his hands and shook his head slowly. "Kath, we've
just got to find those pictures. We've got to."

"Maybe we should ask God to bring them back to us," Kathryn
said, taking Kenneth's hands and squeezing them tightly.

"You think he cares about something like that?" Kenneth asked
doubtfully.

"Of course. He loves us and He cares about everything we care
about."

For the next several minutes the couple prayed that God would
keep their pictures safe and allow them to be returned home where
they belong.

When they finished praying, Kenneth looked up at his wife. "We've
looked everywhere, Kathryn, you know that. It'll take a miracle
now."

Kathryn smiled. "That's all right, Kenneth. I believe in miracles."

Months passed and the following winter Kathryn was sitting on
the living room sofa one evening when she had a sudden strong desire
to check the attic. For some reason she could not explain, she believed
the pictures would be there.

Kathryn reasoned with the idea and thought it a silly one since she
and Kenneth had thoroughly searched the attic several times and
found none of the missing photos. Still, the feeling that she should
check the attic persisted. Finally she stood up and faced her husband.

"Kenneth, I believe I'm going to search the attic for those pictures," she announced.

Kenneth looked at her strangely. "Why, Kathryn, you know we've looked through that attic a dozen times. They're not up there. Besides, it's freezing outside, and you'll catch a cold if you go up there."

"That's all right," she said stubbornly, heading for the attic door. "I'll need some help pulling down the stairs, but I'm going up there right now."

Kenneth glanced at their son and grandson who were visiting with them that evening and shrugged. "Come on," he said. "Let's go give Grandma a hand."

Kenneth followed his wife into the hallway and reached up to pull down the attic stairs. A cold draft immediately filled the hallway.

"Come on, Kathryn," he said once more. "This is crazy. It's freezing up there."

Kathryn pulled her shawl tightly around her shoulders and shook her head adamantly. "No. I need to look right this instant. I just have a feeling about this."

She climbed the stairs carefully, pulled a string that turned on the attic light, and poked her head over the landing. There in plain sight was a beautiful cardboard box sitting an arm's distance from the steps. Kathryn looked puzzled. She had never seen the box before, but she slid it closer to her and saw that it was not covered with dust or cobwebs, as many of the items in the attic were.

Carefully Kathryn lifted the lid off the box, and there packed neatly and in perfect order were Kenneth's World War II pictures and every other family picture that had been missing for nearly a year.

"Kenneth!" she shouted, her voice muffled. "Kenneth, it's the pictures. They were sitting right here near the steps."

Kenneth looked at his son and grandson. "That's impossible," he said gruffly. "We've been through that attic inch by inch. We'd have seen them."

Kathryn tried to lift the box but found it was too heavy to move. She climbed down the stairs and eventually it took her son and grandson working together to get the box down the stairs.

Over the years Kathryn and Kenneth had kept their pictures together but never in a neat, organized fashion. As the couple looked through the box now, they realized that now the pictures were in perfect order according to the date they'd been taken.

"I don't understand," Kenneth said, shocked by the discovery. "They're back in a box we've never seen, in an order we've never placed them in, and put in a spot where neither of us could have placed them. It doesn't make sense."

Kathryn smiled and leaned closer to her husband. "Yes, it does," she said. "We prayed about those pictures and asked God for a miracle, didn't we?"

Kenneth nodded.

"Well, Kenneth," she said. "Sometimes you don't have to understand something. It's enough just to know God heard you and to thank Him up and down. And after that to just believe that once in a while he really does work a miracle."

# NINETEEN

# Timely Assistance

Steve and Charlotte Paulson were a quiet couple, determined to lead a simple life in their hometown of Everett, Washington, a suburb of Seattle. Charlotte was a slim, soft-spoken elementary school teacher who was shy around adults. Steve was much the same way, a quiet man with an athletic build and thick red-brown hair. For years he had run a nursery not far from their home.

Soon after they got married, Charlotte gave birth to the couple's only child, a son named John. Like his parents, John was shy around other people, and he grew up saying little in times of conflict. He learned at an early age the art of cooperation and how to go with the flow of things around him.

So it was that when John was overlooked for a class presentation, or passed by when the time came to choose character actors for the school play, neither he nor his parents complained.

"Sometimes that happens," his mother would tell him. "Don't let it get you down, son."

But as John grew older and began playing sports, he and his parents noticed that he was paying a price for his quiet nature.

"He's as good as any of the boys on the team, but the other kids always get the most playing time," Charlotte complained to Steve one night. "We know it's happening, but we don't say anything and neither does he. Do you think that's right, Steve?"

Her husband shrugged. "It'll have to be all right, Charlotte. We can't change who he is. If they don't play him for his athletic abilities, there's not much we can do about it."

Charlotte began to develop a special empathy for her son since she, too, had been a quiet child. Also, as a teacher, Charlotte was able to see how soft-spoken children were often overlooked in the classroom setting. She was sure that was the reason John had been spending more time on the bench than on the playing field.

Finally, when John entered high school, he was finally given a chance to prove his abilities. Despite the fact that he was not as talkative as the other boys, he became one of the strongest members of the local high school's football team.

Then, during his senior year, everything changed. The team had a considerable amount of talent, and the school administration decided to bring in a more experienced head coach to lead them to what might be a state championship. The new coach watched the boys during practice for one week and announced a new starting lineup. John's name was not on the list.

Although he was bitterly disappointed, he did not complain about the change to his parents. Not until they attended the first game that year did they see how little playing time their son was given. Eventually Steve became so disappointed he rarely attended the games.

"It hurts the boy to have me up there in the stands when he knows

I won't get to see him play more than a few minutes on the field," Steve explained to his wife.

Her face fell and she looked absently out the window. "I know. It's breaking his heart, but even if it kills him, he won't say anything about it."

The redeeming factor that year was the fact that the team was extremely successful under the new coach. The boys were undefeated during the regular season and marched steadily through the playoffs until finally they had just one game left. The state championship. Even though John was sorry he hadn't seen more playing time, he was as thrilled as his teammates with the prospect of playing in the championship. That year the contest was to be played three hours away from Everett near central Washington. Charlotte promised she would drive the Bronco to see the game, but Steve wasn't sure.

"Steve, why don't you join me?" Charlotte pleaded with him. "I know he may not play much, but it's the state championship after all. Just this once I think you should be there."

"I've been to other games, Charlotte. It kills me to watch him ride the bench when I know how good he is," Steve said, releasing a loud sigh. "I just don't see the point of going. Besides, I have to tend to my trees. They need a lot of work, and if this nursery's going to be a success I'll have to put in some extra time."

Charlotte nodded and muttered a phrase she said quite often, "Sometimes that happens." Then she made an effort to smile. "I'll be all right; I'll just go by myself."

When the game day arrived, Charlotte visited a friend and asked her to pray for a change in attitude.

"I can't help but feel resentful against the coach, Mary," she said. "I know he isn't keeping John for personal reasons, but if John was outgoing and popular like the other boys, I really think he'd be starting."

Mary nodded in understanding. "I'll pray for you, Charlotte. It doesn't help anyone for you to be resentful. It's just one year out of John's life. Besides, he seems like he's having fun."

"He is; that's just it. Now if only I could let it go and accept the fact that even though they're playing for the state title, John probably won't even get his uniform dirty."

"Now, Charlotte." Mary smiled. "What is it you always say? 'Sometimes that happens,' isn't that it?"

Charlotte grinned sadly. "Yes, that's my line. Sometimes that happens."

"Well, it's true. Sometimes that happens and all we can do is go on to the next thing. Listen, when you get home tonight, read *Psalm Thirty-four*. Maybe that'll help you feel better."

Charlotte knew Mary was right, but when she left for the game, she was still distracted, frustrated at what seemed like an unfair situation. Win or lose, it would be John's last football game as a high school player, and Charlotte wanted so badly for John to feel good about his role on the team.

When she arrived she found seats on the fifty-yard line just twenty rows up from the field. But John played only a few minutes, and the Everett team struggled throughout, losing by several touchdowns. After the game Charlotte approached the fence separating the crowd from the field and caught John's attention.

"Good effort, John!" she shouted over the din of cheerleaders and marching bands. "Sorry you lost."

John looked around. "Where's Dad?" he mouthed.

Charlotte felt her heart sink. "Not here!" she shouted back. "Had to work."

John nodded, waving solemnly to Charlotte and then walking slowly off the field alongside several of his teammates.

Charlotte's eyes filled with tears as she made her way back to the

Bronco. She would do anything, she told herself, to ease the disappointment for John. She climbed into her truck and wiped her eyes. But even as she tried to put the game out of her mind, John's pained expression continued to haunt her.

When she arrived back in Everett, she pulled into the supermarket parking lot with her mind on a thousand other things. Because the area was hilly, several parking spaces were on steep slants. Even the shopping carts had hand brakes to prevent them from rolling uncontrollably.

Charlotte chose one of the most steep spots and parked her Bronco. After putting the emergency brake on the truck, she climbed out and began walking toward the market, still preoccupied with thoughts from the day.

Just then she heard several people scream and point toward her Bronco. Charlotte turned around and saw that the vehicle had begun rolling backward and was headed for two parked cars.

"Stop!" she screamed as she ran toward her truck. Without thinking about her actions or the fact that she was merely five-feet-three and without much upper body strength, Christine threw herself behind the Bronco and tried to stop it from moving.

Just before the Bronco would have crushed her, it came to a sudden stop. Realizing the danger she had unwittingly placed herself in, Charlotte stood up straight and looked beside her. There, holding the vehicle in place with their hands, were three men. The tallest of the three smiled and spoke.

"You can get into the car now," he said.

Charlotte nodded and moved quickly into the driver's seat. In her distracted state of mind, she had not applied the emergency brake as tightly as was necessary to keep the truck from moving down the hill. She parked the Bronco once more and put the brake firmly in place.

When she climbed out, the tall man who had spoken to her was no where in sight.

The other two men stood several yards away leaning against a car. Charlotte stared at them and thought they looked unearthly, somehow. They were probably in their thirties and looked like ranchers, but their teeth were brilliantly white and as straight as dentures. There was also something unfamiliar and strange about their eyes, yet their expression filled Charlotte with peace and made her forget the heartache from earlier that day.

Charlotte approached them hurriedly. "Thank you," she said. "I guess I could have been killed."

One of the men nodded. "That truck would have run right over you, ma'am."

Charlotte shook her head. "I had the brake on, just not tightly enough, I guess," she said. "Well"—she looked toward the market— "thanks again. I'm really sorry to bother you."

"Don't worry about it," the other man said, smiling in a way that was both serene and unnerving. "Sometimes that happens."

"Yes . . ." Charlotte was suddenly struck by the man's words. They were the very words that she had used so often in the past. She cocked her head curiously and stared at the men. Then she shrugged and waved goodbye, turning toward the market.

Later that night after she had unpacked her groceries and told Steve about the incident with the Bronco, she remembered that her friend, Mary, had suggested she read Psalm 34. She found her Bible and flipped through the Old Testament looking for the right chapter, and suddenly her eyes fell on these words.

"The angels of the Lord encamp around those who fear Him and He delivers them."

"Angels," she whispered out loud. She thought of her Bronco and how it had almost crushed her that evening. Instantly the problems of the past year fell into perspective, and Charlotte saw the greater picture of their lives as a family. John had been born with a personality that made him less outgoing than other children, but in that instant Charlotte was at peace with the fact.

The important thing she realized was that God had a plan for John and for their family. He wanted them to support each other, encourage each other, and not be frustrated by the things outside their control. And in that plan God would continue to protect them much as He had protected her from certain death at the supermarket.

# TWENTY

# That Special Life

$B$ack then there was no way for anyone in the Oppedisano family to know how special that summer of 1939 would become. It started out like any other and would have been uneventful for the Oppedisano children if it weren't for Catuzza Lizzi. While their mother tended to household duties, eleven-year-old Antoinette was put in charge of keeping her little brother, Joe, occupied.

One morning soon after summer started Antoinette was playing with Joe outside the house in Albany, New York, where their family rented the upstairs when Catuzza walked past with a bag of groceries. She and her husband had no children yet, but that morning Antoinette noticed that Catuzza was pregnant.

"Hey," she called out. "Want some help?"

Catuzza stopped and smiled at the young girl. She had married into the Lizzi family and not long after they had decided to turn the upstairs floor of their trilevel house into an apartment the Oppedisano family had become their tenants. Not until after the families had shared the house for several months did they realize that their ancestors had lived in the same Sicilian village in Italy many years earlier.

"I don't believe in coincidence," the senior Oppedisano would tell his children. "Our families were together back then and we're together now. There must be a reason for that."

Now, as Catuzza looked at the young Oppedisano children, she welcomed their help. After all, they were practically family.

"Sure, Antoinette, I'd love the help." Catuzza set down her bag and watched Antoinette take her brother's hand and scramble to pick up the bag. The children trailed behind as Catuzza entered her apartment.

"Why don't you set them there," Catuzza said, pointing to a small kitchen table. Then she looked at the blond-haired boy peeking out from behind his big sister's skirt.

"Well, hi, there, Joe," she said. Looking at Antoinette, she smiled warmly. "Would you two like to stay for some cookies and maybe I could bring out some paper and colorful pencils?"

Antoinette was thrilled with the idea, and for the rest of the morning the children stayed at the Lizzi house visiting with Catuzza. Just before they left to go home, Joe walked up to Catuzza and stared at her protruding stomach. Catuzza smiled and tentatively Joe reached up, touching her gently with his pudgy hand.

"Ball?" he asked.

Catuzza laughed and her cheeks grew red. "No, it's not a ball. It's a baby. I have a baby inside my tummy."

The child's eyes grew wide. "Baby? Inside you?" he asked.

"Yes." Catuzza held his hand and moved it over her taut midsection. "It's okay to touch it. Maybe you'll feel my baby kicking."

Joe left his hand on Catuzza and continued to stare at her abdomen.

"Love baby," he said softly. "My baby."

Catuzza smiled again. "No, sweetie. It's my baby. But when it's born you can be his or her friend. Okay?"

Joe seemed satisfied with the answer and nodded. Then he leaned over and kissed Catuzza's stomach before skipping away with his sister.

After that, the children returned every morning, and Catuzza was happy to have the company. Her husband was a shoemaker, and she was often lonely while he kept long hours at the shop. She enjoyed visiting with the Oppedisano children, and was especially taken by Joe. Each time the boy visited, he was enthralled with Catuzza's pregnant body. He would pat Catuzza stomach and stare at her, even resting his head on her. Sometimes the child would feel the baby kick and then squeal in delight.

"I don't understand it," Antoinette said, looking strangely at her brother. "Joe has been around other pregnant mothers. We know many pregnant women, even now, and he never made this sort of fuss over her."

"Maybe they're going to be special friends," Catuzza said, patting Joe' golden hair as he laid his head on her stomach.

Joe talked constantly about holding the baby, even though he did not understand how the infant was going to come out of Catuzza's stomach. Then one day Catuzza went to the hospital, and four days later she returned home with a tiny wrapped bundle in her arms.

"His name is Frank," Catuzza said, stooping low so that Joe could see the baby.

The older child was enthralled by the baby's tiny hands and feet and the miniature face. "My baby?" he asked Catuzza once again.

"Your friend, Joe. Baby Frank is your friend."

Antoinette smiled as she watched the exchange and wondered what would happen as the years passed, whether Baby Frank and Joe really would become friends.

But only two months later the Oppedisano family moved away to be closer to the butcher shop where Joe Senior worked. For weeks afterward Joe spoke of Baby Frank and seemed sad that he had moved. But as winter arrived, the child discovered other things that captured his attention and he forgot about the tiny baby.

Over the next seventeen years Joe Oppedisano attended the same school as Catuzza's child, but the two were not aware of each other because of their age difference.

Two years after Joe graduated from high school, he enlisted in the Army and was sent to Panama for two years. There he and his fellow soldiers were exposed to the systemic herbicide, Agent Orange, which the Army used as a defoliant in areas where troops were stationed. Oftentimes Joe and the other young men in his division would get violently ill and have to spend days in the infirmary. But never was a connection made between the harsh chemical herbicide and their sickness.

In 1958, at age twenty-two, Joe returned to Albany and reestablished himself as a student at New York State University. He soon earned his teaching credentials and began working in the same neighborhood where he'd grown up. Eventually he married, had two beautiful children, and gave up teaching for a better salary working with the New York State Labor Department as a training director.

At about the same time, early in 1970, Joe began feeling ill and losing weight. Several weeks after he first began having symptoms a doctor confirmed his worst fears. He had Hairy Cell Leukemia, a rare form of lymphoma that was both painful and deadly.

"Antoinette, please pray for me," Joe asked his sister when he told her the news. "I'm not ready to die yet."

"Ah, Joe." Antoinette could hardly believe that her younger brother had cancer. "Of course I'll pray. I'll pray for a miracle."

For nearly a decade Joe was in and out of remission, but then he began worsening. His spleen was surgically removed, and after the operation the doctor told him he probably did not have long to live. Determined to beat the odds, Joe changed doctors and in 1979 began seeing a specialist in the field of hematology, Dr. Benjamin Norris at St. Peter's Hospital in Albany.

"The other doctor wrote me off," Joe told Dr. Norris. "Now don't you go and do that, okay? I've got a lot more living to do."

Dr. Norris smiled. "You're very sick, Joe," he said. "But I think we can help you here. Besides, I want you to be around for the big test."

"The big test?"

"Yes, Joe. Interferon. It's an experimental drug right now, but it might be just what you need."

"Well, let's get it going."

Dr. Norris shook his head. "Not yet. It'll take a few years before it'll be ready. My job will be to keep you around until then."

Joe's outlook was very positive and his condition improved, but more than a year later in 1980, Dr. Norris phoned him to say he was retiring from his practice.

"But don't worry, Joe. I've got a brilliant young doctor taking my place. If anyone can keep you alive until the Interferon is available, it's Dr. Lizzi."

"Dr. Lizzi?" Joe was puzzled. "That name sounds familiar."

"Well, I think you both grew up in Albany, so you've probably heard his name somewhere. I've set up an appointment for you to meet him right away."

The first meeting between Joe and the young doctor was upbeat and positive.

"Joe, your condition is serious," Dr. Lizzi said. "But I think I can help you stay alive until the Interferon is ready."

Dr. Lizzi was tireless, spending hours with Joe testing his blood and advising him about his condition. Throughout that year and the next there were several times when Joe nearly died. He would lie on a hospital bed clinging to life while machines cleaned his blood. Almost always Dr. Lizzi would sit beside him holding his hand and praying for him. For Dr. Lizzi, Joe was more than a patient with a rare form of leukemia. The two had grown up in Albany and had ancestors who were originally from Italy. Because of that, Dr. Lizzi cared deeply for Joe and devoted himself to helping the man and his family deal with his cancer.

"Sometimes, Joe, all we can do is ask God to take over," he would say occasionally. "We're doing all we can, and now it's up to Him."

Despite his brushes with death, Joe lived and Dr. Lizzi continued to help him fight for time. Then, in the late 1980s when Interferon finally became available, Dr. Lizzi made sure that Joe was one of the first leukemia patients to use it. Almost immediately Joe's body grew stronger, and by late 1989 he was in remission.

"You saved my life, Doc," Joe said to him when he got the news. "I'm supposed to be dead right now, but you never gave up."

"We did it together, Joe. You, me, and God. You've always been special to me. You're a fighter." He paused a moment. "And now I have something you can really fight for."

Joe listened as Dr. Lizzi explained that he wanted Joe to help him with a telethon he was about to do to raise awareness about leukemia and possible chemical causes. He also wanted to work with Joe in filing suit against the U.S. Army for exposing Joe to Agent Orange.

"I'm sure that Agent Orange is what caused your leukemia," Dr. Lizzi said. Both men knew that by then Agent Orange had been partially banned because of its harmful side effects. "Now we need to see that nothing like that ever happens again to a group of soldiers."

Dr. Lizzi's zeal was contagious, and Joe agreed heartily to help in the fight against both leukemia and government-approved exposure to harmful chemicals. The telethon was scheduled to take place the next month, and since Joe would be on television, his sister, Antoinette, working as a reporter in New Milford, Connecticut, promised to watch.

"Wave to me," she told Joe.

Joe laughed. "Oh, sure, Antoinette, you bet."

Then there was silence for a moment, and when Antoinette spoke her voice was serious. "Really, Joe. I'm so glad you're okay. I'm proud of you for being such a fighter."

"It wasn't me it was Dr. Lizzi."

"Dr. Lizzi?"

"You know, the doctor who's been helping me these past ten years."

"I know, I know. I've met him a dozen times when you were in the hospital. It's just that his name sounds so familiar."

"I thought so, too. He grew up in Albany, so we probably went to the same schools or something. Who knows."

Now, as Antoinette tuned in the station carrying the telethon, she was still puzzled by the name of Joe's doctor. Where had she heard the name Lizzi before?

She watched the telethon intently and saw that Joe was looking very well. He had survived Hair Cell Leukemia for nearly twenty years, and because of Dr. Lizzi's tireless monitoring, testing, and cancer-fighting procedures, Joe was the longest living survivor of that form of cancer.

Antoinette watched as the cameras showed Dr. Lizzi standing beside Joe, and suddenly she had a flashback. In her mind she pictured her brother as a three-year-old towhead nuzzling his face against the pregnant abdomen of Catuzza Lizzi.

"My, God, could it be?" she wondered out loud. The Lizzi family had rented a flat to the Oppedisano family when Antoinette was a young girl. Catuzza was pregnant back then, and Joe would have been about three years old.

That night Antoinette called her brother excitedly.

"Joe, do you know your doctor's mother's name?" she asked.

Joe was puzzled at her interest. "Sure," he said. "Catuzza. Sicilian for 'Sweet little Catherine.' "

Antoinette was stunned. "I don't believe it," she said. "I just don't believe it."

She was flooded by a sudden wave of memories.

"What is it, Antoinette?"

"Do you remember when we lived on Irving Street in Albany? You were just a little boy."

Joe thought a moment. "Not really. I've heard about it. An apartment or something, we rented from another family."

"Joe, we rented from the Lizzi family. You and I used to go and visit Catuzza Lizzi, and you would always touch her stomach when she was pregnant. You were in awe over her unborn child, always looking at her and patting her and trying to feel the baby kick."

"Okay, so?" Joe still did not see the connection.

"Don't you understand? That baby was Frank Lizzi. Your doctor. The one who saved your life. You were so taken by the life of that unborn child, and then that child grew up and saved yours."

"Are you serious?"

"Yes. I prayed for a miracle, Joe," Antoinette said confidently. "And God was working one all along."

Joe was stunned at the thought, and within minutes was on the telephone with Dr. Lizzi.

"Yes, when I was born we were living on Irving Street," Dr. Lizzi said.

For a while the two men said nothing, absorbed in the realization of how their pasts had connected.

"It's just about impossible to imagine something like that happening," Joe said finally.

Frank Lizzi smiled at his end of the conversation. "Not really, Joe. You might have been only a child, but children are always closer to God. Somehow you knew back then that the life you touched would one day touch yours. Now it has."

*Author's note:*

*In writing this particular story I worked weeks trying to find Joe Oppedisano and Dr. Frank Lizzi with very little information. One afternoon, the day before finishing this book, I felt something telling me to call the hospital in Albany where Dr. Lizzi might still work.*

*I was thrilled to be connected to his office, and I told the nurse my reason for calling. I then asked if Dr. Lizzi still kept in touch with his patient, Joe.*

*The nurse laughed and said, "In fact, Joe's standing right here." It turned out that Joe still comes in to have his blood checked once a month. His visits typically last about ten minutes and that was the time I had felt driven to call.*

*Indeed, miracles abound.*

If you would like to share an angel encounter, a miracle story, or a story about someone who has been a hero in their home or community, please write to:

Kelsey Tyler
P.O. Box 264
Clarkdale, Arizona 86324-9998

# RUNAWAY

## KRISTINA DUNKER

Translated by KATJA BELL

**SKYSCAPE**

**SKYSCAPE**

The characters and events portrayed in this book are fictitious. Any similarity to real persons, living or dead, is coincidental and not intended by the author.

Text copyright © 2011 Deutscher Taschenbuch Verlag GmbH & Co. KG, München
English translation copyright © 2012 Katja Bell

*Runaway* was first published in 2011 by Deutscher Taschenbuch Verlag GmbH & Co. KG, Munich, as *Durchgebrannt*. Translated from German by Katja Bell. Published in English by Amazon Children's Publishing in 2012.

ISBN-10: 147781034X (paperback)
ISBN-13: 9781477810347 (paperback)
ISBN-10: 1611094275 (eBook)
ISBN-13: 9781611094275 (eBook)

Book design by Paul Nielsen and FaceOut Studio
Cover photos: istockphoto
Cover Design by Katrina Damkoehler

T he chocolate-hazelnut Bundt cake smells yummy, as always. The aroma fills the entire kitchen and gets even more intense when I break a piece off with my fingers. It was ridiculous of my mother to bake this frosted cake ring. As if we're going to celebrate this birthday like any other old birthday. She probably wants to prove to the whole extended family what a great and wonderful mood we're all still in. Me, I stopped being cheerful a good while ago. Honestly, I think a messy, half-smashed cake—not a tidy, perfect Bundt— would have been a lot more fitting.

"Stop gorging yourself on cake already and go get dressed." Mom is all over the place: she's rummaging through kitchen drawers when she accidentally tears a button off of her shirt sleeve—"*Shoot!*"—and hands me a small plastic box. "Let's not forget these."

Little birthday candles. They're pale pink, yellow, baby blue, and you're supposed to stick them into the cake. I start flipping out.

"Mom! Sarah's turning eighteen!" As of late, Mom's had this tendency to make Sarah seem younger than she is. Sarah, my big sister, who is four years older than me, is now "our little one" and I have turned into "our big one." I was okay with it at first, but I've come to learn that all it really means is that I should kindly start behaving like a grownup from now on.

"All this baby stuff is embarrassing," I say a little louder now because my mom seems to have switched off again. "Did you hear what I said?" Yeah, I already *sound* like a grownup. Well, that should make her happy.

Finally, she turns around to me. "Fine, maybe that's how *you* see it. But Sarah wanted a real birthday just one more time. The whole shebang. You know, like before."

Yeah, right. But I know better: Sarah wished for something completely different for her eighteenth birthday. What she wanted was to start partying the night before at the Rock Palace here in small-town Germany and party all the way until dawn. And then, the next day—which is today, the Saturday before the long holiday weekend—drive up to our soccer club's summer vacation camp by the sea in Northern Germany with me and our friends from the club. It's the number-one event of the year, and we've all been looking forward to it for months. And for a while, too, it looked like Sarah would be able to make it. She even borrowed an insulated sleeping bag from our soccer coach, a piece of super-subzero survival gear that you can supposedly use to camp out overnight in the Arctic. Plus, she had spent the entire afternoon with her friend Anna, talking about which of the other girls would be allowed to sleep with them in their tent.

And so I really want to rub it in Mom's face that there was *no way* Sarah wanted a little kid's birthday party complete with blowing out candles and kissing aunts. But I can't, because I find the words "just one more time" so hard to swallow. Just one more time. That's another thing I get to hear a lot these days.

*"Sarah wants to go to the soccer stadium just one more time."*

*"Sarah wants to have pasta at Da Luigi's just one more time."*

*"Sarah wants to go to the theater festival just one more time."*

Doesn't anyone else notice this? What's with this "one more time"? Surely it can only mean "one *last* time." It seems like something you say casually, in passing. Everyone says it from time to time, right? But for us, for our family, these words signify the possible end because Sarah's very sick. We should prepare ourselves for the possibility that Sarah might die, that's what the doctors told us at the hospital. She has only a fifty-fifty chance of recovery.

How could I possibly object to a party?

Mom puts a hand on my shoulder and seems to be reading my thoughts. "I know you don't agree, Florian. But things change. Sarah's changed. And she told me a few days ago that this is exactly what she wants."

That's a possibility, of course.

"Alright. Now, please, lighten up. Pull yourself together. And help us get all this stuff packed up! It's her birthday. And it should be"—she hesitates as if she wants to say *just one more time* again, but she doesn't—"exactly the birthday she wants." A jolt seems to run through her body and she suddenly starts humming "For He's a Jolly Good Fellow."

I feel sick to my stomach. I hate sing-alongs. Besides, I'm annoyed that my mom doesn't seem to understand that I wish Sarah a nice birthday, too. The kind of birthday I would have wanted for myself. But apparently that makes me selfish. At least, that's how it appears to my dad, who is now coming down the stairs while trying to tie his tie: "It's a quarter to ten and you're still in your pj's. Instead of sleeping in, you could have helped me set up the guest beds. Did you spend the entire night in front of your computer again?"

I didn't sleep well, and I can tell he didn't, either. He's been having nightmares lately, which get him so worked up during the night that he doesn't just wake my mom but also me, two doors down. But I'm pretty sure he doesn't want to be reminded of how he's been calling for help in his sleep.

"You guys forgot to wake me up."

"Good grief, there's a lot going on today. We can't constantly be looking after you."

My dad always returns fire when he gets a shot from someone. This time, though, I don't resent him for it, because I know that he really doesn't enjoy having the entire extended family over, and I also notice his twisted face when he hears Mom singing from the kitchen, "*and so say all of us, and so say all of us.*"

I try my hand at the tiniest of jokes: "We'll be singing it in a round next, with Cousin Daniel as our choirmaster."

My dad looks at me with a puzzled expression on his face, undecided if he should allow himself to get drawn in by my little joke and laugh, or if he should yell at me instead. It's entirely possible that he'll call me *counterproductive* again in his loud voice. He starts opening his mouth, but then the doorbell rings.

"The mother-in-law," Dad growls, now too preoccupied to comment on my little joke. "Two minutes, and we're off. If you're not ready, you'll stay at home."

Oh, how I'd love to.

\* \* \*

I almost trip over the bed frames of the two guest beds that are set up right in the middle of my bedroom, still without their mattresses. I'll be sleeping in one and my cousin Daniel in the other. The real bed, my bed, is reserved for my fat uncle Thomas. Thomas, aka The Steamroller, breaks into a sweat just drinking a beer. Even though he wobbles and jiggles and sweats, which is super gross, he's allowed to claim my bed because of his degenerative disc disease. Also, his son Daniel—my cousin—is apparently highly gifted, only nobody's ever noticed it apart from his own parents. To me, the unrecognized genius seems a little, shall we say, less than smart. He's completely useless; you can't even play computer games with him.

I am so angry! The whole house will be full of people—people Sarah doesn't want to see at all. Me neither, by the way. All I wanted was to share a tent with my buddies Nils and Eric, and Ferhad, our Turkish friend. I wanted to play soccer on the beach, throw myself into the waters of the North Sea, and spend the evening dancing and partying. I cuss and check my cell phone. No new texts from Sarah, but I have one from Nils: *Stay strong, dude. See you Tuesday.* Stay strong; easier said than done.

To top it all off, Mom insisted that I wear the dress shirt I wore for my confirmation. Great, I'll look like Daniel's clone. Maybe I should try to spill coffee or bright orange soda on it.

Sarah will probably be asleep when we get to her hospital room. She'll have her eyes closed and will be dreaming of stuffing her sneakers, bikini, and sleeping bag into a duffel bag and making her way to the bus stop by the soccer field. But unfortunately, she's too weak to leave her bed for an extended period of time, and I'm too young to stand up to my parents.

To cheer myself up, I try to imagine my cousin and uncle having to spend the night on empty bed frames, no mattresses. Chained to the metal frame and not allowed dinner. If I were the prison guard, The Steamroller would quickly shrink to the size of a regular person. People would even say that it is a good deed because I would have taken the strain off the insurance company. The insurance company is not really paying up, at least that's what my dad always says. And because they're not paying up in full, not even for Sarah, who has cancer, we have to fork over a deductible, which we pay for from our vacation fund, my pocket money, and of course from what little money I need for my weekend activities and my membership in the soccer club.

O n our way to the hospital my parents get into a fight in the car because Mom is trying to sew the torn-off button back onto her blouse, which makes my dad nervous for some reason.

"Will you stop fidgeting! Do you really have to do this right now?"

"Why does it bother you so much?" she asks. She sounds ready for a fight.

"It's your constant perfectionism. You can never just sit still for a second. You invite a thousand people over . . ."

"Because everything will break apart if I do. Somebody has to make sure that things stay normal. Besides, they're *your* brothers and sisters, and you really could have invited your mother a while—"

"Oh, Sylvia, please!"

Before their squabbling can get out of hand, Grandma Gaby chimes in from where she sits beside me in the backseat. "You're not going to start quarreling over a silly button, are you?"

She really has no idea of the kind of damage a little button can do. When I was very little, I once stuck a button all the way up my nose. That incident led to a panicked visit to the emergency room and ended in a huge scene when we got back home.

I suddenly remember how Sarah had tried to fix the situation. She stood there, blonde hair parted in the middle and braided into pigtails. She grabbed my dad by the arm, pulled him away from me, and held the button out to him: "Look, Daddy, it's a magical button! Nobody can resist it. It's a good thing Flor didn't swallow it, because I probably would have."

"Honey, you don't do stupid things like that," my dad had said, sitting down while shaking his head in disbelief, as she settled onto his lap. Together they had looked at the button like it really was something precious, twisting and turning it in their fingers.

I had wanted to be with them, wanted to be part of their little unit, but I didn't dare try just yet and so sat down on the floor where I pressed myself against Daddy's legs, like a cat. Sometime later he softly and absentmindedly stroked my hair, which I found very comforting given that he had been so angry before.

Suddenly I feel an overwhelming urge to be close to my dad and wrap my arms around his shoulders from behind. But he's driving and trying to pass someone, and he shrugs me off.

"Jeez, do you have to go so fast, Manfred?" Mom says, still a little annoyed. "We're in a 45 zone. The way you're driving, it's dangerous."

"*I'm* okay with it," I say, trying to be supportive. "Because we all want to see Sarah as quickly as possible, right?"

There's silence in the car. Grandma Gaby gives me a skeptical sideways glance and then squeezes my hand. I know what she's trying to say: I'm right and I'm wrong at the same time.

My dad, for example, would love to be by Sarah's side 24/7 and already spends all of his annual leave inside the hospital. At the same time, he always gets very agitated and grumpy just before a visit, because he's afraid the doctor might call him into his office and give him bad news. Mom's been pretty tough up until recently, but I think she's slowly losing her cool, losing weight and getting more and more nervous like a little bird with ruffled feathers that's been disturbed in its nest. My guess is that she's having a hard time with

Sarah turning eighteen today and still being a long way from healthy. You see, Mom "promised" Sarah when her illness started that it would all be a distant memory by the time she turned eighteen. Kind of stupid to make a promise about something you have no control over. And so today Mom didn't spend the day with her in the hospital as she normally does, but instead went grocery shopping like a crazy person and prepped the house for all the guests we invited over.

Which is why I gave Sarah moral support, at least the type that can be electronically transmitted. We texted each other, like we normally do in the evenings.

Unfortunately, we're starting to run out of topics of conversation. For example, we used to have fun just talking about horror movies, but now every little thing gets her scared and worked up. Soccer is another topic which has gone pretty stale for us. She says that she'd be lucky to even play foosball again sometime in the distant future, and that she couldn't care less about gossip and stories from our soccer club, which she used to love. You can't even have a fight with her anymore, because she's so ill and fragile, and because loud noises stress her out too much. For me this means I have to tiptoe around her, like walking on eggshells. Not exactly my strong suit.

So, the question is: do we really want to see Sarah as quickly as possible? The Sarah who's waiting for us?

She's barely recognizable now. Her body all skin and bones, eyes deep in their sockets with dark lines underneath.

Only her cheeks look strangely puffy or bloated, as if she's stuffed her mouth full of candy.

"Will you get me a role in a horror movie?" she had asked me one time when our parents briefly left the hospital room. I had only smirked. "What do you want to be? An alien?" "A mutant," she had whispered. "A bloodthirsty mutant out to destroy the world." Then her eyes closed. She could never play that role, no matter how bad she looked. Even if she sometimes gets on my nerves because she's being so nice all the time, she really is a kind person to the core. I have to wonder if it's any coincidence that something as evil as cancer picked someone as nice as her to be its victim.

For as long as Sarah was the healthy older sibling, she was more than okay as a sister. One of the reasons was probably the fact that she played the outside left position in the girls' soccer team and you could talk to her like she was one of the guys. Of course, she had her mean moments like any other girl, but she was never as bad as our neighbor's daughters. Those two will start snickering and cackling for no apparent reason whenever I walk past, even today and even though they're both in Sarah's class. And so in my eyes they're practically a pair of old hags. When Sarah and I got into a fight back then, it was usually because of her room. I would go into her room when she wasn't around, just for fun and without asking permission, and she would always slap me around for it. Which I guess was justified because I would read her journal. One time, I decorated the photo of Coach Peter, my soccer coach—that she had framed in little pink hearts—with vampire fangs and devil's horns.

The best thing about her as my healthy "big sis" was that she would always be there for me when I had a problem. Spelling or math issues? "No problem, let's do some drills." Trouble with one of my teachers? "Don't worry, I'll talk to him." Grandma discovers cigarettes in my jacket pocket and wants to tell on me? "I'll tell her they were for me."

When our parents almost got divorced three years ago and Daddy didn't come home for a few nights in a row, she let me sleep in her bed. I was eleven then, and Sarah was as fit and healthy as can be.

Two weeks ago, when it became clear that Sarah wouldn't be able to make it to the soccer camp, I asked her if she would mind me going by myself—and having to leave by about noon on the day of her birthday. She just shook her head without hesitating for even a second. "Of course not," she said. "You'll just have to tell me all about it when you get back. Besides, I don't want you to rot away at home."

And still my parents told me that I couldn't go.

Two days ago, I asked Sarah again when our parents were in the room with us. This time, she didn't reply. She pretended she couldn't hear me. I mean, it's true that she's frail and hasn't been hearing well for a few months (one of the side effects of her chemotherapy). But I'm sure that she heard my question.

It was the first time that she ever really bailed on me. So, I need to stay here this weekend. I need to spend time with my stupid cousin who's standing in the hospital parking lot, holding a bouquet of helium balloons and pointing at our car as we pull up to show all our waiting relatives that we've arrived. I need to allow these people to hug and kiss me and listen to them say how "awful" all of this is. I need to fight for breath under Aunt Margaret's perfume clouds and feel the sweat on my fat uncle Thomas's skin. I need to listen to Aunt Katie asking me for the millionth time what I want to be when I grow up. The first time she asked was on my first day of school, and it seems to be the only thing she can ever think of saying. I need to join this group of noisily chatting people, trot after them across the sunny parking lot. I need to walk past the smokers outside with their IV poles on wheels, through the revolving doors, and into the air-conditioned, neon-lit inside of the hospital. I need to take in this smell, the quiet squeak of rubber soles on linoleum floors, get out of the way of a nurse pushing a cart full of breakfast trays. I'm familiar with all of it; I come here all the time. Only today they want me to share my sister's suffering with everyone else we're related to.

My parents feel it's important that the entire family show up together. It's "proper." Besides, they honestly have no money left for my little vacation. We took out a loan to buy a townhouse so that Sarah can sit outside in her wheelchair and in her own garden. We made all sorts of wishes come true for her—we even managed to get a famous soccer player to come visit her bedside—and spent many hundreds of euros on alternative therapies and medicine, so that now we can't even afford to pay the ridiculous sum of eighty euros for my three-day soccer summer camp.

But I'll bet you anything that tonight they will invite all the relatives out to the local Italian restaurant. If Uncle Thomas wants to order dessert, tiramisu with extra whipped cream perhaps, I'm sure they'll pay for that, too—while I have to listen to them whine if I even ask for so much as an popsicle.

Most of the family now spills into the elevator, me included. Only Grandma Gaby patiently waits outside for the next one. I want to go back out to her, but I can't get through. Even though the elevator is quite large, it's kind of overcrowded with a nurse who's pushing an empty hospital bed, plus eight members of my extended family, a whole bunch of gifts, and eighteen helium balloons.

Grandma Hilda takes my hand. Hers is shaking a little and makes mine shake, too. "How do you like the balloons? It's a nice idea, isn't it?"

"I don't know. They remind me more of a funeral," I say, which earns me a scathing look from my dad. Not sure why since *he* was the one who told me only two days ago, while we were out running, that Sarah had wanted to talk to him about her funeral. He told me he'd tried to cut her off, change the topic, assure her that she'd pull through and get well again. He'd then tried to reassure me, too, listing her promising blood levels and the latest survival rates, all details he normally only discusses with my mom. I'm not sure that he realized he was even talking to me. He had started running faster and faster, which was very risky because he didn't even stop when he got to the crossing on the main road.

He just ran across it, while cars were honking their horns and stepping on their emergency brakes.

S arah is awake and politely enjoys her gifts.

The nurse, who stops by a couple of times and checks all the tubes and machines, notices how we all cluster around Sarah's bed and scolds us, seeing nothing more than a bacteria-laden crowd. "Please, no hugging or kissing! Please also tell the rest of your family. And if someone's got a cold, they'll have to stay outside."

My father gives a nod with a defeated expression on his face and tells her, as if to apologize, that it's Sarah's birthday today. "I'm sure you can make an exception."

"Germs don't make an exception," the nurse warns Daddy with a raised finger. "You of all people should know that by now."

I'm trying to become invisible and silently hide behind Grandma Hilda's back. I press myself against the wall and watch how Sarah unpacks a new pajama set sporting a fancy ladybug pattern, oohs and aahs at a stupid bathrobe, and forces herself to give a weak smile about the birthday balloons. Only Grandma Gaby's gift manages to lighten up her face, if only for a second: a set of wind chimes that you can hang from the balcony door and that make a soft ringing sound.

I'm not giving her my little package, at least not just yet, because the longer I stare at the charade that's taking place in front of me, the more convinced I become that I'll get into trouble over my gift. It's only that T-shirt that Sarah discovered in a music magazine a few weeks ago and that she really, really wanted. I must have spent ten hours or so searching the entire Internet because I wanted to make sure that I ordered the exact same T-shirt, but I'm guessing the grownups are not going to be thrilled. What's worse is that I'm not even sure if Sarah's still going to like it.

I think back to her latest texts, and how she seems listless and tired even when I talk about the newest movies and thrillers. I think about how hypersensitive she can be sometimes, and how scared she gets now when we talk about deliciously bloodcurdling things. Dad isn't the only one who's having nightmares these days—Sarah is having them, too.

"Hey, where's my baby brother?"

Grandma Hilda shows no mercy and pushes me to the front. I stand there in front of Sarah's bed, holding my little flat package, and I can't seem to say a word. Sarah's toenails are alternately painted mint green and pink. That must have been the work of Anna, her best friend. If the two of us had made it to soccer camp today, then Sarah and Anna would have pitched their tent right next to mine, I'm sure of that.

The toes in front of me are starting to wiggle and Sarah's high, clear voice says, "Hey, Flor! Did you get me something, too?"

She reaches out her hand, just a little. She stops, though, expecting me to meet her halfway, but I'm holding on to my package. The T-shirt shows the drawing of a skull grinning, with flowers wrapped all around it. Underneath it says in cursive lettering: *Love hard, die young.*

I can't give her that, I just can't. Not now that she's in such horrible shape and that her big, round, hairless head with the huge, deep-set eyes almost looks like a skull itself. What once were full, brightly painted lips are now only a sore, shriveled version of them, and where her piercing used to be is now a tube coming out of her nose. Sarah hates being stared at and I usually try to avoid it, but I just can't help myself today. I keep staring at her face while the seconds are dripping away. So much easier to be texting than looking at each other face-to-face.

"Florian, we're waiting," my dad says.

"Did he pop a pill? Looks like he's stoned or something." Daniel smirks.

"He just didn't get enough sleep, is all." I can tell from my dad's voice that my cousin's remark annoyed him. He seems annoyed at me, too, because he gives me a shove. "Don't just stand there, give her your present already."

I have no choice. In a moment, everyone will see that image on the T-shirt. Mom will be appalled. Dad will once again say that I'm being *counterproductive*. My grandmas and aunts will eat me alive. For them, I'll be the one being negative and taking all hope away from Sarah and reducing her chances of recovery. It'll give them the scapegoat they need. And what about Sarah? How will Sarah react?

But she—good old Sarah—notices my distress and comes up with the best of all ideas. For a moment, her lips seem as full of life as they once were. She smiles at me with her typically mocking Sarah smile, gives me a wink, and says, "Thanks. I'll open it by myself, when you're all gone."

"But why?" Aunt Margaret is disappointed.

"We're all curious what's in it," Uncle Thomas says.

"Because then"—a sudden cough attack—"I'll have something nice to open when I'm alone and by myself again."

That saves my neck. The family quiets down. Mom is full of hope, talking about a new phase in Sarah's therapy, and cuts the chocolate Bundt cake: every cut is as clean and precise as a surgeon's. First, we'll cut out the cancer, but we won't get it all. So then we'll take out more with the knife, but you'll still be sick. You'll go a little bit deaf, too, and you'll look like a zombie in the process, but that's alright, you'll get over it eventually.

Hahaha!

"Florian, you're as white as a sheet, you go first."

Grandma Hilda hands me a plate. I don't want to eat anything. I'm depressed and don't want to hear Aunt Margaret talk about how well Sarah looks and Uncle Thomas claim that she'll be back as her team's goalie by next week. Sarah was never a goalie: Uncle Thomas is misinformed. Most of all, I don't want to see Sarah nod and weakly accept it all. She really doesn't seem to care about the fact that everyone is talking so much baloney. Then she gives me a wink, and I suddenly realize why she had pretended not to hear my all-important question that last time. She probably didn't want to talk back to my parents, she wanted to stay out of it: for lack of strength, or because she's already making such an effort to please everyone all the time.

Just like she's doing right now. I'm pretty sure she doesn't want any cake, otherwise she wouldn't be looking at her plate as if it was full of live bugs.

"Try it, honey," says Mom, who is sitting on the bed. "Just a small piece, come on. You really wanted me to bake it, remember?"

Sarah takes a small piece and swallows it, her neck very long and thin. There is a big blue vein running across her forehead. Then she smiles bravely and looks as exhausted as if she'd just climbed Mt. Everest.

"It's yummy," she whispers, and anybody who can't tell that she's lying must be blind or totally retarded. "I guess I should be blowing out eighteen candles"—a gasp for air—"but why don't we ask Flor to do it for me?"

I look around. My mother didn't even stick the candles into the cake in the first place.

"I've got them on me, but ..."

"Mom, do you remember what you promised me for my eighteenth birthday?"

"And I still believe in it," my mom affirms. "But we need to wait just a little bit longer and be patient." Her voice is breaking. She has no strength left; I've known that for a while.

The other relatives pretend not to notice. On the contrary, they praise Sarah's appetite and Mom's cake; they chew and swallow like a bunch of munching, glassy-eyed cows out on the pasture. I want to kill and slaughter them all, and in my head I play out a first-person shooter game. I can easily imagine what makes some people go on a killing spree—I hate them all, hate this collective helplessness, and I hate Sarah for asking Mom about that promise. It's because of her that I have to listen to these stupid, god-awful, heart-wrenching lies.

The nurse and a young doctor now enter the room and ask my dad to follow them out into the hallway. I would like to run after them but I can't, because Grandma Hilda is grabbing my hand again and croaks into my ear, like an old crow with ruffled feathers: "I would love to know what you're getting Sarah for her birthday. Can you tell me? Will you whisper it in my ear?"

In her ear? With its bristly gray hair, wrinkly skin, and thick coating of earwax? Why does it seem that everyone around me is such a monster? To avoid her, I take an extra-large piece of chocolate cake and shove it into my mouth. It smells of ointment, pee bag, and old ladies' perfume. It tastes of the insects I had imagined Sarah seeing in the cake earlier; I crack their shells with my teeth. I can't breathe.

Sarah seems to feel the same way. She grimaces, screws up her face, gasps "sorry," leans forward—and throws up. She vomits on everyone's feet, on the pretty little bows and paper plates; throws up blood and chocolate, undigested nuts, and gray phlegm.

Out, out, I need to get out! I'll go insane if I have to stay in here any longer.

I bolt out the door, through the ward, jump down the stairs; faster and faster, one more glass door, another one, and I'm free.

The hospital campus is big—all freshly mowed lawns and old trees. I run across the grass, grab a tree branch that's lying on the ground, use it to start thrashing around me and beat up this summer day, these bird songs, and the patches of sunlight that are coming through the tree canopy. I yell and rant and rail, curse Sarah and her illness, curse my parents, my aunts, my uncle, and my cousin. "Crap," I call out. I climb onto the ledge of a goldfish pond and start beating the surface of the water with my stick. "Yes, yes, try to get away, you big, fat, googly-eyed monsters!"

An old married couple with walkers slowly moves past me. "Boo!" I yell when they turn back around after they get a few yards past me. Shortly afterward, a young woman walks by and shakes her head disapprovingly—she looks like a doctor or a teacher or Aunt Margaret; the type who would say, "You should be ashamed for acting like a child." I pull an ugly face, stick out my tongue, raise my arms over my head, and jump up and down like a monkey. That does it and finally chases her away, too. Me too, I would like to run away, first back home to pack my bags and then off to soccer camp, but I'm not allowed. Right. I have to stay here and wait until I go cuh-razy.

Do you have any idea what you're doing to me, what you're asking of me?

These past few times at soccer practice: everyone talking about the trip, making plans for the tournament, allocating sleeping spots in their tents, everyone happy that the girls will be there, too—and I can't come. Instead, that useless Lennart guy will take my place on the soccer field: a loser like my cousin Daniel, a softie, a third wheel, a brownnose.

I keep beating the surface of the water, furious, then the wooden stick slides out of my hands. I see another stick— one some stupid mutt has probably already slobbered on— but I don't bother grabbing it and continue walking instead. I rotate my arms as if doing warm-up exercises before soccer practice. Like a walking windmill, I move along the path next to the goldfish pond, spot an empty beer can down in the gravel, and kick it with all my might. Loose gravel stones scatter in all directions in a cloud of dust.

"Goal," says a small, squeaky voice coming from behind the next rhododendron bush up the path. I get around it and see a little girl's face.

"Nah, I missed." I don't like being accosted. Especially not if the person doing the accosting looks almost like a ghost: a thin little child, all skin and bone, with a gray face and white dress that looks like a burial shroud. What kind of an idiot chooses a ghoulish outfit like that?

She's sitting on a bench all by herself and has cupped her hands together carefully, as if she's holding a very small animal.

"What have you got there?" I ask, suddenly curious, and I think back to the days when Sarah and I wanted to save little baby birds that had fallen from their nests. We usually failed.

"It's a secret."

"I can keep a secret." Determined, I sit down beside her. "Let me see."

"No." She shifts over a little bit—not like she's scared, more like she's angry. "I saved it."

"You know, it's better if you leave little baby birds where you find them. Otherwise its parents might reject it next time."

"Oh, you're so smart." The little girl lifts one of her eyebrows, only one—it looks quite funny. On second thought, she seems pretty much alive after all. "Do you really think I don't know that?"

I consider getting up and leaving.

"Okay, I'll tell you what I fished out of the pond." She gives me a wide, open-mouthed grin and shakes her long, lank hair out of her face. "Because I like you. But, shh"— she lifts her hands to her lips—"don't tell anyone: it's a fairy princess."

"A fairy princess?"

"Yes. She's very beautiful, with a blue-green tummy and golden wings. She fell into the water and almost drowned, but I saw her struggling and flapping her wings and managed to fish her out of the pond and save her life. As a thank-you she said she would grant me three wishes."

Obviously, this girl lives in her own little world. She's probably hospitalized in the same ward as my sister. Next she's going to tell me what she wishes for: being healthy, and a birthday cake.

I get up.

"You know," she says, "I don't really wish for anything. You can have my three wishes. I give them to you. Why don't you tell the fairy princess what you'd wish for?"

I feel relieved and give a small laugh. And because I've got nothing better to do, I decide to stay and play along.

"Alright, so, I wish for . . . I wish I were eighteen already, I wish I had a Porsche, and I wish Ricarda were my girlfriend."

"Ricarda." The little girl rolls her eyes ecstatically. "Is she pretty?"

"Yes, very."

"Like a top model?"

"At least."

"But she's not your girlfriend?"

"Nope, not at the moment." I'm starting to feel a little uncomfortable. What am I doing exactly? I've never told anyone about Ricarda. Nils has an idea, of course, but he never asks me about it. A lot of guys like Ricarda, and Nils probably thinks she's out of our league anyway. This is the first time all day that I've allowed myself to think about Ricarda. So, now I do, and it makes me realize how much I would have liked to go and hang out with her and the others at soccer camp.

The way it stands, Lennart will get to hang out with her instead. That stupid, pale jellyfish of a boy will get sunburned, and I won't get a chance to work on my tan at all. I am completely convinced that being around my family is extremely hazardous to my health.

"I'm sure she'll be your girlfriend one day." The little girl lowers her eyes to her cupped hands and whispers, her voice deep and meaningful, "Fairy princess, hear his wishes."

My wishes . . . I feel nauseous. All this time talking to the little girl and I didn't even think of Sarah at all! This is insane: if there really is a fairy princess, I have just gambled away my one and only chance of saving my dying sister.

"I gotta go." I jump to my feet and break into a run without even turning around once.

I stop in front of the revolving hospital doors. The most sensible thing to do would be to simply go back upstairs. Sarah doesn't know what just happened. Nobody knows what just happened. If I don't give away my dirty little secret, then nobody is going to guess it either. Not even Grandma Gaby.

So, what am I waiting for? I have to go back inside, don't I?

Darn, but I really don't want to. My lips are tightly pressed together, my fists are clenched. I've had it. I *have* a life beside this one. And if I don't grab it, hold on to it now, then it'll just pass me by.

I come to a decision. My whole body is shaking from stress and effort. The smokers outside in their bathrobes are staring at me.

"Hey," one of them says and starts rolling toward me with his moveable IV pole. "You alright?"

"Mind your own business!" I yell at the man. He's startled, backs off, and almost trips. Me, on the other hand, I turn around right on my heel. I walk then run, taking big steps, and I'm not stopping: across the parking lot, past some houses, down the road, all the way to the bus stop.

I left my monthly bus pass at home, but nobody's checking tickets today. I reach a single empty seat and slump down, without anyone trying to stop me or talk to me. I sit and wait with a slowing heartbeat until we get to my stop.

My street is quiet and deserted because of the long holiday weekend. If anyone were to see me and talk to me, it wouldn't matter anyway. Most people don't know that it's Sarah's birthday today and that I should be in the hospital. I almost feel like a common burglar when I grab the house keys from their hiding spot by the tool shed. But it's my—I mean *our*—house. It's perfectly legit for me to go over to the refrigerator and gulp down the rest of the apple juice.

On the other hand, it's quite a different story to go into my parents' bedroom and search for the silver jewelry box my dad gave my mom on their wedding day. I don't normally go into their bedroom, in the same way that they stay out of my little kingdom.

And so I give a start, like I've been caught red-handed, when I hear the mail being noisily pushed through the mail slot in our front door—because I'm normally not allowed to go through my mom's underwear drawer.

But this is precisely where I find the little jewel case. I open it, and the first thing I see is a photo of Sarah. It's the last important soccer tournament she ever played: after the final whistle, she is depicted embracing my parents, all sweaty and full of dirt, while balancing a trophy on the top of her head.

And where am I? It makes me want to puke the way they've yet again picked a photo showing only the three of them. I remember how many times I had been jealous of dear, wonderful Sarah. Before I can mull it over any further, I've already grabbed and crumpled up the picture.

There's a five hundred euro bill in the box, too, the biggest bill there is. Five hundred euros! That's a lot of money. And yet there's never any money left for me. Well, you'll see. It's my money now. I'm *entitled* to this.

My duffel bag keeps filling up, as if by magic. But I do need to hurry, because one look on my cell phone tells me that it's seven minutes to twelve. I quickly call Nils. He's already on his way to the meeting point, of course. In the background I can hear WDR4, a radio station only old people listen to—in this case, his dad. Mr. Wende, Nils's dad, is conservative even in his taste in music. He's not very nice either: a very square, humorless person who never laughs and constantly nags and gripes, always finding fault with his son.

"Haven't you sent your old man to an old people's home yet?" I ask Nils instead of saying hello.

Nils gives a laugh. "I will, as soon as I get my driver's license."

"Alright. Can you make a detour and pick me up?"

"Did your parents give you permission after all?" he says in surprise.

"Yep." Because that's all I say, he doesn't probe any further. And it would be unwise, too, as long as his dad is sitting beside him.

"Awesome, Flor, that's great. We'll be there in a second."

"Yeah, yeah, it's great," I say after he hangs up. Then I put the money in my wallet, grab the duffel bag, walk down the stairs, and let the front door slam shut behind me: freedom.

\* \* \*

Mr. Wende has a grumpy expression on his face but doesn't ask any questions. He just gives me a silent nod as I climb into the back of the family car. Nils turns around and gives me a conspiratorial grin. "Awesome, dude."

"Well, I can't leave you alone, can I? You'll just get into trouble without me," I reply coolly.

"That's true," Mr. Wende cuts in unexpectedly. "I feel so much better knowing that you'll be there, Florian. Without a doubt you're the more sensible and responsible of the two of you."

I prefer not to comment. Fortunately, I don't have to, because Nils starts getting into an argument with his dad now. As usual, it's all about Nils's grades, and as always, Mr. Wende has the better arguments. What do I care?

At the meeting point, I can see about fifty or so boys and girls of different age groups, as well as a handful of youngish-looking grownups running around like sheepdogs counting their flock, handing out instructions. I can see Coach Peter, who is a lot taller than everyone else, which gives him the height to take a good headcount.

"Thanks for the ride," I manage to say to Nils's dad before we're completely surrounded by our friends.

"Hey, Flor! Fantastic," Eric, our goalie, greets me.

"Here, can you grab these? They need to go into the luggage hold." Ferhad thrusts a whole net of soccer balls into my hands and then darts up the steps leading onto the bus to snatch a good seat for himself. Nils is already inside; he spotted Ricarda and Leah and got on right after them. I stuff duffel bags and soccer balls into the luggage hold of the parked bus and suddenly find myself face-to-face with Coach Peter.

"Yeah, so, my parents finally allowed me to come."

Coach Peter doesn't say anything. He looks down on me

like a bird of prey with his height of six foot seven inches, while I quickly pull my wallet from my pants pocket and take out the five hundred euro bill. "Eighty euros, right?" I hold the banknote out to him.

He gives a nod but doesn't take it. "That's no use to me right now. First of all, Trisha's mom from the board of directors handles the finances, and second, I have no change for that."

"Maybe somebody else?"

"For a five hundred euro bill?" Coach Peter wrinkles his forehead.

"You're kidding."

And already I can feel how everyone up in the bus is looking down on me and that stupid purple-colored bill. My palms are getting sweaty.

"That's all your parents had?"

"Yeah." I'm nervously shifting from one leg to the other. "It's because of Sarah," I say, lying and telling the truth at the same time. "It's all about her these days. They don't have time for anything anymore because they're always at the hospital."

The look of doubt disappears from Coach Peter's face. His voice sounds gentle and soft, when he asks, "How is she doing?"

"So-so."

He nods gloomily, stares at the banknote, hesitates.

"Peter," Coach Philip calls out. "What is it? Can we go? Everyone's on the bus except the two of you."

"Yeah, yeah," Coach Peter shouts back and says, turning to me. "You can pay later. Get that banknote changed when you get a chance. What about the note from your parents that you're allowed to go?"

Oh, I forgot all about that stupid note. *Don't let him see how nervous you are. Look confident.* I point at the closed doors to the luggage hold. "In my bag."

"Alright." Coach Peter gives a sigh. "You can give me that later, too. And now let's go."

He pushes me ahead of him into the bus, which pulls out right away.

**T**he atmosphere is awesome. Everyone is wired and pumped and in a good mood, all the latest songs are playing on the radio and thumping through the bus, and someone has already started handing out drinks. Before I even get so much as a sip of something, I feel as if I've had an entire bottle of sweet sparkling wine to drink.

Yes, sometimes you just have to grab control of your own destiny.

Nils has saved me a seat beside him. Eric and Ferhad sit on the other side of the aisle; Ricarda and Leah are in the seats in front of us.

"I like that they allow girls' teams in our club," Nils whispers in my ear and touches a strand of dark brown hair, which spills over the edge of the seat in front of us, with his fingertips. Ricarda doesn't seem to notice. She keeps going on and on about something to Leah, who just keeps saying, "So stupid, totally."

"Yeah, toootally," I mimic Leah; unfortunately, she overhears me.

She turns around and immediately quips, "What's up?"

"Nooothing," I say and smirk as if I'd been smoking pot.

"Hey, stay away from my hair!" Ricarda hisses at Nils, but it doesn't really sound mean at all, it sounds more like she liked it, which I don't like. I was hoping that Nils liked Leah. Leah has platinum-blonde short hair, which sticks up on her head like little spikes. Ricarda's hair is more like a long, brown mane. Also, she's not as angular and thin. Her whole body is soft and round and supple, just like her curved lips.

"I've got vodka-lemon spritzers in my cooler, do you guys want some?" Nils asks the girls.

"Now? It's not even afternoon yet. I'll be tipsy by the time we get there." Ricarda gives a girly, flirtatious giggle and winks at me.

"Get 'em while they're nice and cold," Nils counters.

"Alright, why not?" Ricarda grabs a bottle, touching my face with her hair while she does this, which she's very much aware of. I take in the smell of her shampoo, when suddenly Leah asks, "Why are you here, Florian? I thought you weren't allowed to come."

"You are misinformed."

"Huh?" She tries to prod me for an answer, and even though everyone is pretending to be busy handing out bottles, I know they're all pricking up their ears.

The less I explain, the better. "I wanted to come, so here I am."

Nils clicks his tongue.

"That's the right attitude," Eric says.

"So they *didn't* allow you to come," Ferhad asserts.

"Which is why I allowed myself."

Everyone is silent for a moment, then Nils thrusts a spritzer into my hands and clinks bottles with me. "We'll drink to that."

"Gosh, Florian, you got it going on!" Ricarda looks enthralled and raises her bottle to me.

Only Leah has this funny look on her face. "So, your parents don't know at all that you're here?"

"Let it go!" Nils says.

But Leah only lowers her voice to make sure that the entire bus can't overhear us. "I don't even want to know what would happen if I disappeared without telling my parents."

"I wouldn't have the guts to do it either." With her bottle still raised to her shiny lips, Ricarda smiles at me. "My parents would go ballistic."

Oh, mine will, too, but it'll take a while for them to figure it out. By the time they realize where I am, we should hopefully be far enough away that they can't make the bus turn around. And I would bet anything that they won't have the nerve or the patience to come pick me up somewhere.

I'm getting cocky, I'm on overdrive. "Better to risk getting into trouble from time to time, than to always put up with everything."

"That's true," Eric says. "You are so right about that."

I'm no longer paying attention to everyone else's reaction: I only have eyes for Ricarda now. She gives a wide grin, lifts her bottle back up to her lips, and keeps her eyes fixated on me. I'm getting hot all over. She really does look like a model from a fashion magazine. And this amazing woman will be pitching her tent right next to ours tonight. . . .

Nils interrupts our little moment before I can get totally lost in my personal nirvana.

"Will you buy us a drink later, Flor?"

"Sure, sure," I say mechanically. "We'll party all night long."

"Fantastic." Nils gives me a slap on the back. He's probably spotted the five hundred euro bill. That much money can get me a long way, and it will. I met a fairy princess today. In my mind I'm eighteen, and I can do anything I want.

I relax and enjoy the ride until we stop again about two hours later: we've arrived in Holland. I approach the cash register in the gas station, groceries in hand—chips, ice cream, drinks—and I just can't seem to get rid of that cursed five hundred euro bill.

"Maybe this guy thinks it's a fake," Nils whispers in my ear.

"He says he can't check whether it's a fake or not," Leah clarifies.

"Well, what the heck am I supposed to do? That's the only money I have," I call out and point at my grocery bags.

The checkout guy repeats something in Dutch, shakes his head, and hands the banknote back to me.

"Oh man, why?!" I complain loudly.

"Don't worry, I'll pay for it, you can pay me back later." Nils takes care of my bill.

I'm a little mad and a little rattled, and I trudge back to the bus with my grocery bags. Stupid parents. I see Anna, my sister's friend, run toward me, and she immediately asks about Sarah.

"She's doing pretty good. She can't wait to see you on Tuesday."

"I haven't even wished her a happy birthday yet. I wanted to call her earlier, but she didn't answer her cell phone."

"She probably didn't hear it. Our whole entire family is there with her."

Anna gives a small laugh. "Poor thing! I hate family gatherings. I always put on five or six pounds. But I'm surprised that your parents let you leave."

I remember what the hospital nurse said earlier and claim, "Well, all the people were too much for Sarah anyway: lots of germs."

That seems to work. Anna nods gravely and gives me an encouraging slap on the shoulder. "I'll call Sarah later, when she's by herself again. We often call or text each other in the evenings."

"We do, too."

Anna pauses, looks for a second as if she wants to ask me something important, and then stops herself as some of her girlfriends walk up to us.

"That's good," is all she says. "You do that, so the change from having all the visitors to being alone again doesn't feel too hard for her."

"Yeah, and she still has my birthday present, which she can open tonight after everyone leaves." As soon as I say this I'm not even sure if it's such a good idea for Sarah to open my gift alone. The skull on the T-shirt might shock her, it might remind her: maybe this is what you'll look like pretty soon. It will tell her: well, already you're no longer pretty. All the wigs and makeup in this world aren't going to change that. The boys wrote you off a while ago—even Coach Peter, who you liked and wanted to hook up with.

Yes, even *if* she remembers that she was the one who picked and wanted that T-shirt, she's not going to be happy. Sarah has changed. That's what my mother said, and she's right.

A few days ago I held that music magazine, the one showing the T-shirt, in my hands again. Somebody had written 'Help, help' with a shaky hand on one of the pages. At first I thought it must be some old lady with Parkinson's, but then my mother assured me that Sarah wouldn't let anyone borrow her magazines.

A truck drives past, pretty close behind me, and it's not just the breeze that follows in its wake that gives me goose bumps.

I would really like to call Sarah right now and tell her to wait to open her present the next time I visit. Then I'd be able to buy something else instead and secretly swap the two gifts. But that's not an option right now. I can't call her. My parents and everyone else will still be there by her bedside, and instead of getting to talk with Sarah I'd probably speak with my dad the entire time anyway.

I'm lost in thought as I get on the bus then I remember to look back for Nils. He has one arm around Leah and the other around Ricarda. They're pretending to be drunk and staggering across the parking lot.

Fat Lennart, the least athletic soccer player of all time, who hasn't really made friends with any of us, follows them like a little puppy. Originally, Lennart was supposed to stay at home. Not so much because his parents didn't give him permission to come, but more because we all thought that he wasn't a good fit for our team.

Shoot! I remember about the permission slip from my parents. I quickly tear two pages from the spiral notebook sticking out of Leah's backpack and start writing on the paper in block letters: "We hereby give permission to our son Florian to travel to and attend the soccer summer camp." When Nils finally slumps into the seat next to me, I'm still practicing my mom's signature on the second page. He notices, raises his eyebrows, gets up, and whispers in my ear, "I'll cover for you. Don't want anyone to see you."

"Thanks," I say. "Also, thanks for paying earlier."

Nils just grunts and tells the girls in a low voice to get rid of Lennart who is lurking nearby. "It'd be real stupid if he were to pick up on anything."

I can feel Leah's critical eyes on me, and I hear Ricarda blowing a bubble with her gum. When I'm done and satisfied with my work, Ricarda says in an admiring tone of voice, "Wow, you're pretty brave."

"I'm not so sure," Leah disagrees. "I don't think it's very well thought out. Your parents are probably already looking for you."

"I don't think so. They're by Sarah's bedside and think that I've gone to the café. Or," I add ironically, "to the playground."

A smile flashes over her face, but it's gone again in a split second. "I think my parents would panic and call the police. Maybe you even have to pay for them to come out and look for you."

"They don't start looking for boys as quickly as they do for girls," Nils interrupts her.

"Huh? Why, how do you mean?"

"Just the way it is."

"Boys can take better care of themselves." Ferhad grins.

I burst out laughing, too, when I see the outrage on Leah's face. But she's already preparing her counterattack: "You guys are all so dumb. And that stupid piece of paper, you're only attracting attention, Florian. Nobody's going to buy it. It has to say that you can swim, remember?"

"Everyone knows I can swim."

"Still. It says it on the preprinted forms. And a few other things, like that we can't drink alcohol, that we won't have sex"—Ferhad and Eric chortle in their little corner—"and everything else you're allowed to do and stuff." She's slowly getting on my nerves.

"I don't have to write it all down. They're making an exception for me," I explain. "Because my sister is sick."

Leah exhales noisily through her nose. "You seem to be very sure of yourself," she says and turns back into her seat. Unfortunately, Ricarda does the same, and even Nils puts on a closed-off face and starts searching for something in his bag. Weird. It is as if mentioning Sarah has suddenly caused everyone to be in a foul mood. The bus is full of everyone's chatter; only the four of us are silent and absorbed in thought. This is so noticeable that Coach Peter, who is counting heads to make sure everyone's on the bus, even asks us if we're okay.

"Everything's fine, boss," Lennart calls out. He is sitting by himself in one of the rows in front of us and trying to make us like him. "Totally hunky-dory, dude."

But who'd listen to Lennart? He has no clue whatsoever, does he? He's even worse than Cousin Daniel.

But it's Lennart of all people who manages to get rid of our bad mood—by spilling his Coke and ruining his light-colored shorts, which makes everyone burst out into cheers and laughter.

The next person to make us laugh is Eric. He uses the toilet on the bus but can't get the door to open from the inside after he's done. It takes a half hour before somebody hears him knocking and another half hour for Coach Peter to force open the door, which had jammed, with a screwdriver.

"Boy, I thought I was suffocating in there." Eric is exhausted and slumps into a seat.

"Poor thing." Ricarda hands him something to drink.

"I would sue the bus company," Ferhad suggests.

"Right," Nils calls out. "We can be your witnesses. We can share the compensation money between us. You thought you were going to die, that should be worth quite a bit."

"Nobody dies that quickly," Leah says, and for once she's right. I just about manage to hide the fact that I agree with her from the others.

I wonder what Sarah is doing. It's almost three o'clock, time for her afternoon nap. The family is probably strolling through the park or sitting in the café right about now. I wonder if they're missing me yet. Are they looking for me inside the hospital? Are they calling me? I check my cell phone to see if I missed anything in all the excitement. No missed call and no text message. They probably haven't noticed that I'm gone yet.

On the one hand, that's good; on the other, it's a little disappointing. It was before eleven when I ran out into the park. Somebody could have kidnapped and murdered me four hours ago, and my parents wouldn't even have noticed. I'm angry and think back to the time when they forgot to pick me up at the train station after a school field trip.

Sometimes they look right through me, like they don't see me. It's been ages since they last asked to see my grades. And for my birthday all I got was a shopping voucher, hand-scribbled at the last minute, which they haven't even taken me to cash in yet. Sarah, Sarah, Sarah. It's all they ever think about: Sarah. Of course I don't want to trade places with her—of course she's had really bad luck, and she's very sick.

But what about me?

After another two hours on the bus we finally reach the North Sea and the campground, which looks over the dunes. It's sometime after four o'clock, and we head to the large grassy area under tall pine trees that's reserved for our group. All around us are the soccer clubs we're friends with, the ones we'll be meeting at the tournament tomorrow. In fact, the campground is full of soccer players. You see teenagers everywhere playing soccer in small groups. Some of them are wearing their own jerseys, others sports-fan wear of their favorite German soccer team. Music and the smells of barbecue and sunscreen are all around us. Yes, this is where I want to be.

Eric, Ferhad, and Lennart will be in the tent with me and Nils. That was Coach Peter's decision: we have to share because my presence was so unexpected.

Nils is complaining because he really dislikes Lennart, but Ferhad and Eric are enjoying this.

"Fill up the air mattress, Lennart, that's your job."

"Hey, and what about you?"

"We'll check and make sure you're doing it right." Eric is swinging a tent pole high up in the air. "Serf, here's the whip!"

"Hahaha," Lennart gives a hesitant laugh.

"No laughing," Ferhad calls out. "Or else you'll be sleeping alone under the awning, got it?"

"Sure, and where will you sleep?"

"In my girlfriend's tent." Ferhad makes a point of looking toward the girls' tents. Leah is busy pushing a tent stake into the sandy ground; Michelle and Nathalie are unfolding a tarp; Ricarda is nowhere to be seen. Who is Ferhad thinking of?

"Didn't you hear, sex is forbidden, as is alcohol." Eric grins widely and starts horsing around with Ferhad.

"The only thing that's forbidden is attracting the grownups' attention," Lennart says, trying to sound cool. He must have picked up on how I reacted to my parents forbidding me to come, and he's now trying to imitate me. But it doesn't work for him, because his face has turned bright red from the effort of using the foot pump, and with every step on the pump he's making a fart noise.

Because nobody else is paying any attention to him I feel it's not worth my time getting annoyed with him. I have more important things to do: I have to give Coach Peter my fake permission slip. Now seems like the right time. Our chaperones' tent is being put up. Coach Peter has a hammer in his hand and no time to take care of paperwork. He asks me to put the permission slip on a big table nearby.

This suits me perfectly. The table is cluttered with tools, coffee mugs, cookies, and lists, and my piece of paper will easily get lost in all the mess. The one important thing is that Coach Peter sees that a piece of paper exists.

I'm in a fantastic mood after this genius move, and it gets even better when I see Ricarda walking toward me. She is wearing a red sundress and asks me, "Are you coming to the beach with us?"

This question is exactly what I want to hear.

And it's okay with me that a whole group is going. If I were alone with her I probably wouldn't know what to say.

I've never seen her in a dress: she normally wears a pair of jeans, or soccer gear. She looks strange now, different, more grown-up. But wasn't it me who had wanted to be older?

"Should we take the ball with us?" Eric asks. "Could be fun playing soccer in the sand."

"Nah, let's see what's going down first." Nils has pushed his hands deep into the pockets of his shorts and wiggles his arms, like he always does when he's getting impatient.

He pulls me aside and says, "If we take any longer, the retard might want to come. At least Coach Peter set him straight and told him that he'd be sitting on the bench during the tournament. You'll be playing, of course, Flor."

Ah, that's music to my ears. Especially because Ricarda overhears us and says, "Flor's the best soccer player there is."

"That's true," Leah agrees unexpectedly. "I'm not really happy with the game you're playing with your parents, but it's still nice that you're here." She flashes me a grin, and I'm surprised that she's being so nice.

The six of us start making our way to the beach, through the small spaces in between the tents and then up the walkway over the dunes. About halfway I stop and turn around to look for Lennart. He looks like an abandoned pet, standing there in front of our tents and following us with his eyes. Before, when we used to go on summer vacation—when Sarah was still healthy—our cat would always sit in front of our house by the curb, its eyes following our car as we drove off. Sarah and I would speculate about how long the cat would sit there. The entire three weeks of our vacation, with exceptions of eating and sleeping, was Sarah's opinion. "If I missed someone that much when they left, I would wait and wait and never ever give up."

I turn back around abruptly and hurry to catch up with the others.

"The sea, the sea!" Ferhad calls out and throws his arms up in the air. Then he starts running. The vast white beach lies before us, and the deep-blue waves roar toward us. There's no stopping the others now. I take a deep, deep breath, let out a howl to greet the lovely, welcoming sea, and start running after them. My feet sink in soft, white sand as my body's momentum drives me forward, on toward the vast open space and the horizon; overhead, the seagulls make me feel as if I, too, could become light as air and fly.

We're like young dogs, chasing each other up and down
and along the water.

What could be more fun than jumping into the North
Sea on a bright, warm day in early summer? I can't think of
anything. I'd almost forgotten about something as great as
this during these last few weeks and months.

That the water is cold? Doesn't matter.

Today I even enjoy our jellyfish fight, and I don't mind
Leah slipping one of the jellyfish (the nonstinging kind)
down my oversized T-shirt, even though it slowly slides
down my back, all cold and squidgy, and I want to outscream

the seagulls from the top of my lungs—if only for the fact that Ricarda wraps her arms around me afterward and hollers, "Oh, poor thing," before we topple and fall into the next oncoming wave.

Ricarda looks even prettier than usual with her long, wild hair flying in the wind. In my happy, boisterous mood, I think to myself that I should follow Ricarda around with a wind machine all the time. Then she would earn a fortune as the most beautiful woman on the planet. I could invent the wind machine and have it patented, and then sell it to all those top model shows on TV and make a small fortune. I feel silly and wired, like I haven't felt in a very long time.

"Hey, look!" Nils grabs my arm and point to two boys who are each riding on the beach on some type of small, four-wheel ATV. They're going pretty fast and seem to be enjoying themselves enormously. "I would love to ride around on a thing like that."

"Riding a Jet Ski over the water would be cool, too, they're even faster," Eric says.

"You'd need a special license for that. Besides, those are super expensive." Ferhad is standing right beside Ricarda.

Nils gives me a look. "If only we had money."

"Ah! You don't need a lot of money to have fun." Ferhad makes a pair of crab pincers appear from inside his pant pocket and pretends to pinch Ricarda on the nose.

As the two of them start horsing around, I say, "Well, I do have a little bit of money."

"You're not going to spend your money on those, are you?" Leah asks.

Sure I will, since I can't impress Ricarda with a pair of crab pincers. I figure I have a pretty good shot at making it work with the ATVs, because the two boys earlier didn't seem that much older than us. Maybe you don't need a driver's license to ride them.

"Let's see how much it costs."

The price—at least that's what the man from Beach & Fun tells us in his Dutch accent—is a real bargain: forty-five euros for fifteen minutes.

"It's up to two people per ATV. There are six of you?" He leans over the counter in his little hut with an almost greedy expression on his face. "Okay, so if you take three, three, yes,"—he holds up three fingers—"then I'll give you a discount. Let's say 120 euros."

"You don't have to pay for us, Florian," Eric says. I wave my hand dismissively, trying to look all resolute and generous.

"Jeez, 120 euros." Leah shakes her head. "You should reconsider."

"It's cheaper than a Porsche."

"What?" the girls and Nils ask simultaneously, but I don't feel like telling them about my encounter with the little girl and her fairy princess and how I had wished for a Porsche.

The Beach & Fun guy opens his eyes wide when I show him the five hundred euro bill.

"Is it a fake?" he asks, grins, and holds the banknote up against the sun.

Why does everyone seem to think that I'm someone who would counterfeit money? Do I really look like a thief? Is it even considered theft if you're stealing from your own parents?

"Okay." With one swift move the banknote disappears into his pants pocket. Then he firmly motions us over to the ATVs and explains how they work.

"What about the rest of my money?"

"Let's call it a deposit."

"You didn't mention anything about a deposit." I can feel the muscles in the back of my neck tighten. Damn, this guy is trying to rip me off!

"You better give him the rest of the money right now." Nils plants himself in front of the Beach & Fun guy who looks like an old hippie with his long hair. Nils may be younger, but he's also tall and does a lot of weight training. "You don't want any trouble with us now, do you?"

The guy gives us a wide, open-mouthed grin, and I can see that he has a big gap between his teeth.

"Looks like this wouldn't be the first time that someone smacked him right on the kisser," Nils says casually, almost in passing. I nod and step up and stand right beside my buddy. "Give it!"

Ferhad and Eric, too, step up to us so that we're almost forming a wall between the guy and his bikes.

"Chill out, boys, seriously! You will get your money, I just need to get change for the big bill."

"If not, you're not getting your ATVs back, simple as that." Leah smiles coldly.

"Exactly," Nils and I say simultaneously.

Ricarda ends the discussion by climbing onto the first of the three bikes. "Okay, guys, who wants to come with me?"

"Me!"

The engine sounds pretty good and the wheels have decent oomph as they chew through the deep sand. Ricarda is sitting very close behind me on the ATV. She has her hands wrapped around my belly, her chest pressing against my back. Her legs behind mine look strong and athletic; they're long and tanned, and her toenails are painted pink and mint green. Like Sarah's. What a stupid coincidence.

The ride is awesome. And Ricarda is enjoying it, too. She snuggles up to me and calls out, "Faster, Florian, they're catching up!"

"We'll see about that."

"Whoa, careful! Don't run over the dog!"

A Labrador, who is obviously blind, is crossing our path. Someone is screaming something in Dutch. I brake. We start skidding; sand scatters in all directions. Eric and Ferhad whiz past us from the left, Nils and Leah from the right—but it doesn't matter, because Ricarda is enjoying herself. She smells like vanilla ice cream with hot caramel sauce and cherries on top, and when she leans forward and I turn around, I can see right down her magnificent cleavage.

Because I'm paying more attention to Ricarda than to the path in front of me, the engine suddenly turns off and our faces and noses touch. Like in the movies, or as if a fairy princess had her hand in it.

She says, "Oops! Hahaha! Hey, you."

I say, "Hi, Ricarda. Uh . . . Thank god we didn't run over that dog." It's just about the stupidest thing, isn't it?

She laughs. "Don't worry, it's gone." Ricarda runs her eyes over the beach then over me, puckers her lips, quietly blows a bubble, and puts her index finger on the tip of my nose. That must be how hypnosis works. "Whatcha thinking about, Flor?"

"Vanilla ice cream with hot caramel sauce and cherries on top."

"Are you asking me out for ice cream?"

"Anything you want. I met a fairy princess today, and she granted me three wishes. Two have already come true;

well, at least kind of. If I can make one of *your* wishes
come true . . ."

I don't think I've ever seen Ricarda make such a confused
and puzzled face. Well, I guess I've never said such weird
things before.

"Are you trying to pull my leg?"

"Yes—no. What I mean is: This morning at the hospital,
with Sarah—"

The expression on her face changes abruptly. First, there's a
tiny touch of irritation, then pity is shining through. Ricarda
looks at me like one of my aunts. She sighs like them, too:
joyless but sympathetic at the same time. "I know that her
being sick is really hard on you."

That's not what I want to talk about right now. I want
to tell her a nice story, a fairy tale with a happy ending. But
there's nothing I can say against this look of pity in her eyes
that I've seen a thousand times lately.

"Look," Ricarda says gently while she pulls away from
me, lifting one of her knees and showing me her toes. "It
was Anna's idea. Take a look around: most of us on the all-
girls soccer teams have painted our toenails like this. They're
Sarah's favorite colors—it's a sign of hope and solidarity, like
the pink breast cancer bow."

What a load of crap. Great, now I'll think of Sarah when
I lie on the beach with Ricarda. And I'll have to ask myself
if I'm even allowed to make out with a really hot girl while

my sister is suffering alone in her hospital bed. Is anybody showing *me* any solidarity? Like, ever?

"What do you think?"

"It's stupid."

"Why?"

Ricarda waits for my answer. But I can't bring myself to say what's on my mind.

The silence between us is getting longer, grittier, deeper—it's like a toxic river between us.

Sarah's illness is such a mood killer. If I told my love interest that I had a criminal record or a diaper fetish, it wouldn't be half this bad. Ricarda might have laughed, yelled, or ignored me from then on; but she wouldn't have given me that empty, dispassionate look—like the way you look at a piece of toast when you're no longer hungry.

I feel pretty bland and floppy myself. Where did my energy go, my spark?

Suddenly, a little plastic sand toy hits me on the head from behind.

"Hey, what are you guys doing? Move, don't groove!"

"Leave them alone, Nils! Don't disturb the little love birds." Leah pulls on his sleeve and looks over to us with a provocative expression on her face. I am sure she's happy to butt in on us like that. She's probably thinking that she stopped us from kissing. Wrong! On the contrary, she only improved the odds.

My dark, depressing thoughts fall off me like a wet beach towel. I will put some gas mileage on this beach Porsche of ours. "Engage!" I holler and start the engine.

Ricarda screams as we take off at full speed. Nils screams even louder. "Oh, you just wait; I can do that, too!"

The beach is big and empty and so inviting for a race against my best friend. We give each other friendly, open-mouthed grins. Our girls are squealing.

"I'm sure she'll be your girlfriend one day," the little girl in the park had said this morning. She's right. Nothing and nobody can take this away from me.

The speed of the race inspires me, gives me wings. Anything is possible if I only want it. I can beat the strong headwind, chase away the people and seagulls in our way, and steer Ricarda's lips closer to mine. I can even buy nail polish remover for everyone.

The beach is almost empty, so the shape that appears immediately catches my eye: Lennart. He has spotted us and flails his arms like a traffic patrol officer.

But we have no intention to stop. I'm in the speeding mood, and Nils is not going to allow some clown to tell him which way to go.

"Move!" Nils yells and aims directly for him. How fun to see pasty-white Lennart go even paler, and then, with a reaction time that is way too long, stumble, stagger out of the way, and fall over in the sand.

"Hey, retard, you really need to work on your reaction time!"

"Look, he's trying to fly!"

Eric and Nils's remarks are drowned out by everyone's laughter. In his desperate attempt to escape, Lennart has managed to knock down a sand castle. Three little kids are screaming and crying.

Lennart wipes sand off his face. The six of us on our super-cool ATVs come to a stop in front of him and look down.

"And how exactly were you planning on replacing me at the tournament tomorrow?" I ask Lennart.

"I would have tried my best."

"What a stupid answer, you idiot," Ricarda throws back at him. "Florian is irreplaceable." She embraces me—thankfully, very unlike my aunts—and wraps her arms and legs tightly around me. Then she whispers into my ear in a husky, sexy voice, "Come on! Let's keep going, I'm loving this."

I'm also loving that she's playfully biting my earlobe. I feel a tickle, and not just in my ear.

"Can I ride with you?" I can hear Lennart call behind us.

He really doesn't get it, does he?

11

Even though we return the bikes a few minutes late, the Beach & Fun guy doesn't make a fuss. He hands me my 380 euros without me having to ask for it. Because it's all smaller bills it's quite a bundle—even after I buy everyone ice cream and pay Nils the money back that he lent me earlier.

"Out of curiosity, where does all the money come from?" Ferhad asks.

Once again I'm playing it cool. "It's an all-inclusive trip."

Ferhad laughs. "So you stole it, or what?"

I click my tongue. "Sponsored by Daddy."

Leah butts in and is probably going to yell at me again. But this time, surprisingly, her criticism is aimed at Ferhad. "Seriously, didn't you guess? You should have asked Florian that *before* he paid for your ATV ride."

"You let him pay for yours."

"But I warned him. Florian might pay dearly for this little joyride."

I'm on overdrive. "Every rebel takes a risk."

"Five hundred euros is no pocket change."

"Oh, Leah, you're always so terribly sensible. You worry too much." Ricarda links arms with me and her friend. "Don't you see that Flor's parents are pretty relaxed about the whole thing? They haven't even tried to call him since this morning, right?"

When I reply I sound a little disappointed. "I've been gone seven hours, and nobody's even surprised."

"Parents!" Eric slaps his hand against his forehead. "My mother is pretty senile, too. She's always coming into my room, saying, 'Oh, now I forgot what I came in here for.'"

"But seven hours?" Ferhad recaps. "Somebody must have noticed."

"Somebody probably already did," Leah says. "The police have already taken the whole hospital apart, helicopters are circling the city, and if you turned on the radio you'd hear the missing person report repeated every five minutes or so."

"Hogwash!"

Leah has found my Achilles heel, of course. What's the point of being a rebel if nobody notices?

"That's impossible," I say with a sharp tone in my voice. "Switch on your brain, will you? They would have tried to reach me on my cell phone first."

"Maybe they forgot your number." Eric laughs and so does everyone else—with the exception of Leah. She's the only one who stays serious, holding my gaze like she's ready for a fight, and says very calmly, which gives her words all the more impact: "I think we can exclude early onset of Alzheimer's. So there's only one possible explanation of why they haven't been in touch yet."

"Which is?" I snap. "Alright, let's hear it."

Leah hesitates. Her face becomes serious, her tone of voice careful. "It's obvious: your sister isn't well."

"My sister's never well!" I yell.

This gives Leah such a fright that she trips and almost falls. Ricarda lets go of my arm. Everyone's laughter dies down, and I'm getting startled looks.

"It's not my fault, stop picking on me," Leah says. Tears are welling up in her eyes.

Crap, this is embarrassing. Why do some girls always have to cry so easily? "I'm not picking on you. I'm just under a lot of pressure, don't you get it?"

"But it's not *me*. I'm not putting this pressure on you." A sob escapes her lips. She's mad at herself. She pushes her clenched fists deep into her pant pockets, turns her back, and walks a few steps away from us. She reminds me of a hedgehog who's scuttling across a busy main road. A skinny little hedgehog who, even if it doesn't get run over by a car, doesn't stand much of a chance to survive the winter.

"I'm sorry," I call after her, and she pauses. I realize I shouldn't have lost it with her, so I tell the others, "You guys have no idea. Just before I left the hospital this morning, Sarah puked all over her bed."

"Hmm, yummy," Eric comments.

I feel the need to explain myself, even though I hate doing it. "Okay, it's now after six," I start, gritting my teeth. "Which is dinnertime for Sarah. But because she constantly pukes it all up anyway, they have to drip-feed her some of the time. She doesn't use the toilet anymore, either. It's all done with tubes."

"Eeeww, that's enough now, Flor," Ricarda says and caresses my arm. "We believe you that this is a really screwed-up situation to be in."

"And I don't want to be reminded of it constantly, especially not here."

Everyone accepts this for what it is, but Leah, of course, is not finished yet. She turns.

"Don't think I don't care about your sister, because I do. But it's not my fault that you have this problem, Florian. I was just trying to help. I'm sure there'll be others who'll bring up your situation back home. And they won't be as nice as me."

As soon as we're back at the campground, Coach Peter calls me over to him. "Florian, come here for a second." He's waving the permission slip. "Is this the permission your parents signed?"

My friends stop in anticipation, while I walk up to our coach. Okay, this is going to be hairy.

"Why?" I ask as coolly and calmly as I can. Has Coach Peter guessed that it's a fake? Or did my parents maybe call him instead of me? In that case it's probably best to stop lying so he doesn't get too mad at me.

He looks at me with his eyes squinted. I'm starting to feel really small, and not just because of his height. "We specifically ordered preprinted forms. I mean, your parents could at least have made a little bit of an effort."

I breathe a silent sigh of relief. Coach Peter has nothing on me. I mean, it would have surprised me if my parents had remembered his full name and researched his cell phone number before they tried calling me directly. Yes, Coach Peter still thinks that I'm allowed to be here. He's just mad that my parents didn't use his preprinted form.

I guess my usual, well-worn excuse will have to do. "Sorry, my parents don't have time for minor details like that."

"Still." Coach Peter shakes his head.

"No, they really don't!" I say defiantly, feeling pretty irritated. Suddenly, I would prefer if he saw right through my lies. Then he could just yell at me and rip my head off. He could make me call my parents immediately, threaten to never take me along on another team trip, and slap me with some decent punishment—something stupid and tedious, like cleaning the dirt and grass off our tents at the end of this weekend.

Yeah, that would be okay. At least I'd know where I stand. I wouldn't have to dwell on the idea that Leah brought up earlier. I'd be a rebel who'd had his punishment, but a proud rebel nonetheless.

But I just can't bring myself to tell him the truth. Instead, I launch a counterattack. I hand Coach Peter my eighty euros and say, "By the way, it's Sarah's birthday today. Did you wish her a happy birthday? I'm sure it's important to her, you know how much she likes you."

Coach Peter's eyelids flicker nervously. "I didn't get a chance because I was too busy preparing this tri—"

"See?"

Coach Peter can tell that my defense is holding up. He quickly changes the subject. "I heard you guys rented ATVs. Remember you need to ask us first, if only because of the risk of an accident. It seems there even was a potentially dangerous situation?"

Lennart, that little toad.

"No, nothing happened. *Somebody* was jealous because *somebody* wasn't invited to join."

"This is a sports club. We should all remember to be fair and cooperative!" This wasn't just addressed to me; it was addressed to my friends, too. "You all know what I'm talking about. Nobody will be excluded from this team, am I making myself clear?"

I can hear murmuring and complaining and can't help but visualize a pack of stray, growling dogs. Even Coach Peter has to realize that he can't force us to make Lennart part of our team. He pockets my stupid permission slip and grumbles, "Alright, everybody try to make yourselves useful. Somebody might give Coach Philip a hand with the barbecue, for example."

"Lucky you," Nils whispers in my ear. "I thought your parents had called Coach Peter already and you were done for."

"No, they probably think I went home to watch TV."

"Yeah, you're right. My parents would call my cell phone or your parents, even, before they turned to a complete stranger. But they would do something. You know what my dad is like."

"Of course." All this talk about my parents being so hard-boiled suddenly washes over me. Sure, Nils's dad bugs him with his constant nagging and his ambitious desire for Nils not to drop out of high school. Sure, his dad is a control freak and all. But my parents paying no attention to me whatsoever is just as bad; it just hurts on a different level. I thought that if I suddenly disappeared they'd miss me. That maybe they'd notice that I exist. But I guess I was wrong.

"My parents treat me like an unwanted child. Their son who's fourteen—fourteen!—has been gone without a trace for an entire day, and they couldn't care less. I could be the perfect victim for a sex perv. All he'd have to do is throw my dead body in the backyard, and they'd just mow around me with their stupid lawn mower."

Nils is signaling me like crazy to shut up.

I realize too late that it's not only my friends who are listening, but also Lennart. And he's got that look on his face like he's planning on using everything he has heard against me first chance he gets.

I am furious at my own stupidity, at Lennart, and at the entire world—and I storm off.

Because I don't know where else to go, I make for the campground showers. My heart is pounding as if I just finished a marathon run. I feel nauseous from all the lies. I imagine them squirming in my stomach like snakes.

But my queasiness might also come from all the hair collected in the drains of the public sinks. Somebody forgot their toiletry bag on a window ledge. It tipped over, and the toothbrush slipped out and fell into the sink, with the bristles facing down. I stare at it for a little while before turning on the cold-water faucet and sticking my head under it.

Ah, that takes the edge off. Alright, I will stop acting like a child. I will be patient and wait for my parents to decide to pick up the telephone. When they call, my plan is to take their angry outburst without argument while keeping an expressionless face so the coaches won't notice. Then I'll enjoy the rest of the trip as if nothing has happened and hope that by the time I get home the worst of it has blown over. That's got to work. Other teenagers rebel against their parents, too, and they get away with it with a slap on their wrist. Right? I'm entitled to these three days. Which is why I will stop thinking about what Leah said: that Sarah might be getting worse.

I will simply delete this possibility from my hard drive. This suddenly seems easy, as a soccer ball somehow finds its way to me through the open doors near the sinks. I kick it back out into the open, skillfully returning it to the players who sent it astray. This is a round I win.

13

Nils and Leah wave at me from their table. I squeeze myself onto the wooden bench and into the space between them that they have preheated for me with their backsides. Then I shoot Lennart a warning look.

Everyone has contributed something to our dinner: people have brought soft drinks, country bread, salads in plastic containers, different types of meat for the barbecue. Except me, of course.

"Oh man, I'm not exactly keeping a low profile," I say, trying to sound witty. "I didn't bring anything for the dinner and now you guys have to feed me."

I glance over at everyone. All of my friends are keeping a straight face. Lennart raises his eyebrows but doesn't dare say anything.

Only Coach Peter, who is just passing behind Ricarda at that moment, overhears me and grumbles, "Sure, Florian, you're getting extra special treatment again. We'll just raise your membership fees. Don't worry, we'll make the money back in no time."

"Hahaha," I say, feeling relieved, because I know that he has a soft spot for me. As long as Coach Peter is joking around, he's not holding a grudge.

The food is excellent, especially because it's only now that I notice how hungry I am. I dig in and really stuff my face, cracking jokes with Nils about Eric's habit of drowning everything he eats in ketchup. I love it when I hear Ricarda telling the other girls how much she enjoyed our ride on the beach.

Then a cell phone rings. It's my ringtone, that's for sure. My face instantly turns red. This is it. The shit's hitting the fan. I jerk sideways to come away from the table first, phone tightly clutched in my hands—but I can't get away. A sudden, stabbing pain runs through my forehead, and for a moment I almost black out. My head has crashed into Leah's who turned in my direction at the exact same second I turned.

"Ouch! Watch it!"

"You watch it!" she shoots back. "I can answer my phone, can't I?"

Her phone. The screen flashes: *7:21 PM, Daddy calling*.

I feel dizzy. That's impossible.

"We have the same ringtone." It's not my parents.

"Yeah, so? It's the only thing we have in common, too."

Truth is, my parents still haven't called me.

Leah massages her forehead and turns her back to me to answer the call. I listen absentmindedly to her conversation as she complains to her dad that "Florian, that dope," almost knocked her out with his "thick skull." And I can't help but overhear her dad's deep baritone voice—although it's muffled—through the telephone. "Oh, honey, I'm sure you can take it," he says with a laugh. "That's the boy you like so much, isn't it?"

Leah's face turns bright red, like a tomato, and she quickly glances over at me. I am way too confused to even pretend I didn't hear anything. She jumps to her feet and hisses into her phone, "I never said that, Daddy! Him, of all people . . ."

Yeah, why not? I'm a first-rate defender on the soccer field, and besides, I'm pretty okay overall. At least I'm not as tall and scrawny as Coach Peter or as fat as Lennart; I'm not all pimply like Nils, and I most certainly don't have bad breath like Coach Philip—people say he can knock out his opponents just by breathing on them. At any rate . . .

I follow her with my eyes and suddenly I have this nice,

warm feeling in my belly. Being liked boosts my self-confidence. It's kinda nice.

"You alright?" Nils gives me a nudge.

"Except for a small concussion . . ." I reply, still a little numb and light-headed but with a big, happy grin on my face. Compared to Ricarda, Leah is only half as pretty and twice as difficult, but she's also nothing to sneeze at. She's smart and unique, that's what she is. Wow, who'd have thought that this feisty little beast had a crush on me? She, of all people?

"Hey, Flor," Ricarda grumbles, probably because she's noticed my sudden interest in Leah. "I've been wanting to show you something this whole time, but you're not even looking my way. Here, why don't you try this garlic herb baguette my mom made."

"Mmmm, thank you." I give her a smile, which I hope will calm her down. Listen, girls, don't fight over me, we have the whole weekend still ahead of us!

"There's a ton of garlic on that baguette," Eric warns me. "I'm just saying, in case you want to make out with someone later."

"Who would you want to make out with?" Nils asks.

"Look over there," Eric replies, lifts his glass of cola, and drinks a toast to Nathalie. She beams at him and starts giggling.

I'm as puzzled as Nils. Nils is even more surprised when Eric tells him, "Did you know that Michelle is into you?"

"Huh?"

"At least she used to be. It's quite possible that she changed her mind in the meantime, given that you really don't have a clue."

"Boys always take a long time to notice these things. Sometimes way too long," says Leah, as she sits back down beside me with a disgusted look on her face.

I'm feeling playful and laugh in her face. "Are you trying to tell me something?"

"Would you like me to head-butt you again?"

"Nope." My grin is so wide right now that I could fit a banana in sideways.

Ricarda gives me a probing look, but then turns to Nils and says, "Don't get too attached. You're not even Michelle's type. You're much too . . . childish and irresponsible for her."

Nils, who has no idea that this phrase was aimed more at me and Leah than at him and Michelle, crosses his arms over his chest and settles back into his seat. "Hmm, I beg to differ. Let's see what this evening brings."

"Definitely," I say.

"I'm thinking we should play a training game later," Ferhad whines.

"Sure, whatever, you do that. We didn't sign up, though," Ricarda replies. Then she slides her bare foot, which she has slipped from her sandal, against my leg under the table. "Party on the beach. Still looking for a date?"

"Sure, yeah, of course."

"Party sounds good," Nils agrees. "We've got plenty to drink."

"There'll be a lot more than just grape juice and cola." Eric laughs and wipes ketchup off his mouth with both of his hands. "You can be a true sportsman tonight and give Lennart private lessons if you want," he says to Ferhad who then makes a face as if he'd just bitten into a bad burger. Mr. Bad Burger himself, aka Lennart, overhears the phrase "private lessons." He also overhears what Nils mumbles with his mouth full, which is: "special gymnastics for a retard."

For a moment we look at each other—he, the total loser, and me, the cool, hard-boiled hero of the day. Nobody's given me any hell *yet*. My parents are still having dinner in some Italian restaurant, feeding relatives, and they're going to look real stupid when they get home and realize that Florian is not sitting on the couch watching TV.

Then Lennart says, just to me, "You're not allowed to be here."

His threat, if he means for it to be a threat, sounds more like a question. He can't even blackmail properly.

"So?" I counter with some force. "You're not supposed to be here, either, right?"

"Why, what do you mean?"

I really want to limit my answer to a firm look, but Nils, who is now tuned into our conversation, never skips a chance to come down on Lennart.

"Why? Are you serious, you really have to ask? Because you're useless at soccer, you retard. And because nobody wants you here. Is there anything you can do except blackmail people, huh? So we should have paid for an ATV for you, too? Are we the social welfare office, or what? Don't even think about getting on Florian's nerves!"

Lennart opens his mouth but no words come out. His lips open and close, like a fish.

"Just take care of your own problems, I think that's what's best for everyone," I say and generously try to insert some warmth into my voice. Better to defuse the situation. It's bad enough that I don't know what level of anger is waiting for me at home. There's no need to aggravate someone who might blackmail me and add one more thing to my pile of problems.

Lennart nods—it's crazy, but he looks oddly appeased—then bends over his dinner plate and starts shoveling potato salad into his mouth.

Nils gives a satisfied grunt and turns his attention back to Michelle. Ricarda's foot touches my knee for the second time. A second foot—I'm guessing Leah's—kicks me, but it doesn't hurt and I'm sure it wasn't supposed to hurt either. I find whatever is going on under the table between these two girls very amusing, but it's even more fascinating to watch Lennart, the relentless destroyer of potato salad. A few more mouthfuls and he could be serious competition to my uncle

The Steamroller. He doesn't even chew, he just swallows. When he swallows, I picture the unchewed mash pouring into his gullet like lumpy cement coming out of a truck.

"Do you ever stop eating like a pig?" My question seems to surprise him. My next question seems to surprise my friends. I'm thinking out loud when I turn back to them: "I wonder what he'd wish for if he ever met a fairy princess?"

"What do you mean, a fairy princess?" Leah asks.

I sip my glass of cola. "A fairy princess," I say as if it's the most normal thing in the world. "You know: you save her, and she grants you three wishes."

"You're weird. What makes you think of that?" Nils wants to know.

"I had the pleasure of meeting one this morning."

"How fun! And what did you wish for?" The two girls hang on my every word.

I'm trying to sound casual while counting down the answers on my fingers.

"First, to be eighteen years old, so I can do what I want. Second, to drive a Porsche or maybe ride an ATV. Third . . ." I hesitate. Maybe it wasn't such a good idea to raise the subject after all.

"Third?" Ricarda digs deeper. "Has it come true already, too?"

"No, I'm still working on it."

"Oh?" She gives me a deep, meaningful glance.

Nils mimics her and leans over to me. "We're listening."

Leah doesn't say anything. Somewhere a cell phone rings, but again, it's not mine. Those stupid, hardened douche bags. It's been nine hours since I met the fairy-princess girl. In nine hours you could kidnap a boy, ransack a house, commit a murder, remove all traces of the crime, and leave the country in no hurry whatsoever. Of course, in that same amount of time, a cancer patient could also undergo emergency surgery. Crap! I wish my parents would call me already. I wish they'd give me an earful, yell at me until my cell phone battery gave out. Then I'd get some peace and quiet afterward. Then I could stay here and have fun without constantly having to worry.

I also hope that I won't have to hurt Leah's feelings now.

"Come on, Truth or Dare!" Ricarda leans forward.

"A girlfriend," I say offhandedly and am trying my hardest not to turn lightbulb red.

Ricarda is delighted. She guesses what my full answer would be and says with a smile, "We might be able to do something about that."

But Leah, who is sitting on my left, abruptly gets up. "Did you wish for any girlfriend at all, or did you wish for Ricarda?"

It's not fair to tell the truth. The truth always sucks. Back home, the truth is downright illegal.

"I'm not telling."

"Coward," Ricarda says in a honeyed voice.

"You really are a coward," Leah hurls at me and storms off.

"Sheesh, what's up with her?" Nils asks.

"Bitch alert," I claim and am immediately embarrassed.

But not a second later I practically lose control because Ricarda leans over to me and presses her lips against mine. If only the truth were always rewarded that way.

A nd so my third and final wish is granted.

"Hehe, what's up, you guys!" Nils says.

Ferhad gives a muted laugh. "Smooching is not allowed here at camp."

I hear his voice from very far away. All around me, dishes are clattering, people are laughing, cell phones are ringing—not mine—but my eyes are closed and I'm ignoring, blocking everything out. Ricarda is a great kisser. In fact, she's such a great kisser that I'm sure it's not her first time kissing someone. So what? Even if she has twenty ex-boyfriends, the only thing that matters is this: she's kissing *me*.

In the background, I can see that Eric and Nathalie have screwed up their courage, too. They get up, holding hands, and disappear behind the tents. I guess it's just the right moment.

I like Leah, too, but it was Ricarda I had wished for. Ricarda is the perfect woman to make a vacation dream come true. Any travel company trying to sell vacations and using photos of white beaches and palm trees would hire her on the spot.

We get up together, run a few yards away from everyone else, hide behind the campground shower building, and keep making out like crazy. Ricarda is hungry, really hungry. She opens my mouth again and again, rushes in with her tongue, lifts and bends her leg, presses her knee against my hip. Oh boy, this girl is a lot hotter than I thought. But I've never really been with a girl before. . . .

A soccer ball hits the wall right beside my head; I don't bat an eyelid. If a bomb were to explode next to me, I wouldn't care.

"Do you love me, Flor?"

"Yes, I think you're awesome," I answer, breathless from her soft body pressing up against mine. My hands wander from her back to her front: the smooth fabric of her dress, the lace on her bra.

Ricarda is coming closer and closer. Inch by inch she presses against me and whispers, "I think it's great how you stood up to your parents, it totally turns me on. I wish I could do that, too. My parents are exactly the same: forever trying to stop me from doing things, always telling me what to do. They say I'm too young to go dancing; too young to go out with Leah, just the two of us; too young to bring home a boyfriend. Just like you, I can't wait to turn eighteen."

"Have you ever had a boyfriend?"

"Yeah." She holds up three fingers and looks proud of herself.

"Like, a real boyfriend?"

"What do you mean, a *real* boyfriend?"

"You know, all the way."

"Oh." She grins and runs her hand up alongside my body—only along the side, but it's more than enough. She stops at the right spot and spreads her fingers. "I'm waiting for the right guy. My last boyfriend said that I should stop playing soccer because it made my legs look too muscular. So I dumped him."

"Oh, I like women who play soccer."

"Well, I guess a daredevil like you would have no use for a fragile little fashion doll or a super skinny witch."

The "super skinny witch" is aimed at Leah. Ah well, I guess she's not listening. And I hope she won't see us once we get cozy in one of those roofed beach chairs. Whose idea was this? Who cares? It's a great idea.

"Shall we?"

"Let's go!"

I try but can't remember the last time I felt so happy, so full of energy—the last time that I enjoyed being alive this much.

"Ahem. I'm sorry to disturb you guys, but ..."

"Then don't!" Ricarda takes my hand and we try to walk past Anna, but Anna blocks our way.

"Oh, don't tell me the two of you are together?"

"I don't see how that's any of your business."

Anna raises her hands. "I'm sorry, milady, I was only asking."

"Get lost and go bother someone else!"

"I can't." Anna pointedly turns her back to Ricarda. "Florian, I have to talk to you."

I knew it: Anna spells trouble.

"Hey, listen, now's not really a great time . . ."

"Sorry, but it has to be now. It's because of Sarah."

I can't help it: my resistance crumbles, falls apart like a house of cards. "Why, what's wrong with her?"

"Nothing, but she's not picking up her phone."

Ricarda gives an irritated groan. "And that's why you come here and make a big fuss?"

"It's so unlike her," Anna defends herself fiercely. "Nobody's picking up at all! Not on Sarah's cell phone, not on your mom's cell phone, and I'm only getting the machine on your landline. I haven't even wished Sarah a happy birthday yet. Coach Peter couldn't get a hold of her either."

My brain is working feverishly. Coincidence? In a dead zone? Broken phone lines? No. It can only mean one thing—something's happened back home. Leah was right after all. I'm getting hot and cold chills at the thought of it.

But all I say is: "The whole family is there. They probably just didn't hear the phone ring."

"But I tried like a million times."

"Is it your sister's birthday today?" Ricarda asks, sounding genuinely surprised.

"And it's not any old birthday," Anna says triumphantly. "It's her eighteenth!"

"So why would you come here? On Sarah's birthday?" Ricarda's eyes express a mix of admiration and shock. Even rebels need to stick to certain rules.

"Sarah's happy for me and wants me to be here," I claim. This is true, at least, it was for a little while. "Besides, I didn't want to miss anything."

It was you, Ricarda, I didn't want to miss. I'm trying to tell her this telepathically, but she's not picking it up. Yep, my girlfriend is upset.

To be fair, I can no longer deny it. The fact that nobody is picking up the phone back home and the fact that nobody seems to be missing me must be related. My parents' stubbornness is no longer just embarrassing and annoying, it's troubling, too. Anna spells it out for me: "I'm worried about Sarah, Florian. I think she's in a bad way, in a really bad way. Who knows, maybe it's already the end." She sniffles and turns her face away. "Sarah was so afraid of today. She even texted me yesterday, telling me how afraid she was."

"She didn't want to see all our aunts and uncles and cousins."

"No," Anna sobs. "It's not that. She was afraid of the actual date."

Keep your cool, just keep your cool! Anna likes to exaggerate and sometimes makes up stories. She likes to drive people nuts. Worst of all, I'm getting the feeling that she knows more than she's letting on. Yeah, Anna should write novels.

Ricarda softly touches my hand. "I'll meet you by the tents, okay, Flor? Also, I have to get ready for the party."

"Alright," I croak, feeling miserable and slumping my shoulders. I understand only too well that she's trying to escape. I would love to follow her. I want to run, run away from everything, in the same way I ran away from the hospital this morning.

As soon as Ricarda's gone, Anna grabs me by the wrist. She got what she wanted, didn't she, and starts blabbing away: "Sarah and I called each other a lot these past few days. She was more up front than I've ever seen her. She asked me which of her dresses I wanted when she dies, and she listed the songs she wanted played during her funeral."

My throat is suddenly bone-dry. "She's talked about that stuff with my dad, too," I say, like on autopilot. "But her chances are still pretty good, I'm sure of that. She's just going through a rough patch."

"Because of her birthday, is it?"

"Yeah."

"She told me that she hasn't had a lot of hope in a while. She's only pretending to believe she might get better out of consideration for your parents."

I feel like I'm being punched in the stomach. I can't take it anymore. It hurts so much that I double over with pain. Because this rings true, because this is so typical of Sarah: always being nice, always pleasing everybody. This is what you get for being so nice all the time, Sarah—the short end of the stick, that's what.

"I'm so sorry for your mom, too."

I'm really hating Anna's crybaby face right now. This stupid cow has absolutely no idea what it means to be putting on a happy face all the time. All Anna does is play the Good Samaritan, mount the Help-Sarah-Fight-Cancer Club, and try to recruit new members with slogans like the one she's now aiming at me: "Sarah is such a good person, she's like an angel."

"Whatever, she's not dead yet," I say, and I really hope it's true.

Anna seems to be reading my thoughts, her eyes are open wide.

"No, thank god, Florian, but"—she pauses and I can really see how the wheels in her brain are turning and churning—"maybe I shouldn't tell you this . . ."

I feel like yelling, Then don't! Stop constantly doing something you say you don't want to do! Instead, I just stare at her.

"But somehow she has started believing that an angel of death is coming to her room to come and get her."

Okay, that's it. "What a load of hogwash! She got that from some movie that I bet you probably watched with her. You shouldn't have. You're talking her into all this angel crap! And of course, she jumps on it, no wonder with all the strong medications she's on. She's so doped up, she'd believe anything."

"But isn't that terrible?"

"Why are you telling me this?!" I yell at her. I can't and I won't pretend to be nice anymore. She's really getting on my nerves. She could be Sarah's best friend ten times over for all I care. "As if I don't know this myself! I'm in contact with my sister, too, you know."

Anna's eyes flash at me angrily. Great, now she's offended.

"So you know what the angel of death told her yesterday?"

"Nobody told her anything! She had a nightmare, and you two got worked up over it." I walk away and leave her standing right where she is. This gets her even more riled up.

"Okay, so you don't know what the angel told her," she calls after me. "But I do."

"Well?" I turn around. Bad mistake. Even though I know what's coming and that she's going to say something very nasty I am completely at her mercy.

Anna walks up to me, grabs my arms, and hisses with an urgent look in her eyes, "The angel of death said to her, 'Tomorrow will be your last birthday.'"

That's heavy. For a moment, it knocks the ground from under my feet. I have no idea what to say. I also wonder if maybe she's telling the truth—despite being mad as hell at her right now. All I can bring myself to say is, "That's not true."

"Of course it's true."

"Never in a million years."

Is she hesitating? Her eyes are flaring up as if she is.

"Anna, you're lying, you're just making this up to mess with me."

Now she's really flying off the handle. "I'm not lying! I can only hope that today isn't Sarah's last birthday after all. That she doesn't die while you're out here having a good time and picking up girls. Because if it does happen while you're here, you'll never forgive yourself."

With that she storms off, and all I can hear is the blood rushing in my ears.

16

After the fight with Anna, I promptly get a headache. Intense pressure on my left and right temple, as if a medieval torture instrument is clamped around my head. I massage my temples with both my hands, but it doesn't help.

Then, like a condemned criminal, I pull out my cell phone and dial our home number. It rings. I wait for my dad's voice to grumpily mumble our last name or for my mom's startled and anxious "Yes?" In fact, I'm waiting for the biggest blowup in history—but more than that, I'm hoping for my own deliverance.

But there is no deliverance. Anna was at least right about one thing: nobody's picking up. Not on our landline and not on any of our cell numbers either.

I grit my teeth and trudge back to our tents. Ricarda's cheerfully coming toward me, but she quickly notices my grim face. "Trouble?" She seems like she wants to kiss me, but she doesn't.

"I'm having an especially lousy day today."

"Oh," she says and sounds miffed. "So the day of our first kiss is an especially lousy day."

"No, no, that's not what I mean." I make an effort not to get annoyed and hold that remark against her. "The kiss was awesome. It's just . . . something's up. I can't get a hold of Sarah on the telephone."

It seems that Ricarda is making an equally big effort to stay calm and friendly. "Can't you put that out of your mind for even just one second? You decided to come here and party with us. You yourself said that she's happy for you to be here." Ricarda wraps her arms around my neck. "And now look at you. You took a stand against your parents just to be here. You're free. You should enjoy it!"

"Yeah," I say, feeling exhausted. "I'll try." Then I plant a quick kiss on her mouth and, full of envy, peer over at Eric and Nathalie who are playfully squabbling. How cool and relaxed they are. How free of any problems. Nobody is giving them attitude. Nobody is trying to scare them. And they're certainly not feeling guilty about anything.

"Florian, here, you look like you could use it." Nils walks up and hands me his half-empty bottle of beer.

"Oh yeah, thanks. That *is* what I need right now." I break away from Ricarda and start drinking.

Next thing I know, Ferhad offers Ricarda a bottle of beer, too. "So you're not feeling left out."

"Thanks—how nice that someone's thinking of me."

"Well, if your boyfriend is not taking care of you . . ."

I don't like the way he's grinning at her. All I need now is for him to tell her how pretty she is. And she really is. While Anna was pestering me, Ricarda got changed, put on makeup, and put up her hair. I should make an effort, and be attentive and funny. But I can barely pay any attention to Ricarda. That stupid Anna with her scare tactics and her talk about the angel of death. Well, she got what she wanted, didn't she? It's all I can think about now, even though I'm sure it's only half true. Anna's just a big fat liar. But what if she's telling the truth for once?

"Your hair looks amazing today, Ricarda."

Ferhad is really ticking me off, too. "Hey, didn't you want to play in the coed game?"

He dismisses this categorically. "Nah, there's no point, and besides, hardly anyone signed up for it."

"So, can we go now?" Nils asks and grabs the three plastic bags that contain our evening's provisions. He hands one to Eric and another to Ferhad. Then he scans the area with his eyes. "All we need is Leah. Has anyone seen her?"

Ricarda shrugs her shoulders as if her friend was no concern of hers. "Haven't seen her in a while. She's been in a pretty foul mood all day. If you don't feel up for vacation and if you're constantly preoccupied with something else, then you should just stay at home, that's what I always say."

No doubt about it, that was meant for me. I'm miffed, but I'm trying not to show it. After all, I want things to be okay again between Ricarda and me as quickly as possible. I want to drink myself into oblivion, have a nice make-out session, and forget about everything else around me.

Julia and Karen are walking past us, each carrying a plastic dishpan full of clattering dishes. "You lazy douche bags, you could have helped us with the dishes," Karen says with a sullen look on her face.

"Oh, so sorry, but we're allergic to dish soap," Ferhad counters and puts his arm around Ricarda. He's so busy trying to impress her with his stupid lines that he doesn't notice Karen putting a bottle of dish soap in his plastic bag and grabbing a bottle of vodka lemonade in exchange.

Whatever. She might as well steal his wallet, too, for all I care.

"So what should we do now?" I ask Ricarda. "Should we leave without Leah?"

"We would already have gone to the beach earlier if it were up to me."

"Just because we didn't doesn't mean we shouldn't."

"We'll see about that," she snaps. I nudge her with my foot. That finally seems to patch things up, and she gives me a smile.

"Leah? Leeeeeah?" Nathalie calls out beside me. She sounds bored, and it's totally useless, too. How's Leah going to hear her? The only results of Nathalie's screaming are that my ears start ringing and that Lennart crawls out of his hiding spot. He's got the upper hand, though, because for once in his life he knows something we don't.

"I know where she is," he calls out. The only thing missing is him raising an arm and snapping his fingers to get the teacher's attention. "She's feeding a squirrel."

Eric gets a case of the giggles. "A squirrel? *You're* a squirrel!"

That sounds almost friendly by his standards, and Lennart gobbles it up greedily. "Come on, guys, she's over there."

We get a move on. Ferhad pushes ahead to catch up with Ricarda, but I'm on to him. I stay close, skillfully jumping over tent cords, and I draw a smile out of Ricarda when I manage to snatch and steal a burger off someone else's table in passing.

Leah really is crouching down by the side of the campground in front of a hedge, holding a piece of nut bread out on her outstretched arm, and clicking her tongue to get the attention of the local wildlife. She reminds me of that little girl in the park, but when she turns around and gives us a wide-faced grin—all silver dangle earrings and sassy short hair—she turns into Ricarda's wisecracking friend all over again. I guess she's nice in her own way, and for a second I'm actually really happy that she likes me.

"The squirrel can't move. I think it's sick or maybe hurt."

"Hey, be careful!" Eric grabs her shoulder, wants to pull her back. "I got bitten by a squirrel when I was a kid. I'm serious! You never know if they carry rabies or something. My mom was super worried that I caught something."

"I'm sure you did." Ferhad gives him a slap on the shoulder. "That would explain a few things."

Eric laughs and tries to chase away the squirrel, waving his arms. "Shoo, shoo, away with you!"

"Hey, Eric, stop it," Leah objects. "I've been trying to get it to come closer and now you're scaring it away. . . ."

"No, no, I'm all for making it go away, too," Ferhad says. "I mean, if it's got rabies or some other disease, it better not come too close."

"That's right," Nathalie calls out, sounding excessively scared. Ricarda doesn't make herself heard, but she backs off a little, just in case.

I guess they're right to a certain degree. This is not normal behavior for a wild animal. It really could be infected. But in spite of this, or maybe precisely because of it, there's no need to taunt the squirrel or chase it away. Everyone can see that it can barely move. It's about to die, anyone can see that.

"Leave it alone," I call out, and I can feel my heart pound in my chest all the way up to my brain, which is about to explode. I want to keep my mouth shut, I really do, but I can't help myself and the words are bursting out of me, "Just let it die in peace!"

Ricarda gives me a startled look. Nils puts a hand on my shoulder. "Hey, Flor," he says in a friendly tone of voice. "It's only a squirrel, dude."

"That's right," Eric jumps in, trying to be very pragmatic about it. "Maybe we'll do it a favor if we put it out of its misery. We had to put our cat down, too, when it got too sick."

I can't breathe.

"No!" Leah calls out at the same time. "You have no right!"

But Eric gives her an innocent look. Eric with his stupid, ridiculously long hair that he constantly has to blow out of his face. "It was better for the cat, Leah, honestly. It was in pain the whole time."

"Why are you telling us all this bullcrap?" I bark at him. My face feels really hot, my heartbeat roars through my head. My arms dart forward, and I hit him hard right against the chest.

"What the heck is the matter with you?" he pants angrily.

"I just want to be left alone, okay?! And so does that squirrel there."

"Are you out looking for trouble, or what?" Eric's eyes flare up furiously. "Dude, you're all over the place."

For a moment it looks as if we're about to charge each other, throw ourselves to the floor, and beat the crap out of one another. But then something completely unexpected happens.

Somebody laughs out loud. It's Lennart. Not only is he laughing, he's also rubbing his hands together and calling out, "Come on, come on, we want to see blood!"

I no longer feel up for a fight. The quarrel between Eric and me disappears as quickly as it has started, like a puff of smoke. I remember that Eric is my friend, and that he's a little naïve and clumsy and slow. And he remembers that I'm considered temporarily insane.

His raised fists drop. I breathe out at the same time.

"I'm sorry," I say, and it's not as hard as I thought it would be. "I'm sorry about your cat."

"Esmeralda." Eric relaxes. "She was quite the party girl. Out hunting every night. All the male cats in our neighborhood had a crush on her and always peed on our doorstep. She only had three legs—can you imagine?"

Yes, I can smile about this. It's crazy, but I manage. Even though at the same time I smile, I have to make an extra effort not to burst out into tears. My jaw muscles hurt as if smiling is something that can only be achieved with great effort.

Lennart, on the other hand, seems to find it very easy to laugh. He even keeps on laughing when everyone around us stares at him with contempt. Only when Nils calls out: "Hey, retard, enough already!" does he finally stop, with his mouth still open.

Nils gives us a nod. "Come on guys, let's go. This is going to be one hell of a party."

Our group leaving the campground is quite large. Aside from Nathalie we also have Finn, Jaffa, Luca, Schnitzel, and—as the only person who's neither invited nor welcome—Lennart. He probably thinks that it's safe to join just because there's so many of us.

And that's true at first. Out on the open beach we all walk pretty far apart. Nils, Schnitzel, and Luca set the tone and walk ahead of everyone else. Ferhad and Ricarda follow directly behind, then there's me—alone and preoccupied with my cell phone. A little distance away are Finn, Jaffa, and Lennart, who are chatting about tomorrow's soccer tournament. Very far on the left is the happy couple, Eric and Nathalie. Leah, who's collecting seashells, comes in last.

My head hurts with every step I take. Maybe a few sips of beer will help. After all, they say beer has a calming effect. The sun is setting behind the dark, towering clouds, giving them a bright, shiny outline; they look like monsters with halos. The seagulls are pretty aggressive tonight, too. Feathers flying, they're wrangling over small pieces of bread that Luca is throwing their way. A wave hits the beach and washes over my sneakers. Water soaks my jeans all the way to my knees. I hate getting wet socks. I also hate that wet, sloshy sound of water inside my shoes. Sure, I could take them off, but then I'd have to stop and bend down now . . . nah, I'd rather drink a little more.

Up in front, Nils picks up his cell phone and starts talking to someone; I have no idea who it is. My feet destroy dozens of light-colored, longish seashells: crunch, crack, burst, crumble. I leave behind a long, white, thin trail of destruction. I turn around and start walking backward for a little while. That way at least the light of the setting sun, which suddenly slants through the huge clouds, won't hurt my eyes. Sure, I like a pretty sunset, but does anyone ever consider that you're blinded by the sun when you look at it?

Eric seems to have forgotten everything around him and focuses on smooching. Lennart stares at me with a dimwitted expression on his face because I'm walking backward. Jaffa breaks away from his little gang of three and kicks a stray soccer ball back to its rightful owners with some oomph. They're a bunch of unfamiliar players wearing red headbands.

A minute later—I'm back to walking forward—the same soccer ball covered in wet, heavy sand rolls in front of me. I do what I've never done before in my life: I walk around it.

Ricarda is being entertained by Ferhad. I had no idea he could talk so much. He's really sticking his chest out, that stupid horny show-off. My mood is a flatline. I'm not even jealous anymore.

*　*　*

"So, what do you think, Flor?" Ricarda suddenly asks, turning around to me with a cheerful tone in her voice. She takes my hand and swings it back and forth.

"What do I think about what?"

"You know, getting Lennart real drunk and then stealing his clothes." Her face radiates glee.

"Whatever, do what you want, I'm sick of him anyway."

"So . . . is there a special someone you're not sick of?" She throws back her hair and gives me an open, candid look, once again ready to forgive my mood. Her lips look delicious in the evening sun, just waiting to be kissed (by me)—and she pauses for two seconds.

Then her lips curl up like the waves do on the ocean before a storm, and she raises her eyebrows. She pulls me closer to her until my face is very close to hers. "Yes? No?"

"Yes."

"So?" Her voice sounds almost threatening. "There's nothing you want to do right now by any chance?"

"Yeah. Sure. Of course. Sorry. But right now . . . I have a headache."

"Holy crap," Ricarda calls out. She lets go of me and links arms with Ferhad instead. "Can you believe this?"

Ferhad glories in his success. "That's what I've been saying this whole time. Florian is in a foul mood and not up for summer vacation at all."

"That's totally not true," I call after them angrily. "I'm in a great mood. I'll be better in a second, you'll see. I just have to make a phone call."

"All you've been doing is thinking about other things. And even when you kiss me, your mind is elsewhere."

"I'm a little preoccupied right now with my sister!"

"You should have thought of that before you came here."

"Jeez, Ricarda, wait up. Not you, too—give me a break? Besides, I could really use an aspirin."

"Then go see a doctor!" Ricarda snarls at me.

"Do I always have to be in a good mood? Am I not allowed to have a down moment?!"

No reply.

My eyes are burning.

I down the rest of my beer in frustration and stick the bottle into the sand.

Finn and Lennart trot past me, and I have to sit through a stupid comment from Finn, who's also our team captain, along the lines of not leaving trash behind on the beach. Finn gets an angry growl from me in response. Fortunately, he ignores it.

Next, Eric and Nathalie pass me by. His chin is red all over from her lipstick. She's making bedroom eyes at him, as if she's well past her actual thirteen years and as if they'd just "done" it. Jeez, get over yourselves already.

"Hey, Flor," he says in passing. "Any chance you can pay for us to get ATVs again tomorrow, after the tournament?"

"Why should I?"

"I told Nathalie about it. She totally needs to try it out." He shamelessly slobbers all over his girlfriend's neck. "It was so much fun . . ."

"I'd rather you give me something from your shopping bag!"

Eric suddenly gets a grim look on his face but then hands me a beer.

I sit down on the beach and open the bottle, which doesn't have a screw top, with my teeth.

"Don't drink too much, huh? We've got a tournament tomorrow."

Yeah, whatever. Get lost, you lucky dog.

At least I manage to keep my mouth shut this time. But only because my teeth hurt now on top of everything else.

Eric and Nathalie clear out; Jaffa is not stopping by, he wound up hanging with the soccer players farther back; Leah is the last person left. She stops in front of me, gives me a squinty smile, and without saying a word sticks her hand out to help me up. I shake my head.

"Come on!"

I grunt and pick myself up. Everyone else is already way ahead of us. The ones out front are now leaving the beach and taking the path leading up into the dunes. I don't even know if I still feel like spending an evening with all of them. Even so, I follow.

Leah keeps collecting her seashells, doesn't say a thing, doesn't ask a thing, only gives me a disapproving sideways glance from time to time.

Suddenly, though, she bends down, calling out, "Hah!" She picks something up, cleans the sand off it—and hands me a bluish spiral seashell.

I look at it in surprise. It's lightweight, perfectly twisted, and completely intact. It looks like it's from a different world, and yet it's just laying here on the beach.

"Pretty," I mumble.

"They say you can hear the sea roar inside one of these seashells." Leah takes the shell out of my hands and holds it up to her ear. "Yeah, I can hear it. It's pretty loud, too."

We both laugh awkwardly.

"Maybe you can use it to communicate?" She gives me a questioning look. "Hello? Hello, Atlantis?"

I feel myself relax a tiny little bit. Atlantis, yes, that sounds like the kind of place this seashell comes from. A quiet, blue world full of wonder.

Leah puts on a voice. "You have reached the Atlantis Customer Service Center. If you would like to speak with the Atlantis Underwater Committee, please press one. If you would like to rent a submarine vessel, please press two. If you are currently drowning, please stay on the line and we will transfer you to the next available professional diver."

I laugh so hard that tears stream down my face. "Atlantis! How do you come up with this stuff?"

"Well," she says and offers me the seashell as a gift. "You're the one who was talking about fairies."

Suddenly and without a warning I have lost all sense of humor. "That stupid fairy princess!"

"What? Why?"

"Because I totally fell for it."

18

We have turned our backs to the sea and are now slowly walking up to the dunes. I talk and talk to Leah, kneading my hands together nervously the whole time. A lonely vacationer is flying his kite, and I follow the kite with my eyes. Then it crashes, the kite string is being rolled up, and the sun sets.

"Do you know what I'm scared as hell of? That they'll say, 'Sarah? Oh, we buried her while you were on vacation.'"

"Come on, you're exaggerating."

"No, I'm not. I have absolutely no idea what's been going on back home. Can you imagine what that's like? It's driving me insane."

Leah reaches out with her hand as if she wants to put her arm around my shoulder, but then she doesn't.

"If you can't reach your family, you'll have to try the hospital. Ask them to put you through to the cancer ward and ask how Sarah's doing. Then you'll know."

My heart starts racing at the thought of it. I can't do it, not now. Have some arrogant nurse scold me. Have someone tell me that they're not giving information to strangers over the phone. Or maybe hear that Sarah's no longer a patient there, meaning she's been released. That's what happened with my granddad. My dad was told at the gate that Granddad had been released, but he really was in the basement below, dead, in a cooler.

"Do you want me to call? Come on, I'll do it for you. Do you have the number saved on your cell phone?" She holds out her hand to take my phone.

I turn away. I don't want to be touched. I feel sick from this headache, woozy from the beer. My feet are firmly and deeply stuck in the sand as if it's concrete. I just want to be left alone, fall down, and die. "No."

"But you're in pain."

"The only pain around here is you."

"Sure, I know, I've been such a pain all day long. I'm not super-awesome, super-beautiful Ricarda, right, who's always playing along without ever using her own brain just for once." She looks disappointed and shakes her head. "I just wanted to help."

"Nobody can help me. Not me, and not Sarah either, not anymore."

Leah doesn't say anything. I don't know if it's true, nobody knows. Our conversation is over and we don't restart it, because we have now reached the top of the dune and meet up with Finn and Luca who are walking toward us.

"If you're looking for the others, they're in the dunes over there." Luca points to a gloomy looking, olive-green range of hills behind him.

"Why aren't you with them?" Leah asks.

"We changed our minds. We got better things to do than to get wasted." Finn is pulling a sour face. "After all, we want to win a tournament tomorrow."

We follow the two of them with our eyes, how they walk away, following our footsteps, talking, hands in their pockets. A few more minutes of daylight, then it'll be dark. Dark, like inside my heart.

"What about us? What do you want to do, Flor?"

I would love to just run after them, back to the camp, into my tent, and pull my sleeping bag over my head so I don't have to see or hear anything anymore.

"Dunno." I take a sip from my beer.

"Call the hospital, try to reach your parents again."

"No, I know it's all for nothing anyway. This morning I should have wished for something else from the fairy princess. It was stupid of me to come here. Everyone else had more fun with the ATVs than me. And the girlfriend . . ."

"Ricarda. You can say it."

I ignore her comment. "That didn't really work either."
And then—I don't know why—I add, "Maybe I should have
wished for a different girlfriend."

"Oh, come on," Leah says harshly. "Don't give me that! Or
I'm leaving."

"I'm just saying. Is it true what your dad said on the
phone?" I carefully reach out with my hand to touch hers—
and get turned down.

"Who the heck do you think you are?! First, you try
getting it on with Ricarda, and when things don't work out
with her you come running to me? Really? I am not your
stand-in, let's be clear about that. You know what, I think
you're bored. You don't really mean it and you're completely
off your rocker!"

And with that, she stalks away—worst of all, she's right
about everything. Which is why I don't follow her. It's too
painful, too difficult, too complicated.

When I reach the others, I can see that hanging out
in a hollow between the dunes has only sped things
up between the boys and the girls. Eric and Nathalie are
completely wrapped up in each other, and Ricarda and Ferhad
are on their way there, which does not improve my mood.

Nils, on the other hand, doesn't seem to mind that
Michelle didn't come with us. He's chatting with Schnitzel,
who is four years our senior and famous for being able to
hold his booze.

"Hey, Florian, where did you leave Leah?" Lennart
asks me. He has managed to force himself into Nils and

Schnitzel's little group and is clearly proud to be in the middle of things for once. "Is she feeding squirrels again?"

"Shut up, or I'll feed you to the crocodiles!"

"Crocodiles. Here in Holland?" Lennart laughs himself silly like a little boy and hands me a bottle of beer. Since nobody seems to have noticed my arrival and because my own bottle is empty yet again, I accept. The sand on which I sit is cold and damp, and on top of everything else the ground is sloped so that I almost slide into Lennart.

The four of us who don't have girlfriends hold on to our drinks—the other boys hold on to their respective conquests. Ricarda half lies in Ferhad's lap, sucking on a bottle of sparkling wine. She has her feet toward the spot where Nils is sitting and her head tilted back. "Wow, so many stars. I can see the Big Dipper."

"Could you please put your feet somewhere else?" Nils complains.

"Aw, don't be like that, Nils. They're the longest, prettiest legs in the world." Ferhad is obviously not just caressing Ricarda's knee, because she suddenly sits up and says, "Hey, hey, what do you think you're doing?"

"Hey, you're practically lying on top of me. . . ." Ferhad laughs and tries to kiss her. I notice the fact that Ricarda very quickly turns away. Huh, she doesn't seem to know what she wants at all.

At the same time, Lennart calls out, buzzed on beer, "You can lie on top of me any time. I can be your pillow."

"Do you think I want to drown myself in blobs of fat?" comes her disgusted reply.

"Hey, retard, you can drink all you want but shut the hell up!" Ferhad doesn't seem to like having Lennart around.

Ferhad isn't done yet. He peels away from Ricarda, jumps up, and kicks Lennart in the side unexpectedly.

Lennart squeals like a pig.

"If I hear you talking to us one more time, frog face, I will turn you into mashed potatoes, got it?!"

Ricarda gives me a glance. She looks like she's trying to check my reaction to the whole thing.

Whatever, if it's a macho guy you need, be my guest.

"Ferhad, stop it," she says to him. "He's not worth it."

"He was coming on to my girlfriend!"

Ricarda and I exchange glances again. I say, "Up until an hour ago you were *my* girlfriend. At least that's what I thought."

"And *I* thought you didn't want a girlfriend, Florian."

"Flor, you missed your chance." Ferhad gives me a wide, arrogant grin. "You go nurse your headache."

"Don't tell me what to do, got it?" I snap at him.

"Hey, you guys, stop it!" Ricarda steps in. "You don't need to fight. Besides, I don't feel like partying anymore." Then she turns to me and asks, "Where's Leah?" It's as if she only just now notices that her friend isn't around.

"She went back to the camp with Luca and Finn."

"Yeah, that's exactly where I'm going, too. Nathalie, what about you?"

"Okay." Nathalie gets up, pulling Eric with her.

"So, is everyone leaving now?" Schnitzel gripes. He's pretty blasted already. "You guys are such sissies. What a crappy party this turned out to be."

Ferhad and I exchange angry looks. "I'm heading back, too," Ferhad says as the other three are leaving. And he gives me this look, just with his eyes, like he's trying to tell me to not even think about joining them.

Still, I do think about following them but not primarily on account of Ricarda. I really would like to say goodnight to Leah and apologize for my weird come-on earlier, and then find some aspirin and close my eyes for a little bit.

"You coming?" Ricarda asks—maybe because she still likes me, maybe because she doesn't like Ferhad all that much after all. Who knows.

I'm just about to say yes, when Nils asks, "Flor, have you heard from your family yet?"

"Nope. Nothing. Nada."

"I've got to tell you something. Come here for a second. Just don't be mad. I should have told you earlier but completely forgot."

"Can you wait for just a moment?" I ask Ricarda.

"I don't really want to wait anymore."

"I see." And I do, I mean I understand what she means,

but I think to myself: *Then you're not the right girl for me.*

"I'm sorry, Ricarda. Somehow everything just seems to be going wrong today."

She shrugs her shoulders and turns to leave. Ferhad raises his hand in a good-bye wave. "Have fun, don't drink too much!" I can hear triumph flowing from his every syllable.

"You'll never get Ricarda anyway, don't flatter yourself. She's only playing with you," Nils snarls through gritted teeth and quiet enough so that only I can hear. Then he clinks his bottle of vodka lemonade against my beer. "Nobody here is getting lucky, except for Eric. Oh, and I need to fess up to something."

"**Y**our parents know where you are. They've known all day."

"What?" Furiously, I jump to my feet. "How's that possible? I thought I could trust you!"

Nils swallows hard, coughs. "You *can* trust me! My dad told them. How could I have known that he'd drive to the hospital together with my mom right after he dropped us off to visit my aunt. Yeah, and in the doorway they ran into your mom who was completely distraught. She was just about to have you paged. You know, like in the shopping mall: Little Florian has been reported missing. . . ." Nils chuckles to himself, but I don't think this is funny at all.

"Oh crap," I cuss.

"I went missing once in a mall," says Lennart, who has scuttled up to us and has been listening to our conversation.

"So, who realized you were missing?!" I bark at him and suddenly I feel like kicking him, like Ferhad did before. But I manage to control myself and turn back to Nils. "How long have you known?"

He looks completely overcome with remorse. "For about an hour or so." Very carefully he tries to bring me back down to earth. "I'm sorry, but when I got the call I didn't have time to think about you and your problems. Michelle was being pretty weird earlier. She's not into me at all. Eric gave me grief about her liking me. I really put my foot in my mouth when I asked her if she wanted to come to our party. And then you and your ladies . . ."

"What's that supposed to mean?"

"You've got this extra-special status because of that thing with your sister, and you can pretty much take your pick."

"That's not true."

"Is too! First, you hit on Ricarda with all your cash, then you look all sad and lonely and hook up with Leah. And me? Did you ever think about me in all of this? Even our team captain asked me to look after you. Am I your dad? My old man told me that if I ever did anything like what you did he would throw me out of the house and I would never be allowed to come back. So, you see, now *I'm* in trouble because I'm partially responsible for getting your family all worked up and worried out of their minds." He imitates his dad's voice, "Did you ever even consider them?"

"But there's nothing I can do about this stupid situation!" I'm screaming now. "It's Sarah's friggin' cancer that's screwing everything up."

Tears well up in my eyes. I can't take this anymore. My head feels like it's about to explode. For a while I just sit there, trying to get my headache under control. Which is why I don't hear my cell phone ring at first.

But then I realize what's going on—*Home calling*—and I rush off to the side. I don't want anyone to listen in. "Yes?"

"Florian?" It's a quiet, creaky voice. "Dear boy, is that you?"

"Grandma???" Seriously? They're sending Grandma Gaby to check on me?

"Oh, thank god. It's you on the line. I've been worried sick. Are you at the sports club?"

"Soccer camp, yes." I walk between the dunes in disappointment. I mean, I like Grandma, don't get me wrong—but the fact that my stupid parents don't even bother to call themselves, that's rich.

"Your parents are very angry with you. I told Manfred, 'Leave the boy be, you're just as hot-headed as he is, I'm sure you were exactly like him when you were younger,' but he didn't even want to call you. Nor did your mom, but she wouldn't have had time after everything that's been going on today."

"So, what happened?" My heart clenches up, my hand is clutching the cell phone. In the end, I guess it doesn't matter who tells me first.

"It was a terribly stressful day. It still is. I can't stand this any longer. My old ticker isn't strong enough to take it anymore. I'm getting old, you know."

"Grandma! What happened?"

"You went missing. Cousin Daniel thought maybe you got sick. He went to look for you. And then he didn't come back for the longest time. I guess he got lost out on the hospital grounds."

"What a dork."

"And then your mom ran into your friend's parents downstairs, and your dad got furious and drove home to see if it was true and if your duffel bag was really gone. I told your mother that she should call you on your phone but she didn't have hers with her and she was too worked up to remember your number. There are always so many numbers these days. And they didn't want Sarah to find out, and— listen, did you steal money from your parents? Honey, you can't do that. You should have just asked me."

"Would you have given me money? Now? For my vacation?"

Grandma doesn't say anything for a little while. "Hard to say. I am so glad that I don't have to make those kinds of decisions anymore. Anyway, so your parents were having a big fight. All this trouble in front of all these people. There were a few girls from Sarah's high school, and even one of the teachers. They didn't need to know that you ran away. And then to top it all off your Grandma Hilda fainted from all the excitement. That was the last thing we needed. And Sarah . . ."

"What about Sarah?"

Her voice gets all small. "I don't know."

"Why, why don't you know?"

"Your parents are still at the hospital. She was suddenly in a really bad way, and so they sent everyone away except for your parents. And they're running all these tests right now." Grandma sighs a deep, tragic sigh. "This stupid birthday. It was a mistake to make all this hoo-hah about it. All these people wanting to wish Sarah a happy birthday, it was lovely and touching, and she was real happy about it, too, but it was also really stressful for her. Besides, I think it only made her understand her situation even more clearly. Especially when she was chatting with her girlfriends from her school. They're all talking about getting their driver's licenses and she . . . turning eighteen, coming of age . . . that's when your life is supposed to start, not when it's supposed to end."

"But she's going to make it, right? She's not going to die?" I'm no longer talking, I'm begging for mercy. "Grandma?"

"No, I don't think she's going to die. I guess nobody knows for sure. The doctors say it's normal for her to have such episodes of sudden weakness. The important thing now is for her not to give up on herself. Florian, dear, take care of yourself. Your granddad would have said you should also enjoy life, although . . . well, whatever: I'm glad you're healthy and well taken care of and that nothing happened to you. Bye."

And with that, she hangs up the phone.

I run through the dunes. Then I let myself fall onto the
sand and close my eyes. I can see it all.

\*   \*   \*

Nils's dad telling my mom where I am. "You didn't know?
He's got some nerve, your son. What kind of parents are
you?!"

My mom standing there like a little schoolgirl being
yelled at. Her noticing how Nils's parents stare at the puke
stain on her blouse that she had tried to wash out in a hurry.

Her looking down on herself and at the stain, trying very hard not to burst out in tears.

Then my dad joining them, quickly realizing the situation, and pretending he gave me permission to attend the soccer camp. He lies because he's ashamed, which confuses my mom who doesn't catch on quickly enough. Him being unable to explain it to her, grunting and grumbling, taking off his glasses only to put them back on a moment later. While he's doing all that and breaking out in a sweat, he quickly comes up with another lie, which is that he needs to go home to make an important phone call to his employer.

It slowly dawning on my mom why he really has to go home. "Manfred, you're too worked up, I don't like you driving like this!"

Which makes things even worse because he hates being treated like a child.

"Don't tell me what I should and shouldn't do!"

"You're in a rage, Manfred, you're scaring me. Besides, your driving has cost us a lot of money already, money we could have used for other things."

Now they're really getting going, in the middle of the hospital hallway, in between the cancer patient zombies and our relatives who are hungry for some gossip and scandal. And then, suddenly, fear: Sarah being wheeled out of her room in a hurry.

\* \* \*

That's how it went down, something like that anyway. But it's no excuse for them not calling me. I need them, too. I want them to stay strong and stick together, and I want them to take me in their arms, right now.

I also want them to make things easier on Sarah. I don't want Sarah to know how much we worry because of her.

I sit on the beach for a long time, thinking. With my fingers I caress a gnarled root that is shaped like a hand. Somewhere out in the marshy brush I can hear a seabird wailing. It sounds like crying.

A light rain starts to fall. I can't see the stars anymore. Do our souls really rise up to heaven? Even in bad weather, when flights are grounded? I blow my nose.

Then I catch rain drops with my tongue and come to a reluctant decision.

*   *   *

When, almost an hour later, I'm ready to hit the road back to the campground, a big, bulky shape stumbles toward me: it's Schnitzel.

"Whoa, Florian," he roars and tries to slap my shoulder, but he misses and topples to the side so that I have to reach out and grab him to stop him from falling. "You're not going to believe this: Nils and the retard want to be blood brothers." He belches, and the booze smell coming from his mouth almost knocks me out. "They're drinking whatever they can get their hands on now." He raises his voice without sounding particularly interested. "They're toasting to not having a woman in their life and to being true friends." Schnitzel has the hiccups. He tries to laugh but it sounds more like he's whining. "Blood brothers! Them! Isn't that sad?"

"More like scary," I mumble and abandon Schnitzel to his fate. "You better go find your sleeping bag."

The party—if there ever was one—is well over. Only Nils and Lennart are left in the hollow between the dunes. They look like a pair of idiots who have collapsed right where they were standing. Lennart has his chin on his chest and is babbling to no one in particular. Nils has slumped into himself. He's got a distrustful look in his gray eyes with one arm outstretched uneasily, as if he isn't sure whether he should shoo me away with his hand or ask me to pull him up to his feet.

Schnitzel was right: it's sad.

"Nils, get up! It's starting to rain and it's already past twelve. Coach Peter said we all need to be in our tents by midnight.

Come on, guys, pull yourselves together. Let's go back to the campground. Otherwise there'll be trouble."

"Oh, my friend, this is the end," Nils slurs and in mock misery, gives me a sly smile.

"Okay, no time for talking." I bend down, pick up a few empty bottles, and put them in the plastic bags we brought.

Nils gives Lennart a slap on the back. "Hah, look at that. Florian is all envi-envi-environmentally conscious. Did you know that, retard?"

"I thought you were blood brothers now," I hiss, surprised that Lennart doesn't seem to have noticed me being here. While I had stuck to beer all night, he must have been drinking the hard stuff. He lifts his head very, very slowly. "Florian? Florian who?"

"You know, Florian: Leah and Ricarda's boyfriend. One of them he'll marry and one will be his lover. Or maybe he and Ferhad can share, I heard he likes having two wives, too."

"You're talking horsecrap!"

"Then they can have a threesome, no . . . a, a foursome." Nils holds up four fingers of his left hand and then the middle finger of his right hand and moves his hands together in one sudden move.

"You are completely drunk, Nils." I take the bottle, which has slipped out of his hands, away from him and put it in the trash bag.

"And you can't stop hitting on people." He takes a loud, deep breath through his nose. "Just like Ricarda."

"That's what a trip like this is for, isn't it? But don't you worry, there's definitely nothing going on between Ricarda and me. There's also nothing going on between Leah and me. It's just not the right time right now."

"Not right now," Nils sneers. "See? That's what I mean."

"Look, I have a whole lot of other problems on my mind at the moment."

Lennart briefly wakes from his slumber, lifts his head, and asks, "Florian who?"

Jeez, they're pathetic. And to think I went looking for them just so I wouldn't be alone.

"And what sorts of problems could you possibly have, Mr. Womanizer?" Nils's voice is getting loud, and he flails his arms.

"I give you three guesses!" I reply angrily, and that's when my friend has a lucid moment in his drunken stupor and realizes what kind of a dumb question he's asking.

"Yeah, sure, Sarah, but she's going to make it, she's always pulled through," he says quickly.

"I don't know." Suddenly my legs seem to be made of Jell-O, and I sit down in the sand beside Lennart.

"I've got a bad feeling this time. Apparently, she's had a real bad breakdown today."

"How do you know? Did they—?"

Nils can't finish his sentence because Lennart interrupts him. "Now I know who you mean! Florian." He turns to me and lifts a bottle of vodka to his mouth.

"Cheers! To your sister!" And then, stupidly drunk and completely insensitive, he starts singing, "Happy birthday to you . . ."

I think of my mother who is desperately trying to hold on to a normal life and yet seems so pathetically helpless.

"Happy birthday to you . . ."

I think of my dad who gets heart arrhythmia before every single doctor's appointment and yet is making a point to demonstrate his toughness by not calling me.

"Happy biiirthday, dear Sarah . . ."

And I think of Sarah who bears it all, who takes it all: every treatment, every visitor, every song—right up to her last second.

"Happy birthday to you!"

Stop!

I slam the bottle out of Lennart's hand. It hits his teeth with quite a bit of force.

Lennart screams and trips, falling backward toward Nils, who jumps out of the way without trying to catch him and who lets him crash into the shopping bag full of empty bottles. Glass is breaking.

A bottle rolls to the side, a strangely formed bottle. Made from plastic. Nils holds it up to show me. "Florian?" he asks. "Should we have him drink this?"

"Whatever, I don't care. As long as he shuts the hell up."

Nils unscrews the top, hands Lennart the bottle.

Lennart, who's whining: "I'm bleeding."

"Crybaby."

"Shut up and drink," Nils orders him. Our eyes meet. "Florian?"

"Bottoms up," I say, even though I should say something else because I realize, of course, that this is wrong.

Nils stares at me, then at Lennart. Lennart says, "Hmm, smells soapy."

Then he tilts his head all the way back, lifts the bottle, and opens his mouth wide.

I watch every single one of his movements like in slow motion. Simultaneously, another image slides on top of what I'm observing: Julia and Karen playing a prank on us and swapping the bottles. I can sense, I know what's about to happen. And for a brief moment I feel something like satisfaction because if there's something I know for sure, it is this:

No matter how hard I try, I will never be able to enjoy myself here during this soccer camp vacation. So, why should others be able to enjoy themselves?

On the other hand—

"Stop!" I burst forward to snatch the bottle from Lennart's hand. Too late. He's already poured a big swig down his greedy gullet. Not a moment later he makes a weird gurgling sound and touches his throat.

"Lennart, spit it out," I yell.

Lennart spits and gags. He opens his mouth wide and sticks out his tongue. He extends his neck as if he's trying to stretch and stretch it and separate it from his body. He groans and grabs my arm in desperation.

My heart is pounding. Damn, what have we done?

Lennart's fingers pinch and dig into my arm. It hurts—but watching him is a lot worse.

"Nils, give me water so I can rinse his mouth!"

"Bah, no."

"Drink!"

I leave him no choice. All we have is seltzer, and he guzzles it down.

And then, just as the rain gets going and it really starts pouring down, there it is: the first delicate soap bubble coming out of Lennart's mouth.

"It's the fizz in the water," Nils says, but he's wrong of course. It's that thing that you get when you mix liquid dish soap with water: bubbles and fresh lemon scent.

"Oh, crap," I whine and lower my voice so that Lennart can't hear me. "Nils, what have you done?"

"So, this is my fault?" Nils calls. "You were okay with it, remember? This was supposed to be your revenge. You were the one smashing his face in in the first place. Besides, he drank it himself. We never forced him."

I thrust my cell phone into Nils's hand so he can call for help, and at the same time I yell at Lennart to keep drinking water.

But this turns out to be not such a great idea. Quite the opposite, in fact.

When Finn, Leah, and Coach Peter join us a little while
later, we all watch by the light of our flashlights as
Lennart throws up dish soap. He's got both his hands
clenched around his throat, and I try to imagine how harsh
that stuff must be on his esophagus. My own throat is getting
raw and sore at the thought of it.

"What on earth is going on here?"

Coach Peter gets no reply from either Nils or me, and as
for Lennart . . . he *can't* reply. Tears are running down his
face. When he is finally trying to say something, he gulps,
spews, gags, gurgles, and spits out a single comprehensible
word, "Di-di-dish so-soap."

"Spitting it out is exactly the wrong thing to do," Coach Peter says firmly. "We need to get you to a hospital right now." He dials a number and talks into his phone in an animated, agitated voice, then makes a second call to order a taxi. Meanwhile, Leah tears open a pack of paper tissues and wipes Lennart's mouth.

"Florian, give me a hand!" Coach Peter is trying to get Lennart to stand up, but it's not working too well because Lennart's legs keep giving out.

Finn is looking after Nils. Leah is showing us the way back through the dunes with her flashlight.

Fortunately, there is a bench by the pathway leading down to the beach. There's also a gravel road right next to it. We let Lennart slump down on the bench, then we lift his legs so he can lie down and turn his head to the side so that saliva, soap bubbles, and whatever else is coming out of his mouth can drip down onto the sand.

"It's not exactly recovery position, but I think it'll do," Coach Peter says. Then he starts yelling: "How could you not have noticed what bottle he's drinking from, boozed-up as he is? The two of you aren't that trashed yet!"

Nils looks at me with fear flashing in his eyes. No, we're not *that* trashed, and we're also not completely crazy.

"It was a mistake," I reply quickly, and I can feel Coach Peter eyeing me up very skeptically.

"A prank," I add, even though I know it's not the exact right answer either.

"A prank," Coach Peter repeats ironically. "I see." Then all hell breaks loose. He's letting us have it so unexpectedly that we cringe. "Well, I thought it was a prank, too, when I heard you'd gone to get hammered! Jesus Christ, this is soccer camp, not a frat party. There are rules, just like during a game. We thought we could trust you. We are responsible for your safety, we have to get you back home safe and sound. How the hell are we supposed to explain this to your parents?"

"At least he seems to be breathing a little easier now," Leah whispers and strokes Lennart's sweaty hair, just like my mom often does with Sarah.

"Well, I guess that's the only positive thing about tonight," Peter grumbles. He cusses, looks at his watch, and nervously walks up and down until the taxicab he ordered finally shows up.

Hospital is "hospitaal" in Dutch, easy, but our cab driver understands German as well. Coach Peter takes the bottle of dish soap with him so that the doctors know right away what they're dealing with. He lets Finn, Leah, and Nils walk back to our camp by themselves. But me, he takes along with him in the cab.

While we're in the cab, Coach Peter holds his questions and accusations. The three of us are sitting in the back with Lennart in the middle. The cab driver tries to start a conversation with Coach Peter, but he's in no mood to talk and neither am I. I glance outside, even though I can't make out any details in the rainy darkness. A song is playing on the radio that Sarah likes and that I always thought was cheesy. But right now the cheesiness of the song has a different effect on me: I'm about to start crying again. I guess I'm just a bag of nerves.

And I have every reason to be, because as soon as Lennart is admitted to the emergency room at the hospital and we sit down in the waiting room, Coach Peter starts with his interrogation.

"Alright, Florian, the truth please, and quick! What happened?"

*I snapped, and for a second I wanted Lennart to really suffer just this once*—that's the answer I should give Coach Peter if I want to be honest. But I can't, and so I try to make excuses and talk about an accident.

"We couldn't really tell what was in the bottle, it was too dark already. It wasn't intentional."

"You've been picking on Lennart all day."

"That's not true. That thing with the ATVs, that was supposed to be a joke. Plus, nothing happened, he just fell into the sand without hurting himself."

"But now something did happen. Who of you beat him up?"

"Beat him up?"

"Do you think I'm blind and didn't notice his busted lip?"

Right that second—thank god!—his cell phone rings and interrupts our conversation. His ringtone's been the team song of his favorite soccer team, FC Schalke 04, for the longest time. It's a silly song, more like a drinking song, but I don't dare to crack any jokes about it right now.

"Hi Trisha," Coach Peter says, and I overhear Trisha telling him how Julia and Karen had planted the bottle of dish soap on Ferhad and slipped it into his bag.

"Okay, so at least the boys didn't plan this." He gives me a nasty look. "That's some consolation. Okay, Trisha. You do that. Send everybody to bed and make sure that they stay quiet. Bye."

He turns back to me. "This does not clear you, not by a long shot. So, again: who beat up Lennart?"

"It was me. He sang the happy birthday song for my sister. I couldn't take it. It was like he was mocking me. I'm so worried that Sarah might die soon. She's gotten a lot worse since yesterday."

"Really? Are you sure? You're not just making this up? Why wouldn't your dad tell Trisha that? He called her today around lunchtime and asked how you were. He was really weird on the phone, but there was no mention of Sarah at all."

"Hah. So he called, did he? Well, that was for something completely different."

"And what other reason would he have to call? Why would they even allow you to come?" While he's asking me this, the answer dawns on him. "Oh. I don't believe it."

I just shrug my shoulders.

It's pretty obvious to me. In front of all these people running the soccer club, Dad didn't want to stand out as someone whose son doesn't take him seriously or whose rules can be disobeyed. For a split second I even toy with the idea that Dad might not have mentioned anything so I could enjoy my time here. But I immediately drop the idea, because as soon as he and Mom knew for sure where I was and that I was okay, they stopped picking up the phone—because they felt hurt in their stupid pride, or maybe because they thought it was fair punishment for my running away. How very understanding and gracious of them.

Of course, another reason why my parents didn't get in touch was because Sarah was in a particularly bad way. It was all so typical. Unlike me, my parents are allowed to make all the mistakes in the world because they always have an excuse. "I didn't think you had it in you," Coach Peter says.

"Me neither."

I glance around the waiting room. There were well-worn newspapers and tired, gray, hopeless faces: a scene I'm all too familiar with from my thousands of hospital visits to Sarah. And then I spot—or am I imagining things?—a tiny, skinny girl wearing a cream-colored sweat suit who peeps around the hallway corner, winking at me.

I stare at the little girl in fascination. Then I abruptly get up from my chair, but Coach Peter grabs my arm and stops me in my tracks.

"Are you kidding me? Do you think I'm an idiot?"

"Whatever. Throw me out of the club if that makes you feel any better."

I break away from him. Then, with determination, I walk up to the girl.

"Hi," I say and don't feel stupid at all about saying it.

"We had an accident with our car," she tells me right away in German and points behind her to the second waiting room, where I can see a husband and wife waiting. They look like they're on vacation, too. The dad has buried his face in his hands, the mom is watching us with tears streaming down her face. "All I remember is a really loud crash! I just don't know where my brother is. And I'm missing my teddy."

I pull the seashell from my pocket, the one Leah gave me as a gift, and hold it in my cupped hands as if I'd caught something.

"I just saved a fairy princess," I say and show the little girl my hands. "As a thank-you she has granted me three wishes. I'll give them to you, you can have them."

The little girls opens her mouth excitedly as if to speak, but I quickly interrupt her, "Shh! You can't say your wishes out loud."

She thinks for a moment. "Okay, I made my wishes. Now show me the fairy princess."

I open my hands and offer her the seashell. It looks all polished and shiny because my palms are so sweaty. The girl looks surprised. "That doesn't look like a . . ."

"It was a fairy princess a second ago," I insist. "But now that you've made all your wishes she's turned back into this."

She smiles, grabs the seashell, and runs over to her parents. I can hear her call out, "Mommy, look," while I turn around and walk back to Coach Peter who now looks more puzzled than angry.

"What the hell was that all about?"

He wouldn't understand, nobody would understand. I ignore his question completely. "So, back to the point, Coach. Yes, I forged the permission slip from my parents, and I hit Lennart because he was getting on my nerves. And I'm sorry about that thing with the dish soap. It just happened."

Suddenly, my mind is very clear. I don't feel tired or in pain anymore, not even confused or scared; I'm determined and self-confident in a way I haven't been in a long time.

"Leave Nils out of it, alright?" I say to Coach Peter.

"You want me to leave Nils out of it? You're making this way too easy for me." Coach Peter is getting all worked up again. "I don't believe you. Nils is constantly picking on Lennart. You can't tell me that he didn't have something to do with this."

"Nils was drunk, that's all. It was me Lennart was trying to tease. You know how Lennart has this talent for putting his foot in his mouth and how he's constantly getting people pissed off."

Peter doesn't know what to say. "This is going to have consequences," is all he can manage. Then he gets up because the doctor is stepping out of the treatment room. He is followed by two nurses who hold and support a very pale, very pasty Lennart.

"He can leave now," the Dutch doctor says with a slight accent. "But the boy needs some rest. It would be best if you could take him home to his parents."

"I'm leaving in the morning anyway," I say. "I can take him."

I 'm so exhausted that I fall asleep right away. But morning comes too soon. At six o'clock, Eric gets up to use the bathroom and trips over my legs in the tent; at seven, I can hear the first dishes being banged together; at seven-thirty, some idiot turns on his radio at full blast; and shortly thereafter, Coach Peter tears open our tent zipper and calls, "Everyone up! Get some fresh air! Up, up! Florian, Nils, come here. I've got a bone to pick with you two."

Nils and I are a little hungover and shuffle over to the wooden table outside, where Trisha is just spreading Nutella on a breakfast roll. Lennart is sitting beside her on the bench. He slept in the coaches' tent last night—under supervision, so to speak—and you can tell he's had a rough night. His face looks ashen, his lips and nose are swollen, and he's got a long, knitted soccer scarf wrapped around his neck. He peers at Trisha's breakfast with a disgusted—but at the same time hungry—face. He's got only a weak smile for us.

Then he asks in a voice so hoarse that it is barely recognizable, "So, you want to play a practice game after breakfast?"

Nils and I exchange glances. Doesn't Lennart realize that him drinking the dish soap was no accident? Or is he being extra cheerful just because he's trying to suck up to us?

Coach Peter seems to have similar questions on his mind. "I've already heard Florian's version," he opens the debate. "Now I would like to hear your version of last night's party. Who wants to start? Nils?"

Nils opens his mouth. He's never been very good at talking, and so he seems appropriately relieved when Lennart jumps in with his raspy voice, "Look, it's very simple. I can't hold my liquor, and I accidentally grabbed the dish soap."

"And who then slapped your face, smartass? Was it you? Did you accidentally slap yourself, too?" Coach Peter's voice is dripping with irony. All around us the benches are filling up with curious spectators. Everyone wants to be a witness to this tribunal.

"Coach, we've been over this. It was me," I say firmly. "Lennart sang a bad song and I blew a fuse."

A few people laugh. Nobody here really likes Lennart, nobody appreciates him being here, and he knows that, as well as I do.

"Well, I guess I can't sing to save myself," he says in his raspy voice, and for once he is making a comment that sounds appropriate, funny, almost nice—and everyone gives a friendly laugh.

Coach Peter wants to continue with the trial, but I interrupt him, "Coach, it was exactly as I told you. I also told you that I'm going home. Not because I'm feeling super guilty or anything, but because I shouldn't be here right now. I wanted to leave my family's sad, depressing faces behind me and have fun with you guys, but I can't. After breakfast I'll take the next train home."

Leah opens her mouth as if to say something. For a moment I think she wants to come with me. And in actual fact I can hear someone say, "I'm leaving, too." But it isn't Leah who says it, it's Nils.

"Well, I guess I see that as an admission of guilt." Coach Peter just can't seem to let it go. Well, he's not totally off with his assumption. No wonder he's going to law school. "You're not getting away that easily, boys."

"What else do you want, Coach?" Trisha is now getting involved in the discussion, too. "Just leave it be. Can we just change the subject? I think we've spent enough time on this."

Coach Philip and Coach Christoph, the other two coaches, agree. Outvoted, Coach Peter falls silent but keeps muttering to himself the entire time while we're having breakfast. After I'm done packing my things, he says, "But you have to pay for your own ticket back, Florian."

"That's okay, I've got money. I'll also pay for Nils and Lennart."

"Seriously, you don't have to." Nils is embarrassed.

"You'll get into even more trouble with your parents."

"I'm just as mad at them as they are at me. Because they never called me."

I still don't know how Sarah is doing after everything that happened yesterday. I hope everything is alright. . . . I mean, as much as things can ever be alright with her.

Nils doesn't say anything. Coach Peter gives a nod and leaves me alone from then on.

Everyone comes to say good-bye.

"It's a shame you're leaving." Ricarda gives me a spur-of-the-moment hug.

"Yeah. Sorry it didn't really work out between us."

"Oh, that's okay." She kisses me square on the mouth, flashes me a big grin. "I still think you're sweet."

"So are you," I say, but only to myself because she's already turned away from me and is now hugging Nils. "And you're leaving, too. This won't be a proper vacation without the two of you."

Nils is obviously enjoying her hugging him. "Maybe we can make up for it sometime," I hear him say.

Leah wants to come to the train station with us, which is only a little over a mile away. Ferhad and Eric say good-bye with a firm handshake, and so do Coach Philip and Trisha who I really didn't expect it from.

Coach Peter is of course coming with us, too, because he needs to make sure that we underage boys are at least getting on the right train if we're to make our long way home, all alone and all the way from Holland.

As the five of us are leaving the campground, Anna comes running after us. "Florian, wait up!"

I'm still mad at her. "There's no time," I say bluntly.

"Please! I'm sorry about all the things I said to you yesterday. I think I overreacted a bit. Well, I guess I was worried, I mean, I'm still worried, because Sarah's just not picking up her phone. But I hope she's okay. That's all we can hope, right? Could you give her this when you see her?" She thrusts a cardboard box into my hands. The sides are covered in postcards, and the bottom is filled with sand and seashells. "So Sarah has a little bit of the sea in her room."

"Alright."

"Thank you." Anna nervously shifts from one leg to the other. "As I said: I'm sorry."

"So, you only made up that story with the angel of death?"

She squirms. "Not entirely. We really talked a lot about angels since we watched that movie. But that the angel said something to her, well ..."

I nod my head. That's what I've suspected all along.

"I'm sorry, Florian."

"It's alright." I point at Leah up ahead, who has stopped and is looking back, waiting for me. "Listen, I've got to go."

Anna's face suddenly lights up. "By the way, did you know that Sarah and I made a bet a few weeks ago that you'd find a girlfriend on this trip? I thought it was going to be Ricarda, but Sarah was sure it would be Leah."

For a second I'm stumped. Yep, that's her, that's my sister: always a surprise in store.

When the train pulls up into the tiny train station, Leah gives me a big hug to say good-bye. "Call me when you get home and know what the story is, okay? I cross my fingers that everything's going to be alright."

One more time I wave at her from the open door. Then I get into the carriage behind Lennart and Nils, put my duffel bag down on the floor, and look through the dirty window outside. Coach Peter looks grumpy and a little sad as the train is pulling away from the station. Leah has her head cocked to the side, smiles in my direction, and blows me a kiss right before she disappears from my field of vision.

"So, I guess that's it." Nils slumps down into his seat and sighs. "Vacation over already."

"You didn't need to come," I say. "It would have been enough for me to leave. I feel like a lamb going to the slaughter already."

"It was the decent thing to do," Nils asserts.

Lennart clears his throat. "You didn't need to cut your vacation short on account of me. I should have been more careful myself and checked what I was drinking."

We fall quiet. Each one of us knows that it's not quite as simple as that.

"Anyone want to play cards?" Nils asks after a little while.

It's not a bad idea. We shuffle, pick, and play poker while our rumbling old train is making its way east, from Holland back to good old Germany. The once-cloudy sky got clearer the farther we traveled, the morning sun bright and shining warmly on our train car.

"You seem unbeatable at cards, Lennart," Nils gripes. "How about letting Florian and me win for a change?"

"Well, you'll need to try harder then," Lennart croaks with a raspy voice, and laughs.

My cell phone rings at twenty past ten, almost exactly twenty-four hours since I ran out into that hospital park. Green pastures pass us by with cows, fences, and ditches, and the sky is blue with a tiny nest of cirrus clouds.

*Home calling* it says on the display.

I answer the call.

KRISTINA DUNKER is one of Germany's top authors for teens. She was born in 1973 in Dortmund, Germany, and published her first book at the age of seventeen. Since then, Kristina has written many novels for children and young adults and received several awards and scholarships. Her books have been turned into musicals by fans and set to music by the New Philharmonic Orchestra in Düsseldorf. She is a freelance writer based in Castrop-Rauxel and holds regular lectures, discussions, and writing workshops for young people. In total, Kristina has written more than twenty books.

Made in the USA
San Bernardino, CA
06 September 2014